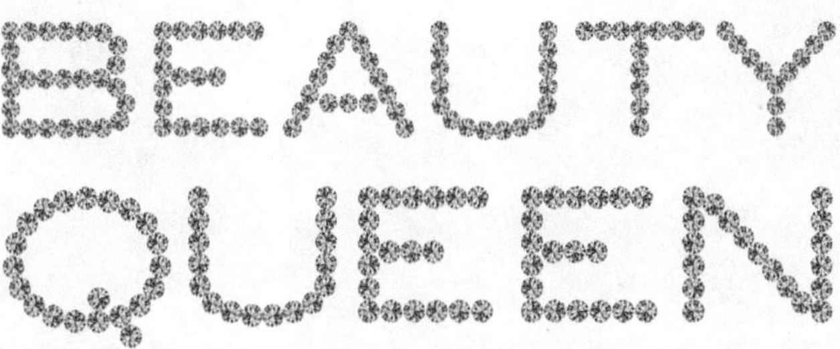

The Pathway to Pageantry

a must-read guide book
for every pageant contestant

The Pathway to Pageantry

ANVITA SUDARSHAN

An imprint of Manjul Publishing House Pvt. Ltd.
• C-16, Sector 3, Noida, Uttar Pradesh 201301, India
Website: www.manjulindia.com

Registered Office:
• 10, Nishat Colony, Bhopal 462 003 – India

Distribution Centres:
Ahmedabad, Bengaluru, Bhopal, Kolkata, Chennai,
Hyderabad, Mumbai, New Delhi, Pune

Copyright © Anvita Sudarshan 2021

Anvita Sudarshan asserts the moral right to be
identified as the author of this work

ISBN 978-93-90924-10-3

This edition first published in 2021

Cover and book design: Supriya Saran

Although the author and publisher have made every effort to ensure that the information in this book was correct at press time, the author and publisher do not assume and hereby disclaim any liability to any party for any loss, damage, or disruption caused by errors or omissions, whether such errors or omissions result from negligence, accident, or any other cause. This book is designed to provide information to readers. The content of the book is the sole expression and opinion of its author, and not that of the publisher. No warranties or guarantees are expressed or implied by the publisher's choice to include any of the content in this volume. Neither the publisher nor the author shall be liable for any physical, psychological, emotional, financial, or commercial damages, including but not limited to, special, incidental, consequential or other damages.

The advice and strategies found within may not be suitable for every situation. This work is sold with the understanding that neither the author nor the publisher are held responsible for the results accrued from the advice in this book.

All rights reserved. No part of this book may be used or reproduced, stored in or introduced into a retrieval system, or transmitted, in any form, or by any means (electronic, mechanical, photocopying, recording or otherwise) without the prior written permission of the Publisher. Any person who does any unauthorized act in relation to this publication may be liable to criminal prosecution and civil claims for damages.

To all those who will read this book.

Contents

Foreword

Every girl aspires to be a beauty queen at least at one point in her life. India's rapid success in international pageants like Miss World and Miss Universe in the nineties has etched India's name prominently in the annals of pageantry worldwide and made this dream seem more achievable to young girls all around the country. Young minds are now au fait with the awareness that pageantry is an enjoyable and rewarding path to pursue for a career. A number of small and big contests have mushroomed all over India and the quality, competitiveness and expectations have risen too.

The pageant scenario in India is constantly changing. From a perception of it being a mere celebration of beauty, to being recognised as an amalgam of competitive excellence that encompasses beauty with talent, intelligence and grace, to it being seen as a stepping stone to Bollywood, pageantry has come of age. Irrespective of the motivation, a crown is always a step in the right direction in a girl's aspirations. Unfortunately, it is not possible to aim for a title without meticulous physical and mental preparation.

India, unlike countries like Venezuela, does not provide strong institutional support to help prepare aspirants for the big stage. Most pageant aspirants make their own modest preparations by collecting information from dispersed sources, and at times undergo training from loosely organised 'sponsored' programmes. As such, most aspirants compete without a clear idea of what is expected and how to harvest their own untapped inner potential.

At a juncture like this, Anvita Sudarshan's book *Beauty Queen: The Pathway to Pageantry* attempts to fill in a genuine vacuum – that of non-availability of a wholesome guidebook that includes everything a pageant contestant needs to know about pageantry. In a very simple and lucid manner, *Beauty Queen* explains the meaning of pageantry, its exciting history, the constituents of beauty, required preparedness, and provides a number of insights drawn from personal experience.

Anvita Sudarshan's personal journey in participating in pageants attempts to turn the preparation of beauty pageant contestants into a well-informed, well-guided and well-coordinated effort, enhancing their chances of winning and excelling on the world stage. It is laid out in ten chapters and is systematic and analytical in its approach. The book is a handy primer for pageant contestants, pageant managers and to all those who have an abiding interest in beauty, grace and the development of a wholesome personality.

I wish Anvita every success and the readers of *Beauty Queen: The Pathway to Pageantry* happy reading.

Pradeep Guha,
CEO, 9x Media

Prologue

Beauty pageants have existed for as long as we can remember—from the time of Homer's *Iliad* to the 21st century. Sure, they've changed a lot, become more structured and streamlined, but essentially they are the same.

Someone once asked me, 'So you think you are the most beautiful woman on earth?'

I was like, 'Excuse me?'

'Of course, you participate in beauty pageants. You must think you are the most beautiful woman on earth.'

Well, you know what? That's not really the case. I do not think I am the most beautiful woman on earth. That would be an extremely narcissistic thought. I look around me everyday and there are zillions of beautiful women everywhere. I would have loved to be the most beautiful of them all, but, I am not. And I have to accept that. However when I go on stage, I know I can convince the judges that I am the most beautiful woman—at least among all the contestants, if not the world! And that modesty and confidence, sweetheart, are the only secrets to winning a pageant. Everything else in this book is meant to help you bolster that confidence. Trust me, it does need assistance or else, you'll end up looking overconfident. And that is certainly not the best way to win a pageant!

I have been associated with pageants for quite some time now. My tryst with pageants started when I was four years old. No, I wasn't a child beauty pageant contestant (thank god for that!). On the contrary, it began when I saw one beautiful woman become the first ever Indian to win the Miss Universe crown and then went on to see another equally beautiful woman win the Miss World crown. I was sitting there, watching them on TV and like any other four-year-old, I was mesmerised by the glamorous gowns and the crown. At that moment, all I wanted was a crown for myself.

...it didn't matter that I was much more highly trained than any other aspirant in the city. There was just so much competition around that all my classical and Stanislavskian training in acting didn't ensure I stood out. I needed something much more, something that would help me catch the public eye.

Over time, I forgot all about this temporary fixation I had with pageants, but only until I was seventeen. That was around the time I decided I wanted to be an actor. Soon after moving to Mumbai, I found out that it didn't matter that I was much more highly trained than any other aspirant in the city. There was just so much competition around that all my classical and Stanislavskian training in acting didn't ensure I stood out. I needed something much more, something that would help me catch the public eye. A lot of careers are about visibility—it's that plain and simple. The career I had chosen was one such.

Take the life of most aspiring actors. From morning to evening, you attend some ten auditions. The problem? Ten thousand other people have also attended those very same auditions. How do you stand out? The easy answer is by attaching a few laurels to yourself. So, like most aspirants, I fell back on the Miss India pageant to provide me with those laurels, to add that little extra to my CV that would ensure I distinguished myself in the world of acting and modelling. After all, pageants are to acting/modelling what a reputed fellowship is to, say, writing or journalism, to put it a little more in perspective. Little did I know that it would soon become a passion of mine.

Today, at the time of writing this book, I have participated in three national pageants and one international pageant and have won two of them, including the international pageant. I have been very lucky and hope to be luckier still. But I have also found that luck only favours those who work hard. You might be beautiful, talented and the most enchanting woman of them all, but without hard work, that crown is nothing but a pipe dream.

You might be beautiful, talented and the most enchanting woman of them all, but without hard work, that crown is nothing but a pipe dream.

Pageants today have become so structured that in order to excel in them, you need something of a curriculum. And that is why this book exists. So that you can homeschool yourself in that curriculum. But just reading it will not suffice. You must also practice it. Regularly. You do that, and I promise you, you will do well.

You know, the thing about pageants is that they are just so captivating. I still can't understand why I am so riveted by it all. Part of the reason I wrote this book was to understand that, but I still don't—despite all my years of experience as a beauty pageant contestant.

The truth of the matter is, pageants draw us into a fantasy where anyone can be a queen for a day. And that is very alluring. This is also a reason why people run away from it. The idea of being queen and then having it all taken away from you the very next year is scary. Also, pageants, much like modeling, draw you into a world that is not real. It's a world where physical beauty is everything. But you know what? Beauty fades! It doesn't exist forever. And to believe that it will, is imprudence. Don't fall prey to that. Pageantry is fun and if you succeed at it, it will take you places in life, no doubt about that. But it is not and will never be a wholesome career path. You can participate in pageants till you're about twenty-seven, but then when you turn twenty-eight, what happens?

What next?

That is a very important question to ask yourself. What next? There will come a day when you will be done with pageants and you will need something more. Me? I have my writing, film-making and acting to fall back on. Have you figured out what you have? Because if you haven't, drop this book at once and think about it. Once you know the answer, then and only then are you ready to pick this book up again and to participate in pageants. Even beauty queens need jobs and university degrees! You would do best to take care of that first.

It is not about having a plan B. It is not even about having a backup. There are no backups in life; there are only options. Pageantry is a tactical career move. Let's keep it at that.

But it is a career move that can provide you with a lot of standing if used right. It is not the be-all and end-all of your career, any more than a scholarship might be. What pageantry does is that it gives a platform. And that platform can be very useful indeed, if you use it right. Use that platform to launch yourself. Use that platform to put yourself in a higher position, whatever your chosen career may be. Some examples of how you can use that platform? Well, there is Irene Saez who won Miss Universe 1981. She later ran for the Venzuelan presidential elections in 1998 (which she lost to Hugo Chavez, but that's another story). Then there is Shandi Finnesey who won Miss USA 2004 and went on to become an award-winning children's writer. There is Sarah Palin (yes, Sarah Palin) who won Miss Wasilla in 1984 and later went on to become the youngest governer of Alaska in 2006, which is quite an accomplishment regardless of what you or I might think of her. Closer to home, we have Aishwarya Rai Bachchan, Priyanka Chopra, and also Smriti Irani, Union Cabinet Minister for Textiles and Woman and Child Development, Government of India, who was a finalist in Miss India 1998. That's quite a list.

Winning a beauty pageant will not launch you to the moon. Nothing can ever do that, except you. But like many other things, it will give a platform (there's that word again) for you to launch yourself to the moon. It won't make you shine. But it will help you make yourself shine. It will raise you, but it won't take you to the very heights. It will propel you to those very heights. You just have to be smart about it.

The History of Beauty Pageants

Contrary to popular belief, pageants are by no means a modern invention. Like democracy and the Olympics, the first time beauty pageants were held (as far as written history tells us) was during the reign of the ancient Greek Civilization. The first ever recorded mention of pageants is in Homer's *Iliad*, during which, prizes were given out to the 'fairest'. According to mythology, it is a beauty pageant that caused the Trojan War.

Looks like times haven't changed at all! Even today, beauty pageants and international politics are often intermingled, although they haven't yet caused a war, thank god! Take for example Miss World 1968, during which Miss Spain chose to withdraw from the pageant saying she wouldn't participate alongside 'that girl from Gibraltar'. She further accused Miss Gibraltar of making unacceptable political statements about the territorial status of the Rock of Gibraltar (the Spanish government, at the time, did not recognise Gibraltar as a separate nation).

The first ever recorded mention of pageants is in Homer's Iliad, *during which, prizes were given out to the 'fairest'. According to mythology, it is a beauty pageant that caused the Trojan War.*

Countering that, Miss Universe 1969 saw two contestants try to make amends for the way their countries had been treating each other. Miss Tunisia (a Muslim) and Miss Israel (a Jew) professed their desire to be roommates for the duration of the pageant saying, 'Perhaps if two individuals can be happy together, two countries could be happy together.'

Miss Universe 1969 saw two contestants try to make amends for the way their countries had been treating each other. Miss Tunisia (a Muslim) and Miss Israel (a Jew) professed their desire to be roommates for the duration of the pageant saying, 'Perhaps if two individuals can be happy together, two countries could be happy together.'

Of course, those outside the pageant are no less averse to trying to cause war either. Remember 1996? I'd be surprised if you don't. That was the year Miss World was held in Bangalore, India. While women inside were preparing for what might be the biggest step of their careers, women outside were threatening to burn themselves to death. Oh don't get me wrong, it wasn't just women. Men were involved too. For once, we were united. But why on earth, you ask? Well, their answer was: to defend a 5,000-year-old culture that pitted apsaras such as Rambha, Tilottama and a few others against each other—until Urvashi was ultimately declared the winner, against a modern culture that pitted Rani Jeyraj, Ana Cepinska and eighty-eight others against each other until Irene Skliva (Miss World 1996) was ultimately declared the winner. Yes, that logic is confusing, but then, we live in a confusing world.

So, as you can see, beauty pageants and politics have always influenced each other.

We've diverted from the topic of the chapter. Let's get back to the point.

The Judgement of Paris

The Judgement of Paris is an ancient Greek mythological tale that describes the cause of the Trojan War. Most of us know of it after reading Homer's *Iliad*, but the tale in the *Iliad* is only a brief allusion to the myth. Fuller versions of the story are narrated in *Cypria* (a lost epic poem of ancient Greek literature of which only fragments exist today) and by later writers such as Ovid, Lucian, and Hyginus. Obviously, each version of the story differs from the other.

But the basic story goes as follows. There was a couple who were about to get married. Their names were Peleus (who was a mortal) and Thetis (who was a Nereid—a water nymph). Every single god and goddess in the Greek Pantheon was invited to this wedding, except one—Eris, the Goddess of Discord. Looking back now, can you really blame them? Who on earth would want the Goddess of Discord at their wedding? Marriages are full of discord anyway. Eris was upset that she was the only one who hadn't been invited. So, she decided to gatecrash and do what she was good at...creating discord.

When the celebrations were on in full swing, Eris snuck in and threw an apple into the midst of the crowd, upon which was the inscription:

To,
The Fairest

No one knew to whom this apple was addressed. And the question remained, who was the fairest of them all? Hera, the Goddess of Marriage, Women and Birth felt that she deserved the apple, being the fairest. Aphrodite, the Goddess of Love, Beauty and Sexuality, and Athena, the Goddess of Wisdom, Courage, Inspiration, Civilisation, Law and Justice, Just Warfare, Mathematics, Strength, Strategy, the Arts, Crafts, and Skill (yes, she was a woman with many talents) also felt the same. So they asked Zeus, the king of gods, to choose the 'fairest' out of them. Now,

Zeus was in a fix. Hera, after all, was his wife and was known for her jealous nature. Therefore, he felt that it would be best if he simply delegated this task to someone else, and let that person take the flak. That is how Paris, a Trojan prince, came to be the judge of the first ever beauty pageant to be held on… well, probably not on earth, since the gods live in their own heavenly abode. This 'beauty pageant', as we put it, came to be known as 'The Judgement of Paris'.

That [The Judgement of Paris] was the first ever beauty pageant to be held, complete with beautiful women, jealousy, rivalry, corruption and to top it all… a war! After that, no beauty pageant has ever matched that dimension of consequences.

Hera, Aphrodite and Athena were all equally eager to win the title of 'The Fairest'. So they bribed Paris. Hera offered to make him the king of Europe and Asia. Athena offered him infinite wisdom and skill in warfare. And the last, Aphrodite, offered him the most beautiful woman on earth: Helen, the queen of Sparta. This turned out to be a tough task for Paris. He no longer had to judge who was the most beautiful; instead, he had to judge which gift appealed to him the most. At length, he decided that the 'gift' (read as bribe) he most wanted was Helen of Sparta. So he crowned Aphrodite as 'The Fairest'. But that wasn't the end of the story. Aphrodite had forgotten to mention one tiny detail in her eagerness to win the title. Helen, Queen of Sparta, happened to be married! Her husband was Menelaus, the king of Sparta. But the way Paris saw it, Helen was rightfully his. He had won her fair and square. So, he decided to kidnap Helen in order to make her his own. And, well, the rest is history, err… mythology! Menelaus wasn't happy to have his wife kidnapped obviously, so he sent an army after Paris, and that's how the Trojan War officially started.

That was the first ever beauty pageant to be held, complete with beautiful women, jealousy, rivalry, corruption and to top it all… a war! After that, no beauty pageant has ever matched that dimension of consequences.

May Kings and Queens

And then came the May Kings and Queens. Crowning May Kings and Queens during the May festival is a tradition that dates back to the High Middle Ages, during which, May queens were also known as Summer Queens. In fact, legend has it that when Henry VIII was courting Mary Boleyn, sister of English queen Anne Boleyn, he crowned her 'Queen of the May'. Whether or not this is true is a matter of speculation. The crowning of the May Queen and the May King is a tradition that has been kept alive for centuries, and exists even today in many societies and communities in England.

It is popularly believed that the crowning of the May Queen was originally a heathen tradition which was later adopted by the Roman Catholic Church. Even today, in a practice that is widely reminiscent of modern beauty pageants, May Queens are selected from among young, unmarried girls. They wear white, in order to symbolise purity that is not only their own, but also of Mother Mary.

May Queen from the 1910s

Not much is known about the crowning of the May King. The lack of information on its origins and its symbolic importance leads us to believe that this practice may have simply developed in order to bring about a certain amount of balance. After all, every queen needs a king and every king needs a queen!

This tradition of crowning a May King and Queen is an example of community queen pageants. They are by and large natural pageants.

The Advent of Modern Beauty Pageants

Modern beauty pageants, however, are very different. Components of beauty pageants today, like the interview round, are very recent developments. Also, which beauty pageant today is complete without its swimsuit and evening gown rounds?

The point of the swimsuit round is not to induce a meat market, as many feminist critiques have interpreted.

So, how did beauty pageants develop these components which were earlier very alien to them?

Well, the swimsuit round is, really, nothing new. The point of the swimsuit round is not to induce a meat market, as many feminist critiques have interpreted. Instead, it is to appreciate and evaluate the physical beauty of a person. Behind it lies the thought that facial beauty is only a part of a person's beauty. A person is considered truly beautiful in an aesthetic manner only when she or he is beautiful from top to toe, whatever the standards of beauty are during that particular era and in that region. This is not a modern school of thought. Not at all! This is a thought that has been consistent throughout the ages, though, of course, the standards keep changing from time to time. Therefore, the swimsuit round can actually be dated back to the Judgement of Paris.

According to a few popular versions of the myth, Hera, Athena and Aphrodite undressed and presented themselves to Paris, in order to show off their flawless beauty. In one version, Zeus allowed Paris to set any conditions he wanted and therefore, he requested to see the goddesses in the nude. In other versions, the goddesses themselves chose to undress! This can be compared to the swimsuit round today.

However, this tradition was lost with the puritanical values of the Middle Ages and Victorian times. So how exactly did it make a comeback? Also, neither in Ancient Greece, nor in the Middle Ages were the contestants required to prove their talent or intelligence. Their only requirement was beauty—physical beauty. So how did pageants evolve into the multifaceted and terribly complicated things that they are today, complete with not just a swimsuit and evening gown round, but also an interview round and talent round (not to mention Miss World's responsibilities towards the 'Beauty With a Purpose' non-profit organisation)? For this we need to look at the last 150 years of pageantry.

Miss United States 1880

P.T. Barnum was an American showman. Today he is considered the father of modern beauty pageants. Quite ironic when you think of the fact that this was a guy who rose to fame with something called the 'Museum of Freaks' where he would showcase Siamese twins, dwarfs and simple plain hoaxes for a small fee.

This guy hosted the first ever beauty pageant in the modern sense in 1854. However, it turned out to be just a one-off event. Reflecting the conservative values of the day, this pageant was soon shut down due to a series of public protests. Barnum continued hosting pageants for babies and even dogs, but he never tried to host a beauty pageant for women again.

According to Elissa Stein, author of *Here She Comes... Beauty Queen*, in 1880, a pageant called Miss United States was conducted at Rohoboth Beach, Delaware, almost three decades after Barnum's unsuccessful beauty pageant. While it might not be the very first pageant, it was definitely the first ever beauty pageant to be held at a national level. The mission of Miss United States was also very similar to the missions of most commercial beauty pageants today. The judges were looking for 'the most beautiful unmarried woman in our nation'. The pageant lasted a week and the women were judged upon, in Stein's words, 'face, figure, hands, feet, hair, grace and costume.' With the possible exception of hands and feet, these are more or less the components of judging even today.

Margaret Gorman, the winner of the first Miss America pageant in 1921.

You might be surprised to know that this pageant was judged by none other than Thomas A. Edison. Yep, the same guy who invented the light bulb.

Miss America

But then there was a long break again. It was 1921 when pageantry was revived in Atlantic City in the form of Miss America. The first crown was won by sixteen-year-old Margaret Gorman from Washington, D.C. She competed along with eleven other finalists, who had been selected from over a thousand applicants. Her prize as a winner was a trip to the Second Annual Atlantic City Pageant as a guest. Compare that to prizes offered to beauty queens today!

The pageant was actually not supposed to be called Miss America. That title was not part of the agenda at all. In fact, this longest-running pageant in the world was meant to be a one-off promotional gimmick staged by Atlantic City hotel owners in order to induce tourists to stay past Labor Day. But it was a phenomenal success, I guess, so they decided to make it an annual thing. The mission was to select 'the most beautiful bathing beauty in America'. But, when the pageant had taken place and the winner had been chosen, a local reporter called Herb Test gave Gorman the title of Miss America. From then on, the pageant has been called Miss America pageant, although for many years, it continued to be officially recorded as 'The National Beauty Tournament'.

It is actually interesting to note that by 1929, the Miss America pageant was considered a crucial part of American culture. During World War II, pageant officials considered discontinuing the pageant for the duration of the war. But the motion was rejected on account of the belief that Miss America strengthened the nation and gave it hope. It was a source of strength, not weakness.

Today, Miss America is known as a 'scholarship pageant'. But it was never originally that. This change was instated in 1945, by the then director of Miss America, Lenora Slaughter. I used to assume that this was to legitimise the idea of beauty pageants both in the eyes of conservatives and feminists. The interview round, after all, was the result of trying to appease feminists who seemed to balk at the idea of the appreciation of female beauty (although pageantry, technically means both male and female pageants). But it does not seem to be so. Slaughter (despite her unfortunate surname) genuinely seemed interested in awarding the winners with something that would help them build a life for themselves. But as she approached various sponsors and businessmen, she found that no one was interested in awarding a scholarship to women just because they were women. Yet, undeterred by the lack of enthusiasm on the part of sponsors,

Bess Myerson, Miss America 1945

she managed to raise a $5,000 scholarship for the winner. Bess Myerson, Miss New York 1945 and later Miss America 1945, became the first to win this award.

Yolande Betbeze, Miss America 1951

Miss America had been one of the most popular pageants so far, but something happened in 1951 that changed the entire history of pageants. In fact, if this hadn't happened, we would probably never have had Miss Universe. In 1951, the reigning Miss America, Yolande Betbeze refused to pose in a swimsuit. She insisted that she was an opera singer, not a pin-up and should be treated as such. Fair enough. But the problem was that a lot of money for the pageant came from a swimsuit company called Catalina. And they were offended. So offended in fact that they parted ways with the Miss America Pageant and started a pageant of their own, a pageant that we know today as Miss Universe.

International Pageant of Pulchritude, 1926-1935

But Miss Universe doesn't really begin there. In a way, it began much earlier with the International Pageant of Pulchritude. The International Pageant of Pulchritude (IPP), which was popularly dubbed by the local media as Miss Universe or the International Beauty Contest, was first held in 1926. Although pageants had been held at a local and national level until then, this was the first time a pageant was

During World War II, pageant officials considered discontinuing the pageant for the duration of the war. But the motion was rejected on account of the belief that Miss America strengthened the nation and gave it hope. It was a source of strength, not weakness.

held at an international level, with participants from across the border. Twenty-two-year-old Catherine Moylan from Dallas, USA, won the first crown, thus becoming the first person to be awarded the title of Miss Universe. After being crowned, she did two movies under the MGM banner. We know that she passed away in 1969, and somewhere down the line, she changed her last name to Singleton (probably because she got married) and she used to perform at the Zeigfeld Follies before winning the Miss Universe crown. But that is about all we know about her. The rest of her life remains a mystery.

Although technically, this Miss Universe is an international pageant, it wasn't what comes to mind today when we talk of the same. Today, international pageants have participants from some fifty to sixty odd countries. And more importantly, each country sends only one representative. But it didn't begin like that. The first annual International Pageant of Pulchritude had thirty-nine contestants. But only two of them were from outside the USA. They were Miss Mexico and Miss Winnipeg (from Canada). That means there were thirty-seven Misses USA, and among them were eight Misses Dallas. But the practice of calling a contestant, or delegate, as is the preferred term today, by the name of the region they represent is a fairly new practice. Those girls weren't representing anything or anyone apart from themselves. International pageantry hadn't yet taken on the form that it has today.

Lisl Goldarbeiter, Miss Universe 1929

However, the most popular title-holder from the IPP remains Lisl Goldarbeiter, Miss Universe 1929.

Hers is a true rags to riches story. Lisl Goldarbeiter was born in 1909 in Vienna to an average middle-class family. She grew up in modest circumstances. In 1929, at the age of twenty, she participated and won the Miss Austria pageant, beating 600 other contenders. From Miss Austria, she went on to participate in Miss Europe, as a representative of her country, where she was awarded the first runner-up position. The crown went to Boske Simon, Miss Hungary.

Having made a mark at Miss Europe, Lisl took the next step forward—Miss Universe. The pageant, which was supposed to be the most competitive in the world, proved to be a cakewalk for her as she walked away with the coveted Miss Universe (International Pageant of Pulchritude) title. As part of the prize offered to her, she received $2,000 in gold and a large silver plaque. But the best wasn't over yet. As the first 'foreigner' to win the Miss Universe title (in fact, many believe that she was the first to be called by the title of Miss Universe, and in effect, was the first ever Miss Universe), she was rocketed overnight into worldwide fame. She started receiving offers from Hollywood. She was even offered a theatrical contract worth $15,000 entailing her appearance in a tight bathing suit four times daily, to which she allegedly replied, 'Papa must decide.'

As Miss Universe, she travelled all around the world. She is said to have rejected numerous suitors—this was the 1920s. Beauty queen or not, getting married was often the only career deemed suitable for girls—before finally marrying Fritz Speilmann, an heir to a company that manufactured silk neckties. After having been all around the world, she finally settled down in Vienna, her home town, to a life of ease and luxury. Or so she thought.

The problem was that Lisl and her husband were Jews—Jews who lived in Austria around the same time that Hitler was making his presence felt. Needless to say, Lisl's fairy tale did not really have a happy ending. She and her husband lost everything they had in the war. We don't know what happened to her husband, or to her children, if she had any that is. All those details are lost among many others in the blur of World War II. The only information we have is from 1950 onwards, which is when she finally found a home for herself in Budapest where she lived until her death in 1997. She had lived till the ripe old age of eighty-eight, and what a life she lived!

Her cousin, Mark Tenczer, faithfully recorded as much of her life as he could on film. The material he had accumulated over the years was finally turned into a documentary in 2006 by director Peter Forgacs. The documentary was titled 'Miss Universe 1929 – Lisl Goldarbeiter: A Queen in Wein'.

Till date, she has been the only Austrian to ever win the Miss Universe crown.

1931 onwards, the International Pageant of Pulchritude ceased to be held in Galveston, Texas, because of the Great Depression. The American markets crashed, and overnight, unemployment, inflation, etc., skyrocketed. The economy was in tatters. So the IPP was then held in Belgium until 1935. However, this did not last long, and the pageant was discontinued from 1935. Although another pageant with the name 'Miss Universe' started in 1952, it had no direct relation to the International Pageant of Pulchritude, i.e., Miss Universe.

Armi Kuusela, Miss Universe 1953

Miss Universe

Remember Yolande Betbeze? Miss America 1951? The one who refused to pose in swimwear and retorted, 'I'm an opera singer, not a pin-up!' Well, if it hadn't been for her, Miss Universe might never have existed!

However validated her reaction might have been, the manufacturers of Catalina Swimwear, Pacific Knitting Mills, were offended and decided to withdraw from Miss America. They decided to set up their own pageants, the results of which were Miss USA and Miss Universe. The first edition of Miss Universe was held at Long Beach, California, on 28 June 1952. Thirty contestants from thirty countries vied for the crown. The coveted crown went to eighteen-year-old Armi Kuusela, Miss Finland. She was crowned by actress Piper Laurie and was awarded a box of chocolates, a gold bangle and a two-way Pan American Airways ticket to and from the USA. She was crowned in her swimsuit, as was the practice until 1960, when Linda Bement became the first Miss Universe to be crowned in an evening gown. Miss World, however, continued crowning their winners in swimsuits till 1976.

Armi Kuusela, Miss Universe 1953

The first woman to win Miss Universe never got to complete her term. She gave up her title, although not officially, to get married, while she still had a few months left to complete her year.

One very interesting thing to notice was that like Miss America, Miss Universe too was post-dated. By this measure, Armi Kuusela was not Miss Universe 1952, but Miss Universe 1953. This practice continued until 1958.

The first woman to win Miss Universe never got to complete her term. She gave up her title, although not officially, to get married, while she still had a few months left to complete her year.

Miss World

Miss World is the oldest surviving international beauty pageant today. It started in 1951, and is nearly seventy years old now. Today, one of the most notable facets of Miss World is its Beauty with a Purpose award.

Beauty with a Purpose, formerly known as the Miss World Scholarship, was instated in 2001 and was won by Piarella Peralta, Miss Costa Rica. With the Beauty with a Purpose award, Miss World has reinvented itself into one of the most wholesome beauty pageants that exist today.

But did you know that Miss World actually started out as a bikini festival? Quite ironic when you realise that just a few years ago, in 2014, they did away with the swimsuit round on grounds of it objectifying women.

It was 1951. Bikinis had just been designed a few years ago. Unable to find a model to wear it, designer Louis Réard finally got Micheline Benardini, a nude dancer from Casino de Paris to model it for him. Understandably, bikinis had already acquired quite a questionable reputation in the short while since their first appearance. In fact, Italy, Spain and Portugal went as far as to actually ban the bikini (and today we're trying to ban the Burkini!). It was under such circumstances that Eric Morley's Festival Bikini Contest was held.

The Festival Bikini Contest was held during the Festival of Britain, on 29 July 1951, as a mid-century advertisement for swimwear. It was not meant to be annual. It, like Miss America, was meant to be just a one-off event. Also, like both Miss America and Miss Universe (the International Pageant of Pulchritude), the title 'Miss World' was given to the winner, not by the pageant itself, but by the media. But encouraged by the national media and by the fact that US-based Catalina Swimwear were planning to start their own international pageant called Miss Universe, founder Eric Morley registered a trademark for the title and decided to hold it annually.

The first edition of Miss World in 1951 housed twenty-six contestants, which included twenty-one from Britain and five from other countries such as Denmark, France, Holland, Sweden and the USA. The winner was Kiki Hakansson from Sweden.

Kiki Hakansson, Miss World 1951

Till date, Kiki Hakansson remains the only Miss World to be crowned in a bikini. It was a crowning that drew angry protests from feminists and a condemnation from the Pope (funny how liberals and conservatives always seem to protest over the same things). The next year, Morley decided to tone it down and the contestants made their appearance in modes maillot swimwear. However, it wasn't until 1976 that winners started to be crowned in evening gowns. Till then, you got crowned in your swimsuit—a one-piece, not a bikini though—that was still too 'immodest' for the times. During the 1960s and 1970s, Miss World was rated as one of the most watched TV programe in the United Kingdom.

Till date, Kiki Hakansson remains the only Miss World to be crowned in a bikini. It was a crowning that drew angry protests from feminists and a condemnation from the Pope.

Miss India

Miss India is a title that is as old as, if not older than, the Miss Universe title (new). However, there is quite a bit of confusion concerning the first Miss India as at least two names have floated before India even started officially holding the Miss India national pageant. The first name is of Esther Victoria Abraham, also known as Pramila, who comes across in some old tabloids as Miss India 1947. Whether she was really crowned or not is a matter of folklore. As it happens, Pramila later went on to be a very successful actress. In fact, it is said that Mr. D.M. Madhok wrote the lyrics of 'Choli ke Andar' for her years before Madhuri Dixit was even born. Pramila, aka Esther Victoria Abraham, was not just a beauty queen and actress; she was also one of the first successful female film producers in India. She produced her own films under the banner, Silver Productions.

Interestingly, in 1952, when she (Indrani Rehman) participated in Miss Universe, she was already married and had a child.

Now, that is an interesting story and Pramila was certainly someone who any woman would look up to. But as of now, claims of her having been crowned Miss India are, to say the least, a teeny bit unreliable, considering the fact that there are no records of a Miss India pageant being held in those days (the Miss India pageant was formally held from 1959 onwards, the winner of which was Fleur Ezekiel), and nor were there any international pageants in which she participated that would document the existence of a Miss India.

It is widely accepted today that the first woman to be conferred with the Miss India title was Indrani Rehman. Now, Indrani never won a national pageant either. She was never crowned Miss India. But she was the first Indian woman to take part in Miss Universe, thus becoming a de facto Miss India. Today, she is known as a highly acclaimed classical dancer of Bharatanatyam, Kuchipudi, Odissi and Kathakali. She played a huge role in popularising these dance forms outside India. In 1969, she received the Padma Shri award from the Indian government. Later in life, she settled down in New York until her death in 1999. She was sixty-eight years old then.

Interestingly, in 1952 when she participated in Miss Universe, she was already married and had a child. Obviously, Miss Universe's rule about letting only unmarried girls participate didn't exist back then, or if it did, wasn't as stringent as it is now, since Indrani Rehman is still officially on the list of delegates.

After Indrani Rehman's participation in Miss Universe in 1952, there was a gap of seven years before India started sending delgates to international pageants again. In 1959, a women's magazine called *Eve's Weekly* took it upon itself to choose a Miss India to represent the country at Miss World. The first woman to receive this honour was Fleur Ezekiel, an Indian model of Jewish ancestry, descending from a Bene Israel family.

In 1964, a rival magazine, *Femina*, started conducting a pageant of its own to send Indian delegates to the Miss Universe pageant. The first girl to have conferred upon her the title of Femina Miss India was Meher Castelino Mistry. However, as noted earlier, she was not the first Indian delegate to Miss Universe. That was Indrani Rehman. Later, towards the end of the decade, *Femina* gained the franchises to both Miss World and Miss Asia Pacific, thus acquiring a monopoly in the Indian pageant industry until 2010.

The next year, in 2011, it looked like things were going to be shaken up quite a bit. *Femina* had decided that from then on, they would send the winner to Miss World and the first runner-up to Miss Universe. Till then, it had been the other way round. Obviously Miss Universe Organization wasn't going to like that. (An interesting point to note: Miss Universe still belonged to Donald Trump at that point.) So they withdrew their franchise from Femina. And who did it go to? None other than the first Indian woman to be crowned Miss Universe—Sushmita Sen. After decades, it looked like the pageant industry in India was going to go through dramatic change. But it didn't last. In 2014,

Femina created a separate pageant for Miss Universe contendors called Miss Diva and the franchise came back to them again.

India has been a former powerhouse, especially in the nineties. India currently holds five Miss World crowns, two Miss Universe crowns, three Miss Asia Pacific crowns and one Miss Earth crown. At Miss Universe, in the fifteen years from 1990 to 2005, India has placed thirteen times, including two crowns and four Top Five placements. At Miss World, in the twenty years from 1990 to 2010, India has placed twelve times, including four crowns (all in one decade) and three Top Five placements.

What is a beauty pageant?

A beauty pageant is a contest where the contestants are judged on the basis of their physical beauty.

Right?

Well, right and wrong!

How, you ask? The thing about beauty pageants is that every contestant there is strikingly beautiful. For a judge to select one woman from a group of around ninety equally beautiful women has to be one hell of a decision, right?

On top of that there is no ideal model of beauty. As they say, beauty lies in the eyes of the beholder. Whom one might consider beautiful may not be as beautiful to another, as can be seen from the diverse notions of beauty from across cultures:

- Until the early 20th century, Chinese women folded their feet into half, crushing their bones, thus binding them to make them smaller. This was done because tiny feet were considered to be the essence of beauty.
- Spray tans are the norm in most western societies, but in the Middle East and Southeast Asia, pale skin is treasured.
- You might be aware that a growing number of models and adolescents suffer from bulimia and anorexia these days. Skinny figures are their idea of beauty, but in parts

of western Africa, you must be pleasantly plump to be beautiful.
- While in most parts of Europe a natural look is considered the most beautiful, men and women of the Māori tribe in New Zealand enhance their looks with spiral facial markings called the Ta Moko.
- Women of the Kaya tribe, an ethnic group from Burma, wrap brass coils around their neck in order to elongate them. The first brass coils are introduced when a girl attains puberty and further more are added as the girl gets older.

Do these measures of beauty match up to what you—or I—think is beautiful? Probably not.

So this is where our question arises—if beauty and its parameters are so diverse, how can a pageant claim to be fair when it picks out one woman from ninety?

This is where the judging system comes into play. Now, each pageant has its own unique judging system but the basic parameters are as follows:

- Beauty
- Fitness
- Intelligence
- Grace and poise
- And most importantly, confidence.

Like the judging system, each pageant has its own structure, but the rounds that you'll most commonly encounter are:

- National costume (only in international pageants)
- Interview
- Swimsuit
- Evening gown
- Talent (but not all pageants have this as part of the judging criteria)

Scores are given in each round, but how the scores are tallied and the final hierarchy of winners is something that differs from pageant to pageant. Usually, after the final three or the final five are chosen, all scores from the previous rounds are erased and the judges are asked to cast their votes for the contestant they feel should be the winner, the first runner-up and the second runner-up respectively, on the basis of this last round only. Depending on the particular pageant at hand, the number of runners-up usually varies from two to four. There is no fixed number. Pageants change this quite arbitrarily, in fact. In the last two decades, for example, Miss Universe has gone from having four runners-up to two runners-up and back to four runners-up quite a few times.

Types of Beauty Pageants

Most commonly, all beauty pageants tend to fall under one of the two following categories:

- Commercial beauty pageants
- Community beauty/queen pageants

Since you are reading this book, you are probably more interested in commercial beauty pageants than in community beauty/queen pageants. Even so, it is important to have a basic knowledge of what pageants are all about, how they work and their characteristics.

All four of the Grand Slam Pageants—Miss Universe, Miss World, Miss International and Miss Earth—are examples of commercial beauty pageants.

Commercial Beauty Pageants

When a person talks about a beauty pageant, usually it is a commercial beauty pageant that they are referring to. In fact, all four of the Grand Slam Pageants—Miss Universe, Miss World, Miss International and Miss Earth—are examples of commercial beauty pageants.

They are, as implied, commercial in nature. The pageant director's goal is to avail a brand ambassador or a spokesperson for the company. For instance, the reigning Miss Universe automatically becomes the spokesperson and ambassador of the Miss Universe Organization, which is a charitable entity. On an average, they tend to be more glamorous than community beauty queen pageants.

Commercial beauty pageants can be divided into five different types:

1. **Glitz Pageants:** As the name suggests, these pageants are very glamorous and glitzy. These are the pageants where anything works. Wigs, veneers, coloured contact lenses, you name it ... actually these are not only allowed, but—expected. The walk might be more stylised than usual and the facial expressions might be exaggerated. Oral communication skills are usually very limited in glitz pageants. The focus is mainly on the drama. Invariably, these pageants are the most expensive. In the words of Rhonda Shappard, a pageant expert, 'The glitz pageant is all about creating an illusion.' An example would be Queen USA. You might not be able to take part in it, but do check it out!
2. **Natural Pageants:** These pageants are the absolute antithesis of the glitz pageant. Natural pageants focus on the natural beauty of the contestant. Unlike the glitz pageant, artificial enhancements of beauty and exaggerated make-up are frowned upon. In fact, in many natural pageants, such additions are banned outright. In order to succeed in a natural pageant, it is important for the contestant to be able to communicate well. They don't seem to be very popular among adults lately, but children's pageants worldwide are increasingly turning natural. An example would be Face of the Globe, which is held in Disneyland every year.
3. **Semi-Glitz Pageants:** Most commercial pageants such as Miss Universe or Miss World fall under this category.

Semi-glitz pageants strive to strike a balance between natural and glitz pageants. The make-up and hair isn't quite as elaborate and the walk is stylised just enough to be graceful, and nothing more. Oral communication skills are usually imperative for the contestant.

4. **Face Pageants:** It is widely debated as to whether or not face pageants are a legitimate type of pageantry. In a face pageant, the judges are usually interested only in the contestant's face. The personality and figure may or may not be judged. The walk is almost never judged at all. A face pageant may be glitz, semi-glitz or natural.
5. **Scholastic Pageants:** These usually require the contestant to work on a cause that she or he believes in. The focus here shifts from the glamour to the personality and intelligence of the contestant. The winner gets a scholarship or grant to either a university or vocational institute to pursue their higher studies. An example that might surprise you here is Miss America, or even Miss Universe! Yep, they offer scholarships to their winners.

However, these categories are formed purely to differentiate one from the other. Most pageants overlap and hybridise between a number of categories. For example, Miss Universe and Miss World, which can both be classified as semi-glitz pageants, can also come under scholastic pageants (Miss Universe) and natural pageants (Miss World).

Community Queen Pageants

Apart from commercial beauty pageants, there are numerous other pageants conducted all over the world. A pageant winner is, first and foremost, the spokesperson and brand ambassador for the firm that owns or sponsors the pageant. Community queen pageants operate in a similar fashion, except that the spokesperson they look for is not for the firm or a company, but for the community itself. Now this is not necessarily a pageant like Miss Chandigarh. A Miss Chandigarh or a Miss Wisconsin is merely a smaller franchise of a larger commercial pageant (like Miss India or Miss America). But community pageants are traditions, usually part of a bigger festival. Imagine, for example, a kanya puja during Navaratri. Now apart from all that halwa, puri and chana they load you with, imagine they chose one of you to represent the festival and gave you a little tiara. That would be a community pageant. Though not very popular in India, these are quite popular in most western countries, and are part of a long-standing tradition.

Community queen pageants tend to be a little more conservative in nature. This means, there is no swimsuit round. This comes as a surprise to most Indians, our perception of the West being what it is. However, community festivals are just as revered over there as a Durga Puja would be revered over here. So, in most places in the world, that environment would not be very conducive to something like a swimsuit round. Also, the judging criteria are never as strict as in commercial beauty pageants. So, if you've got a few extra pounds around your waist, or your walk does not exactly fit the mould for Paris Fashion Week, that's okay! They're not looking for that. They are looking for a person to represent their community—and not just a fashion model (in fact, this point applies even to commercial beauty pageants, though to a slightly smaller extent). Therefore, it is important that you relate to the community and recognise their values and morals, because that is what you will be judged upon. Yes, an angelic face does help, but an amiable personality is much more important in these pageants. In fact, studies conducted by ethnographers like Colleen Ballerino Cohen, Richard Wilk and Beverly Stoeltje on the Minnesota Community Queen Pageant show that girls who were extroverts and possessed an 'outgoing, gregarious personality' were more likely to win than their introvert competitors.

However, the real difference between community queen pageants and commercial beauty pageants are the rituals and traditions involved. Most community queen pageants take place during some festival or the other. For example, the above mentioned Minnesota community queen pageant is held during the Summer Festival while the Queen of the Patios Pageant held in Andalusia is conducted during a festival known as Feria, every year around May.

A community queen is usually also required to demonstrate her ties and closeness to her community by taking part in a popular local tradition. Take, for example, the Snake Charmer Queen Pageant held in Texas. The winner of this pageant, the queen, after her coronation is required to go to a round-up where a few rattlesnakes are placed in a pit. Here, she must 'milk' a rattlesnake, i.e., extract its venom to prove herself worthy of the title that has been bestowed upon her.

In 2017... a thirty-one-year-old man named Darshan Mandhana was crowned Mr. Gay India, which marked the end of a six-year-long journey for him trying to gain acceptance just from his family.

Community pageants are not very common in India. Pageants themselves are a recent import. But increasingly, both in India and abroad, we can see more instances of pageants being held for oppressed communities in order to gain acceptance for them in society. This social side to the entire thing is a very recent development in the history of community pageants (and I count them as community pageants since they don't exactly exist to make money but simply to take their cause further). These are pageants that have more than just a crown at stake. In 2017, for example, a thirty-one-year-old man named Darshan Mandhana was crowned Mr. Gay India, which marked the end of a six-year-long journey for him trying to gain acceptance just from his family. Also in 2017, a Manipuri actor, Bishesh Huirem, became the first ever Indian to participate in Miss International Queen, a pageant aimed towards the upliftment of the LGBTQ community.

It is also interesting to note that most community queen pageants are a form of the natural pageant. The emphasis on glamour here is minimal or non-existent. This shows the overlapping nature of pageants. A pageant is never of just one type. The most important thing to understand about pageants and its contestants is that there are no hard and fast rules. They try to make it neutral, they try to make it the same all across the world, but when it boils down to actually picking a winner, subjectivity rules. It's not maths. Two plus two need not equal four. It could be five, it could be six, it could be twenty and you might still be right.

Beauty

Pageants largely judge their contestants in terms of beauty, and beauty is subjective and provincial. But that is only one side of the coin. The other side of the coin is that beauty can be objective. Beauty, to an extent, can be measured and evaluated in a scientific manner. That brings us to the question: what exactly is this thing called beauty?

What is Beauty?

Beauty is in the eyes of the beholder.

—Plato

Ok... so Plato didn't say exactly that. He said something more along the lines of: 'Remember how in that communion only, beholding beauty with the eye of the mind, he will be enabled to bring forth, not images of beauty, but realities (for he has hold not of an image but of a reality), and bringing forth and nourishing true virtue to become the friend of god and be immortal, if mortal man may.'

And over the centuries, we managed to paraphrase it into eight simple words. It might not be what he said but you get the gist.

We've grown up thinking beauty lies in the eyes of the beholder: how many times have we disagreed and argued with a friend about whether Tom Cruise is better looking or Brad Pitt. How many times have we remarked that Kareena Kapoor looked too skinny to be beautiful in *Tashan* only to have the person sitting across the table launch into a tirade of how she had never looked better?

Certain aspects of beauty are universal. Symmetry, for example.

But still, there are certain aspects of beauty that are universal. Symmetry, for example. A symmetrical face is much more likely to be voted as attractive than an unsymmetrical face is. Seriously. Historically speaking, female beauty can be described as a measure of how fertile a woman is. There are many aspects of our body that reflect how fertile we are, or how healthy we are as women—for example, the waist to hip ratio or the radiance of your skin. These are the scales we use to innately evaluate a person's beauty. We use similar scales to evaluate the beauty of men too. Now, no judge is going to consciously judge regarding these parameters anywhere in the world. This is just to explain to you how we humans are wired to see beauty. Obviously, your judges are humans too (unless you're time-travelling from 52 AD, which I presume you're not) and such unconscious parameters would affect how they see beauty. It is always useful to break down something into smaller bits that we can understand and thus analyse and use to our benefit. Once you understand how beauty works in the human psyche, you will be able to enhance yourself more productively than simply following the latest trends.

The Golden Ratio

The Golden Ratio, also known as the divine proportion, is what many mathematicians believe to be that which determines the beauty of an object, whether it is a tree, a marvelous piece of architecture or even human beauty. To put it simply, the Golden Ratio is a mathematical expression that dictates the ratio things should be in, in nature and otherwise, to be considered aesthetically beautiful. It says that for anything, to be considered aesthetically beautiful, should be in the ratio of 1:1.618.

Now what that means is that the parts of the human body should ideally be in the ratio of 1:1.618. For example, if the distance from the tip of your fingers of one hand to your other shoulder (not the one adjoining that arm) is 1 m, then your height should ideally be 1.618 m. If the distance from the top of your head to your navel is 1 m, the distance from your navel to your feet should be 1.618 m. If the length of your palm is 10 cm, then the distance from your wrist to your elbow should ideally be 16.18 cm. The whole human body is divided into ratios like the above. And the more accurately it follows this ratio, the more aesthetically beautiful we perceive it as.

I'm not going to bore you any further with the maths of it, but the Golden Ratio is not even a modern concept. It has fascinated intellectuals, not just mathematicians, for at least 2400 years, from Pythagoras to Euclid to Da Vinci.

But how does an algebraic expression, a confusing one at that, matter in a beauty pageant? Well, it matters, a lot.

As mentioned earlier, anything in nature and otherwise must accord to this ratio in order to be considered aesthetically beautiful. We humans are no different. Our bodies are made to fit this ratio. And the more accurately we fit this mould, the more attractive we are. It doesn't matter how short or tall you are, or how thin or fat, or whether you have a round face, a square face or an oval one. Do you fit this ratio? If you do, you, darling, are officially, repeat officially, beautiful. Officially, because the human mind is a weird piece of work. Although it does follow the rules most of

The Vitruvian Man by Leonardo da Vinci

the time, sometimes it begs to differ. So, you might fit the ratio like a glove fits a hand, but some people might still believe that the person standing next to you, who doesn't fit the ratio quite as accurately as you do, is more beautiful. That's okay. That's just a difference of opinion. That doesn't mean they're right. And that doesn't mean they're wrong either.

The Marquardt Mask of Beauty is basically a mask that divides the human face into tiny little sections in order to determine the concept of ideal beauty.

Marquardt Mask of Beauty

But how do you find out if your face is in fact 'scientifically' beautiful? Lucky for us, a guy called Marquardt came up with something called the Mask of Beauty. The Marquardt Mask of Beauty is basically a mask that divides the human face into tiny little sections in order to determine the concept of ideal beauty. This mask is based on, no surprise, the Golden Ratio theory. To put it simply, the face that fits this mask exactly is to be considered ideally beautiful. Now, we're humans, not robots, so logically no one face can fit the mask exactly. Then we'd all look alike, right? It is those slight variations from face to face that make us all different. So, let's not say 'exactly', let's say the face that fits the Marquardt Mask of Beauty as accurately as is possible is considered more beautiful than a face that does not fit the mask as accurately. There is even an organisation called the Marquardt Aesthetic Imaging that exists simply to research this phenomenon and understand it better. You might want to check it out actually. There are plenty of impressions of the mask placed upon different faces online

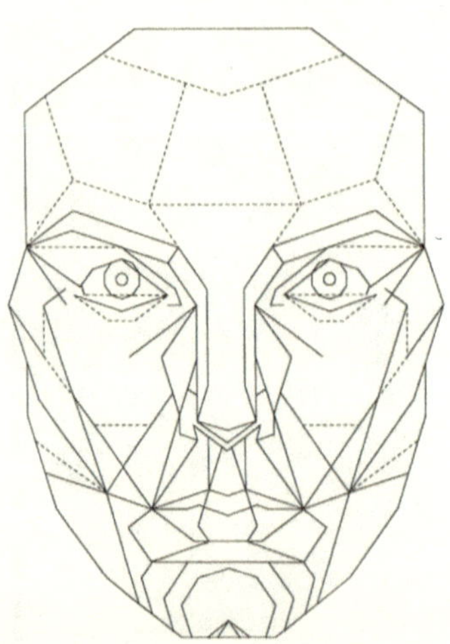

The Marquardt Mask of Beauty

This sculpture of Queen Nefertiti's face fits the Marquardt's Mask of Beauty.

Nefertiti was considered extremely beautiful in her time. (www.beautyanalysis.com)

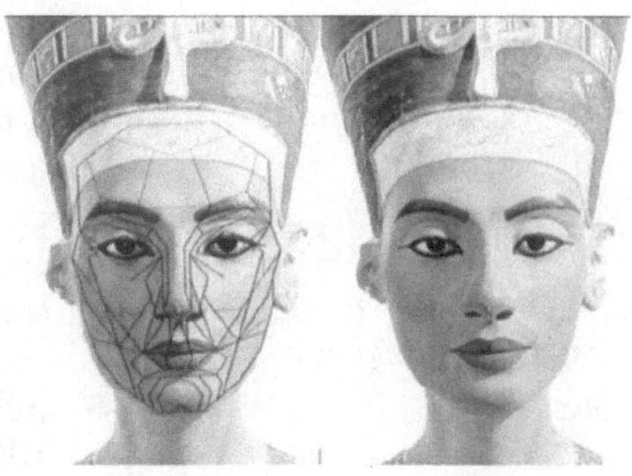
The Marquardt Mask of Beauty on Nefertiti

But this is only one side. The other side is that the Marquardt Mask of Beauty measures the symmetry of a face. The more perfectly a face fits the mask, the more symmetrical the face is.

Human beings are programmed to intuitively recognise a symmetrical face as more attractive than an asymmetrical one. That is because a symmetrical face signals to us that there is no genetic or environmental distrurbance such as disease, malnutrition or any negative genetic mutation in that person. But a symmetrical face need not be beautiful, although a beautiful face is almost always symmetrical (correlation need not always mean causation).

Waist to Hip Ratio

Our opinion on what is beautiful and what isn't has developed over thousands of years. It has developed on the basis of health. Healthy people who have a better chance of survival, are more likely to pass on their genes to the next generation. The waist to hip ratio works on the same approach.

A symmetrical face need not be beautiful, although a beautiful face is almost always symmetrical.

Tell me, who would you say has a better figure, Jennifer Lopez or Kate Moss? They are both incredibly beautiful women, no doubt, but I would probably vote for Jennifer Lopez. Throughout history, women with wider hips have been considered more beautiful than women with slim hips. Why else would corsets have been in fashion for more than three centuries? This is because a woman with wider hips is probably more fertile than the other whose hips are comparatively slimmer. This means that a woman whose hips are wider has better chances of furthering the human race. This is what has led us to appreciate what we call today the hourglass figure.

But like everything else, this hourglass figure also has an ideal, which brings us back to mathematics.

But like everything else, this hourglass figure also has an ideal, which brings us back to mathematics. Don't worry, nothing complicated this time. Just a simple plain number. 0.75, ranging from 0.6 in China to 0.9 in South America.

Fundamentally, the objective is to have your waist and hips in a ratio that is anywhere between 0.6 and 0.9. If you want to know whether you fit this ratio or not, all you need to do is measure your waist and hips, and then divide the measurement of your waist by the measurement of your hips. For example, if your waist measures 26 inches and your hips measure 36 inches, your waist to hip ratio would be 26/36 = 0.722. That's nearly perfect! But very few of us have such perfect measurements. Of course, working out helps, as does eating right. The more toned your body is, the higher the chances are of it falling into this ratio (and the range is pretty wide, so that makes sure most of us fit in). But if it still doesn't, don't fret. Anyone who is healthy and toned looks attractive.

Skin

Skin is one of the most integral parts of beauty. Whether or not you have good skin can change how you are perceived entirely. One of the first things we notice about a person is their skin—not their eyes, not their figure, but their skin, and more importantly, the skin on their face. I've mentioned earlier that there are no hard and fast rules when it comes to beauty, but this is an exception. In order to be beautiful, healthy skin is a must.

That sounds harsh, yes, but it's not really unreasonable. We might not all be able to have those perfect almond eyes, or that perfect 0.75 waist to hip ratio. Those things depend a lot on our build, and that is something we can't change, not without surgery, at least (which, for the record, I do not endorse). But clear skin? That is something most of us are born with!

Have you ever noticed a baby's skin carefully? Have you observed how soft, clear and transparent it is? Isn't it what you would call perfect skin? Wouldn't you want to have that kind of skin? I know I would. But guess what? We were all babies once. We all had that picture-perfect skin. So what went wrong? Why are we afflicted with acne and blemishes now? Why do we struggle with dry or oily skin, when the truth is that we were all born with perfect combination skin?

There are no hard and fast rules when it comes to beauty, but... in order to be beautiful, healthy skin is a must.

Well, we grew up, and made a lot of unhealthy choices on the way (e.g., fast food). Of course, some of it is stuff we don't have direct control on. We can't decide today that there will be no more pollution in the world and expect that to happen. So what do we do? How do we get that perfect baby skin back?

For the answer, we'll have to study a bit about skin, its structure and its configuration. It's biology time.

The Structure of Skin

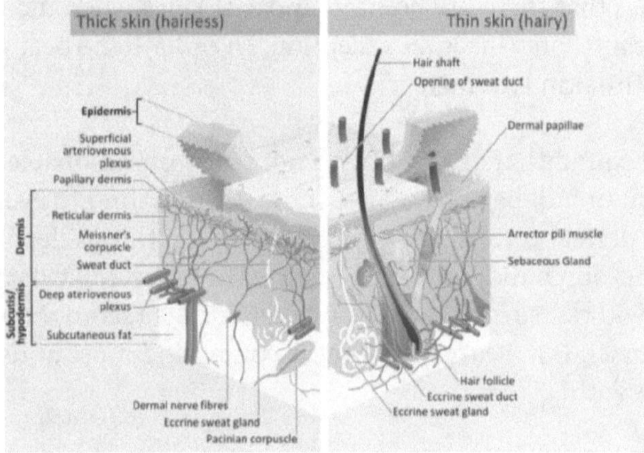

I know what you're thinking. First history, then mathematics, now biology; I need to learn how to win a pageant, not a crash course on what is increasingly looking like a pre-med course. But frankly, this is part of learning how to win a pageant. In order to look beautiful, you need to look healthy. In order to look healthy, you need to treat your body right. In order to treat your body right, you need to learn about how it functions. See where I'm going? Therefore, to look beautiful, and to have beautiful skin, it is not enough to learn about whether multani mitti (Fuller's earth) is better as a face pack or turmeric with besan (chickpea flour) and milk. It is imperative that you understand how your skin works so that you can independently take measures to protect and pamper it whenever it needs it. After all, your skin, just like you, is unique and the person who can understand it best is no one but you.

Your skin is the outer covering of your body. It has many roles. It protects us from pathogens, helps us regulate our temperature, keeps the water and lipids in our body inside our body, keeps dangerous things outside our body out of our body. It helps us synthesise Vitamin D so we don't get rickets. Hey, it even helps us feel! Imagine if you couldn't feel heat, you might have burnt yourself a thousand times over by now!

But on a day to day basis, we divide skin into four types: normal, dry, oily and combination. Now dermatologically speaking, only one type exists, and that is oily. This is because all skin is oily. What differs is the degree of oiliness. You might have skin that has a lower degree of oiliness than mine, but that doesn't mean your skin is dry. It can't be. Oil, after all, still exists in skin. But, we should aim for the degree of oiliness that, in layman terms, we call 'normal'. More on that later.

Coming back to the types of skin, dermatology acknowledges that six different types of skin exist, based on the degree of pigmentation. Recognising and understanding which skin type is yours is the first step towards good skin care. This classification especially helps to understand how our skin reacts to sun and supports us in our effort to prevent skin damage caused by the sun. Exposure to the sun is a dichotomous thing. It is important to expose skin to the sun for the synthesis of Vitamin D to take place. But it is a delicate balance. Too much and the sun can damage it extremely. In some cases, it could even lead to skin cancer.

Recognising and understanding which skin type is yours is the first step towards good skin care.

The different types of skin are:

i	Always burns, never tans	Pale, fair, freckles
ii	Usually burns, sometimes tans	Fair
iii	May burn, usually tans	Light brown
iv	Rarely burns, always tans	Olive brown
v	Moderate constitutional pigmentation	Brown
vi	Marked constitutional pigmentation	Black

This scale was developed in 1975 by Thomas B. Fitzpatrick.

If you want to check what type of skin you have, you can take the following quiz. Just add up the score for each answer you choose and that will lead you to your skin type.

A. What colour are your eyes?

i	Very light	(0)
ii	Blue, grey or green	(1)
iii	Dark	(2)
iv	Brown	(3)
v	Black	(4)

B. How often do you turn brown?

i	Never	(0)
ii	Seldom	(1)
iii	Sometimes	(2)
iv	Often	(3)
v	Always	(4)

C. What is your natural hair colour?

i	Sandy red	(0)
ii	Blonde	(1)
iii	Chesnut or dark blonde	(2)
iv	Brown	(3)
v	Black	(4)

D. How brown do you get?

i	Don't	(0)
ii	Light tan	(1)
iii	Medium tan	(2)
iv	Dark tan	(3)
v	Deep dark	(4)

E. What is the colour of your skin in unexposed areas?

i	Reddish	(0)
ii	Pale	(1)
iii	Beige or olive	(2)
iv	Brown	(3)
v	Dark brown	(4)

F. How sensitive is your face when exposed to the sun?

i	Very sensitive	(0)
ii	Sensitive	(1)
iii	Sometimes sensitive	(2)
iv	Resistant	(3)
v	Never has a problem	(4)

G. How many freckles do you have?

i	Many	(0)
ii	Several	(1)
iii	Few	(2)
iv	Rare	(3)
v	None	(4)

H. How often do you tan?

i	Never	(0)
ii	Seldom	(1)
iii	Sometimes	(2)
iv	Often	(3)
v	Always	(4)

I. What happens if you stay out in the sun for too long?

i	Painful blisters, peeling	(0)
ii	Mild blisters, peeling	(1)
iii	Burn, mild peeling	(2)

iv	Burn, but very rarely	(3)
v	No burning at all	(4)

J. When was the last time you tanned considerably?

i	Days ago	(0)
ii	Weeks ago	(1)
iii	1-2 months ago	(2)
iv	2-3 months ago	(3)
v	+3 months ago	(4)

Answer Key

0-6: Type I
7-13: Type II
14-20: Type III
21-27: Type IV
28-34: Type V
35+: Type VI

(Quiz credits: Australian Radiation Protection and Nuclear Protection Agency)

Caring for Skin Type I

Skin type I is very pale. It rarely tans but burns very easily. It is a type of skin that is mainly found in people of Scandinavian, Irish and Scottish descent. You don't usually come across this type of skin in the Indian Subcontinent. Skin type I is highly sensitive to the sun, which makes it comparatively more prone to sun-induced melanoma cancer. It is also the first to show signs of ageing (photoageing to be precise) and sun damage. Needless to say, this type of skin needs very high maintenance, especially with the environmental changes that are happening presently. With global warming and the depletion of the ozone layer, we have never been as exposed to UVA and UVB rays as we are today.

I'm no dermatologist and I would recommend that you consult your dermatologist before taking any of my advice. But now that the disclaimer has been put up, I would advise the use of a sunblock, rather than sunscreen for this skin type. Sunblock tends to be thicker, more opaque and stronger than sunscreen. Hence, it is able to block the majority of UVA/UVB rays and other radiation from the sun without breaking down in reaction to these rays. That means that it does not have to be applied over and over again to maintain its effectiveness. However, titanium dioxide and zinc oxide are two of the main ingredients in a sunblock; so please check with your dermatologist to know whether it is safe for you. Type I skin is after all very thin and therefore, very sensitive. You don't want to antagonise it. As for SPF, according to Solaveil, a range of inorganic sunscreen actives, you are best off using SPF 50 and above if you possess this type of skin. Also, try and stay out of the sun between 11 am and 3 pm, if possible (since the sun is at its harshest during this time). But yes, that is a bit of an unreasonable demand, so when you're out, try and wear protective clothing, hats and sunglasses.

Sunblock tends to be thicker, more opaque and stronger than sunscreen. Hence, it is able to block the majority of UVA/UVB rays and other radiation from the sun without breaking down in reaction to these rays.

Recommended SPF: 50 +

Caring for Skin Type II

Skin type II is made of tougher stuff than skin type I. It is made for regions where the sun is relatively harsher (this is a pattern, as you will notice). This type of skin is native to countries in Northern Europe. It is still pretty pale in colour but it is not so sensitive. It burns when exposed to sunlight frequently, but not always and sometimes chooses to tan instead. It also ages pretty quickly when exposed to the sun, although the rate of ageing isn't quite as it is in type I. Skin type II isn't as thin as skin type I, and therefore isn't nearly as transparent. This might sound like bad news, but really it isn't, since it means that exposure to the sun will not lead to redness or blotchiness. Redness will be there, yes (I'm type IV and I tend to turn into a tomato when I'm out in the sun) but comparatively less than type I. But the bad news (yes, there is bad news) is that this type of skin is also quite high on maintenance. So you'll want to be careful when out in the sun. Again the advice is the same. Use sunblock whenever out in the sun and if you feel sunblock is too thick, use sunscreen. But make sure you apply it religiously every two hours when you are out in the sun, because sunscreen, unlike sunblock, tends to break down when exposed to sunlight, thus allowing some of that harmful radiation to penetrate through to your skin. So you have to keep reinforcing your troops in order to stay safe. Some dermatologists even advise that not only should you apply sunscreen before you leave the house and every two hours henceforth, but also apply it once more within the first twenty to thirty minutes of being out in the sun. This is mainly to ensure that you have got enough sunscreen on you.

Recommended SPF: 30 to 50

Caring for Skin Type III

Skin type III tends to be darker and thicker in comparison to skin type II. This type of skin is custom-made for areas where the sun can be harsh but not so harsh as to burn. It is native to people of German and Swedish descent. Although this type of skin is comparatively darker, it is not to be confused with dark skin. Type III skin is still quite pale, which does put it at a high risk for sun damage and sun-induced melanoma cancer. You don't see this type of skin very frequently in the Indian Subcontinent, but it does exist, even though it's quite rare.

Now, because of a cultural preference for lighter skin tones in India, you might consider type III to be very pretty. But if you have skin type III, you need to be really careful. We live in a tropical country and this type of skin is made for sub-tropical regions. It does not react well to the harsh sun that we encounter daily in India. Under the aggressive sun, it tends to be very delicate and sensitive. Although it prefers to tan rather than burn, it does burn quite frequently, and you need to guard your skin against that.

If you have this type of skin (type III), you will experience both tanning (which is not really a problem) and burning (which is a problem). So use sunscreen generously, or sunblock if you prefer... and don't forget to reapply every couple of hours.

I have a friend in Dehradun. She is of Garhwali descent. One day, I was talking to her about her sister and we were debating about different types of sunscreen. Both of us have, more or less, the same skin tone, because of which I assumed that maybe we have the same skin type (I'm a type IV); so I went on to recommend the sunscreen I use to her. She looked at it and said, 'I've tried it. But I still burn when I'm out in the sun, regardless. I always burn when I'm out in the sun.' That's when I realised, she must be a type III, because I never burn when I'm out in the sun. I always get tanned, though (so much that both my arms are now two different colours. How? Well, that's a long story. Let's just say it has to do with driving). That's also when I realised that the Indian climate is not very kind to skin type III.

If you have this type of skin, you will experience both tanning (which is not really a problem) and burning (which is a problem). So use sunscreen generously, or sunblock if you prefer (if you live in a tropical country, I think that would be more logical) and don't forget to reapply every couple of hours. Additionally, don't step out without your hat and sunglasses on a sunny day.

Recommended SPF: 30

Caring for Skin Type IV

Now, this shouldn't be that hard. Skin type IV is naturally much tougher than type III. It can generally be identified by the olive or beige colour of the skin. This type of skin is native to people of Hispanic, Spanish, Asian, Portuguese, Italian and Mediterranean descent but can also be found more or less frequently in India. In fact, most of the fairer Indians that you come across will have this type of skin. Caring for skin and protecting it from the sun becomes somewhat easier from now on. This is because this type of skin is made for a comparatively harsher sun and has been programmed to protect itself. It does this by tanning, profusely. Don't get disappointed. That is good. Tanning is good. The more you tan, the less you burn. And people with skin type IV rarely ever burn. I have this kind of skin. I live in Mumbai and I have never ever experienced skin burning.

Skin type IV is naturally much tougher than type III. It can generally be identified by the olive or beige colour of the skin.

But, coming to the other side of the coin, this does not mean you throw caution to the wind and forget about protecting your skin. Although skin type IV is relatively well-equipped to deal with the sun, it is still not tailor-made for the Indian climate. Because we come across this type of skin quite frequently in India, it might once have been, but global warming and the depletion of the ozone layer have made sure that it is not anymore. And it definitely does not provide immunity against sun-induced melanoma cancer. We girls, with skin type IV, need to protect our skin from the sun just as much as any other type. This means regular application of sunscreen, everyday, and use of protective clothing, hats and sunglasses on sunny days, without fail.

Recommended SPF: 15 -30

Caring for Skin Type V

Following the same pattern, skin type V can take a lot more harsher sun that type IV. It usually ranges from brown to dark brown in colour and is native to people of Hispanic, American-Indian, Eastern-Indian (that is us) and mixed African-American descent. In fact, when you look out of the window, most of the people you'll see will have either type V or maybe even type VI skin. As you might have guessed, it is relatively easier to care for type V skin when compared to the types of skin discussed above. That is because this type of skin is much thicker and more prone to pigmentation, aka tanning than the earlier types of skin. Also, type V hardly if ever burns. That would beat the purpose really. After all, this type of skin is made for tropical regions. But instead, it does tan quite a bit.

However, as with skin type IV, just because your skin is capable of protecting itself to a higher extent than most other types of skin, it does not mean that you leave it to its own devices. It is your job to assist it. You have to help it reach its maximum level of protection. And just because you have skin type V does not mean that you are immune to sun-induced melanoma cancer. You still have to use sunscreen (and reapply it every two hours) and other protective materials such as sunglasses and large-brimmed hats just the same as anyone else. Better be safe than sorry.

Recommended SPF: 15

Caring for Skin Type VI

This is the most efficient type of skin, if you ask me. It can survive well under any climactic conditions. It is dark brown to black in colour and is native to people of African, African-American and Southern-Aboriginal descent. It is also quite common in India. And the best thing about this type? It never ever burns. It also has the least amount of susceptibility to photoageing, sun damage and melanoma cancer.

But, as I have said earlier, it is still better to be safe than sorry. Nearly immune does not mean completely immune. You still have a chance of ageing and/or of getting skin cancer. So, on sunny days, be smart, apply your sunscreen (remember, every two hours), and bring out your wide-brimmed sunhat and sunglasses. Don't go anywhere without these.

Recommended SPF: 15

Overview

- Unprotected exposure to the sun can cause photoageing and sun damage including peeling and burning and sun-induced melanoma cancer aka skin cancer, regardless of your skin type.
- Never step out, especially on a sunny day, without having generously applied sunscreen/sunblock, and without wearing sunglasses and a wide-brimmed sunhat.
- If you decide to apply sunscreen instead of sunblock, make sure you re-apply it every two hours as UVA/B radiation has the ability to break down the ingredients of sunscreen over time. Also, within thirty minutes of stepping into the sun, apply one more layer of sunscreen in order to make sure you have got an adequate amount of protection on.
- Contrary to popular belief, there is a vast difference between sunscreen and sunblock. Sunblock is more opaque and stronger than sunscreen and is able to block the majority of UVA/B rays and other radiation from the sun without breaking down. Sunscreen is more transparent and breaks down at a faster rate when exposed to sunlight, thus having to be re-applied constantly.
- Most sunblocks contain titanium dioxide and zinc dioxide as their main ingredients. Please check with your dermatologist to make sure that these are compatible with your skin. Also, titanium dioxide

sometimes gives an ashen, chalky look to the face when the sunblock is applied to the skin.

- SPF stands for Sun Protection Factor, which is only an indicator of a sunscreen's efficacy against UVB rays. Therefore, I suggest you use a broad spectrum sunscreen that also protects you from UVA rays.

Now, despite all that I have said, I must add that the sun is not all that bad. Without exposure to sunlight, our skin would not be able to make enough Vitamin D for us. So once in a while, in the early morning, preferably before the sun's rays turn cruel, go out for a walk or a jog and enjoy the sun without sunscreen. Give your skin a chance to manufacture that much-needed Vitamin D. You don't want rickets or ailments caused by Vitamin D defficiency, do you?

A Little Bit About UV Rays

UV stands for Ultraviolet, which is a type of radiation emitted by the sun. UV rays are of three types:

- UVA, the wavelength of which ranges from 100 to 290 nm (newton meter)
- UVB, the wavelength of which ranges from 290 to 320 nm
- UVC, the wavelength of which ranges from 320 to 400 nm

Without exposure to sunlight, our skin would not be able to make enough Vitamin D for us.

Now, you don't have to worry so much about the UVC rays as much as you need to worry about the UVA and UVB rays. This is because UVC rays are almost completely absorbed by the ozone layer and don't even get anywhere near the skin. That is why you never see any brands advertising UVC protection.

UVB rays are made of tougher stuff than UVC rays. Luckily for us, ninety percent of UVB rays are absorbed by the ozone layer. But thanks to us and our penchant for industrialising the whole world, the ozone layer is not as strong as it used to be. So about ten percent of the UVB rays emitted by the sun manage to get through the ozone layer and hit us. And that ten percent is the current state of affairs. At the rate global warming is increasing, it won't be long before that number goes up. What UVB rays do is that they hit the epidermis, the topmost layer of our skin and cause either sunburn or tanning, depending on your skin type. SPF indicates how much that particular sunscreen or sunblock protects your skin from UVB rays. So here is a reason to choose your SPF carefully. However, if you're sitting indoors with the doors and the window shutters closed, you don't have to worry about it. You only have to worry about it when you're outside directly under the sun. UVB rays cannot penetrate glass.

SPF indicates how much that particular sunscreen or sunblock protects your skin from UVB rays. So here is a reason to choose your SPF carefully.

UVA rays, however, are tricky things to tackle. Not only can they penetrate through glass, most of them manage to get through the ozone layer too. Plus they manage to go much deeper into the skin, going down to the dermis and end up creating trouble that is long-lasting. So if you're sitting inside your house with the doors locked or in your car with the widows rolled up and you think you're safe… I'm sorry to be the one to break this to you, but you're not. You need to go and lather on some of that sunscreen/sunblock in order to be truly safe. And SPF will not help here. Check if your sunscreen has either zinc oxide or titanium dioxide. Alternatively, just check if the sunscreen clearly states that it protects agains UVA rays. If it says so, go for it.

Oily, Dry, Normal and Combination skin

Although dermatology refuses to classify skin on the degree of oiliness, this classification is actually very handy. I can understand why dermatologists might not like this classification, though. It isn't permanent, after all. The degree of oiliness of your skin keeps changing. When I was in Kuwait, my skin was very dry. So dry that whenever I tried to smile, I would feel like I'm pulling my skin in unnatural directions. I would use a moisturiser day in and day out and still feel that my skin wasn't supple enough. In fact, I used to joke back then that if moisturisers were money, I'd have been bankrupt ten times over already!

And then I came to Mumbai. Talk about extremes. I have never lived in a more humid city and frankly, I don't think I ever will. Mumbai changed the whole texture of my skin. From dry and brittle skin, I suddenly got the soft, supple and clear skin that I had always wanted. Even air conditioning here doesn't seem to do much harm. It is so hot and humid outside that I normally have my AC on at home, in my car, basically everywhere. However, my skin still manages to stay soft and supple thanks to all the humidity outside.

But that's how my skin reacts to extreme conditions. Yours might react in a completely different way. Your skin might be normal under dry conditions and very oily under humid conditions. Or you might have some kind of a magical skin, like my mom's, which stays normal, i.e., soft and supple under any type of climatic conditions.

Whatever type of skin you have, the first step to taking care of it is to recognise whether your skin is normal, oily, dry, or combination.

But whatever type of skin you have, the first step to taking care of it is to recognise whether your skin is normal, oily, dry, or combination.

The First Step: Analysing your Skin

Right after you get up in the morning, without washing your face, look at your facial skin in the mirror. Is the overall impression flaky (which means it is dry), shiny (which means it is oily), or smooth (which means it is normal)?

Right after you get up in the morning, without washing your face, look at your facial skin in the mirror. Is the overall impression flaky, shiny, or smooth?

Having made that diagnosis, wash your face with a cleanser. Now how does it feel? The criteria are the same—flaky, shiny or smooth. If you are having trouble figuring out, start making faces at yourself in the mirror, you know, the kind you used to make when you were a kid. While making these faces, observe how tight your skin feels. The tighter it feels, the drier it is.

You're done for the moment now. Your next step isn't until midday.

Come midday, get back to that mirror once again and observe yourself. How does your skin feel now? Does it feel flaky, oily, or smooth? Do you have oil breakouts or does your skin feel dry even though you've lathered moisturiser on yourself as though it is some kind of armor?

Now take an average of your flaky, oily and smooth moments. Whichever has a majority wins. If your skin is mostly flaky throughout the day, it is dry. If it is mostly shiny throughout the day, it is oily. If it is mostly smooth throughout the day, it is normal.

To make it easier, I am including a list of characteristics for each type of skin.

NORMAL SKIN

- Feels smooth and comfortable throughout the day

- Has an even texture
- Pores are small
- The driest areas are the cheeks, although not necessarily and not excessively so
- Once in a while, might experience some shine and/or larger pores on forehead, nose or chin
- Most importantly, water and oil content are balanced

DRY SKIN

- Feels very tight throughout the day, especially after washing
- May look dry or flaky
- Texture feels rough, uneven and dehydrated
- Might be very sensitive
- Pores are small, almost invisible
- Shows signs of ageing and fine lines faster than any other type of skin

OILY SKIN

- Characterised by shiny skin, especially all along the T-zone (which is the forehead, nose and chin)
- Caused by overactive oil-producing glands
- Pores are large and visible
- Breakouts might be frequent
- Signs of ageing and fine lines are very slow to appear

COMBINATION SKIN

- T-zone feels oily
- But the cheeks feel dry
- Spot dehydration
- Comparatively larger pores along the T-zone.

You might have the most fabulous skin, but without care it is not going to go very far.

Now that you know what type of skin you have, it is time to start caring for it. You might have the most fabulous skin, but without care, it is not going to go very far. I've made that mistake. I have been lucky enough to have been blessed with smooth, clear skin. I took it for granted. I just assumed that it would always be that way. Boy, was I wrong! One has to consider, the fact that in this industry, skin is overtaxed. I cannot stress on that enough. Everyone needs to take good care of his or her skin, for the sake of hygiene and health, if nothing else. But *we*, we need that something extra. We need our skin to be perfect on a day-to-day basis. Now, with a disciplined care regime, that is not very difficult to attain. But the truth is that we ruin it almost everyday. In a pageant, you will be using make-up on a daily basis and like it or not, you will not get the chance to wash and moisturise your face from time to time, since washing your face means the make-up either comes off or gets messed up. Most likely, you will only manage to do so once in the morning and once at night, so please do not, repeat DO NOT start feeling lazy and skimp on it during these times. That'll just make matters worse.

We need our skin to be perfect on a day-to-day basis. Now, with a disciplined care regime, that is not very difficult to attain. But the truth is that we ruin it almost everyday. In a pageant, you will be using make-up on a daily basis and like it or not, you will not get the chance to wash and moisturise your face from time to time, since washing your face means the make-up either comes off or gets messed up. Most likely, you will only manage to do so once in the morning and once at night, so please do not, repeat DO NOT start feeling lazy and skimp on it during these times.

On top of it, there are those harsh lights. During a pageant, you will inevitably have numerous photo shoots, photo ops, press conferences and exclusive fashion shows. All these are conducted under harsh lighting. And nothing gets those oil glands working like the heat generated by this kind of lighting. Then you have your frequent make-up and touch-ups. So you have a thick layer of make-up on, then a thick layer of sweat (thanks to the lighting), then a layer of touch-up, then yet another layer of sweat, which means yet another layer of make-up, which means… you get the drift, don't you? Nothing clogs the pores better than this formula. And the worst part? There is absolutely nothing you can do about it. You can't say I won't use make-up. You are a beauty pageant contestant after all, and you need to look good! You can't say I won't perspire at all. If only we had that kind of control on our sweat glands. Nor can you say no to touch-ups. Again, you are a beauty pageant contestant and you need to look good. That is what you are being judged upon. Period.

So what you need is a disciplined and determined skin-care regime, so that despite all this torture meted out daily, you can manage to retain your perfect, flawless skin. As I've said before, no skimping.

Caring for Normal Skin

Normal skin really doesn't need much care. For most of the part, it can take care of itself. You just need to help it a little bit. That is all. Wash it routinely twice a day – once in the morning and once in the evening. Don't take this lightly. Bobbi Brown, renowned professional make-up artist and founder of Bobbi Brown Cosmetics, recommends that you use a foaming cleanser if you have normal skin. However, any cleanser that says it is meant for normal skin should be okay. Also, don't forget to moisturise once you finish cleansing. Preferably, you should use lightweight water-based lotions. Cleansing usually rids your skin of not only dirt, but also essential oils. Your skin needs a thin layer of oil covering it in order to remain smooth. This same oil also acts as a barrier between the skin and external pollutants. But since cleansing strips this oil away from our skin, you need to replace it. You can do this with the help of some moisturiser.

Sunscreen, of course, is a must, but try and use water-based sunscreen so that it doesn't clog your pores, unless of course, you are going swimming. Water-based sunscreen isn't really of any use on the beach. It's just going to get washed away.

Just like taut, botoxed skin without any signs of lines looks grotesque on a fifty-year-old, premature ageing and wrinkling of skin looks grotesque on a twenty-year-old. You need to look your age. That is when you look beautiful, never otherwise.

You must have a lifestyle that includes a healthy diet, full of green leafy vegetables. I cannot stress on this enough. Vitamin A, C and E, especially, help to keep the skin smooth, soft and supple. More on this later in Chapter 3 – Nutrition and Fitness.

Eight glasses of water a day is, of course, a must. It helps in maintaining a sufficiently hydrated skin that is clear of any toxins.

Caring for Dry Skin

Dry skin is, as the name suggests, dry. If you have this type of skin, you need to take extra care, because the dryness of your skin will make it prone to ageing and fine lines much faster than any other type of skin. Ageing and occurrence of fine lines isn't really such a bad thing in my personal view. It makes a person look mature and sophisticated, But, just like taut, botoxed skin without any signs of lines looks grotesque on a fifty-year-old, premature ageing and wrinkling of skin looks grotesque on a twenty-year-old. You need to look your age. That is when you look beautiful, never otherwise. So you need to be careful with dry skin.

The most important thing, of course, is to keep your skin sufficiently hydrated. More than any other type of skin, dry skin needs those eight glasses of water every day. A healthy diet including foods that have a high level of water content like watermelons, tomatoes, oranges, cucumber and all kinds of green leafy vegetables also helps.

Secondly, the reason your skin is so dry is because your oil glands are not producing oil at the rate they should be. So it is your responsibility to aid them. Use a rich cleanser that does not rob your skin of its essential oils and never forget to moisturise it immediately afterwards. Bobbi Brown suggests layering different textures of moisturiser. She recommends beginning with lightweight face oil and then layering a richer cream on top of it. It would help to choose moisturisers that contain alpha hydroxyl acids (AHA) that help in the removal of dry dead skin cells.

Thirdly, stay away from alcohol. Alcohol dehydrates your skin. So does caffeine, in fact. Therefore, you might want to stay away from these two. Even if you don't, the least you can do is limit your intake to a maximum of two glasses a day, MAXIMUM.

Caring for Oily Skin

Oily skin needs a completely different care regime. If your skin is oily, the good news is that your skin will not age as quickly, but the bad news is that you, my darling, are prone to acne and breakouts. And acne, well, is not exactly conducive to the health of skin. As with all other skin types, you also have to wash your face regularly at least twice a day, but unlike other skin types, you have twice as much reason for following this ritual religiously, without fail.

If your skin is oily, the good news is that your skin will not age as quickly, but the bad news is that you, my darling, are prone to acne and breakouts.

Oily skin is caused by overactive oil glands present in the skin. Your skin needs its essential oils, no doubt, but too much of anything is bad. That extra layer of oil does more harm than good – attracting dirt and pollutants and clogging the pores, thus suffocating the skin. The skin also needs to breathe and it cannot do that when its pores are clogged. That is why you need regular cleansing with an oil-control cleanser to prevent the accumulation of dirt and to open the pores. You could also consider using an alcohol-free astringent to remove any excess oil.

After cleansing, you might or might not want to use a moisturiser. That is entirely upto you, since your skin is capable of moisturising itself pretty quickly and efficiently. However, if you do, make sure that your moisturiser is water-based, not oil-based. Using an oil-based moisturiser will only make matters worse.

Regular cleansing is actually a golden rule. It is essential for any and every kind of skin.

Caring for Combination skin

So you have skin that is neither oily, nor dry nor normal. In fact, it is a bit of all three. Well, you have combination skin.

What you need is regular cleansing. Regular cleansing is actually a golden rule. It is essential for any and every kind of skin. Combination skin is no different. But with combination skin, what could help is a combination of cleansers and moisturisers. You could use an oil-control facial cleanser, toner and moisturiser for the oily areas and a milder cleanser combined with a denser moisturiser (maybe even oil-based, if the area is extra dry, but you can be the judge of that) for the dryer areas. Bobbi Brown recommends products containing AHA for this type of skin. You can try her suggestion.

The Ideal Cleansing Regimen for Any Type of Skin

Step 1: Cleansing

Yes, I know I keep going on and on about cleansing. But that is only because it is such an important part of skin care. Without cleansing properly, any skin-care regimen falls to pieces. So please, please cleanse your skin with a suitable cleanser (we have discussed different cleansers for different types of skin. Also, NEVER use bar soaps since they tend to dry out your skin) once in the morning and once in the evening without fail.

During pageants, following this regimen is even more important. Your face will be covered with make-up all day and you would have attracted, thanks to the extra oil, an unspeakable amount of dirt and pollutants that would cosy up on your skin and in your pores. That is why you should, as soon as you enter your hotel room, take off all your make-up and cleanse your skin thoroughly. And don't forget to moisturise. Such a thorough cleansing is sure to strip your skin of its essential oils. Also, never wash your face with water that is too cold or too hot, as that can cause broken capillaries.

Step 2: Exfoliation

Your skin tends to build a certain amount of dead skin cells over a period of time. These dead skin cells are also responsible, in part, for clogging up your pores. By exfoliating your skin twice a week, you will get rid of them, thus allowing your skin to breathe freely.

But, there is a but here, don't overdo it. Once your skin feels clean, rinse off your exfoliating scrub with lukewarm water. Overdoing it can irritate your skin. The last thing you want at a pageant is skin that looks like it has been grated. If scrubs are not your thing, just use a washcloth to scrub your face with your regular cleanser.

Additionally, consider using products that are rich in retinoids. Retinoids are basically Vitamin A derivatives that help you unclog your pores. They remove the top layer of dead skin cells while generating collagen at the same time. Collagens are extracellular proteins that form the skin's structural fibre. They are instrumental in protecting skin from ageing and are even used in plastic surgery (for example, in lip jobs). It is their breakdown that causes the growth of fine lines and larger pores.

Step 3: Moisturising

Dermatologists say that the ideal skin is one that doesn't need any kind of external moisturising. But that's theoretical, not practical. Most of us are not lucky enough. When we cleanse our skin of all the dirt and pollutants of modern life, we end up drying out our skin, despite whatever skin type we might possess.

Whatever you eat does not and cannot have an impact on your acne. The only thing that has any relation to acne is how oily your skin is.

Still, let your skin make the decision. Don't just moisturise it for the sake of moisturising it. Your skin will let you know when it needs moisturising and when it doesn't. Whenever your skin feels tight and flaky, give it a dose of that much-needed moisturiser. But whenever your skin feels fine, stay away from moisturisers. You need to be careful. Over-moisturising can cause clogged pores and breakouts.

Step 4: Sunscreen

I don't think I need to add any more about protecting your skin from the sun. Apply a broad-spectrum sunscreen twenty minutes before stepping out in the sun, apply it twenty minutes afterwards and every two hours thereafter. That's it. Enough said.

A Few Myths about Skin Care Cleared Up

Acne is caused by what you eat

I would really love to know who gave birth to this myth!

Whatever you eat does not and cannot have an impact on your acne. The only thing that has any relation to acne is how oily your skin is. That, and genetics. If your mother and grandmother never had to deal with acne, most probably, neither will you. So enjoy your chocolates and ice creams and rest assured, you will not get acne from it.

That being said, the only time acne can be caused by what you eat is if you are suffering from something called rosacea acne, which is a kind of allergy. If you really feel that your acne is being caused by what you are eating, it is best you go to a dermatologist to have it diagnosed.

A day at the beach or a visit to the tanning parlour will get rid of pimples.

Absolutely not! A day at the beach or a visit to the tanning parlour might dry out your pimple and/or even out your skin tone so that the pimple doesn't look so prominent but it most definitely cannot and will not get rid of them. On the contrary, it will expose you to harmful UV rays which can cause skin cancer, especially if you are a tanning bed addict. Tanning beds radiate UV rays in very high concentrations which are harmful for your skin.

So give the beach and the tanning bed a skip and pick up some turmeric instead. Turmeric is one of the best natural antiseptics out there and it is a drying agent. Mix a pinch of turmeric with some besan (chickpea flour) and milk and apply it on the spot where your pimple has appeared. The pimple will run its course, of course, but the turmeric will make sure it doesn't leave a gift for you (in the shape of a scar) when it finally does leave. Oh and yes, whatever happens, do not pick at a pimple. You might or might not be left with a scar but you are definitely leaving it vulnerable to infections.

Turmeric is one of the best natural antiseptics out there and is a drying agent too.

You don't need sunscreen on a cloudy day or in winter.

I don't think I need to explain this one. You already know. It's utterly and entirely false and has no basis whatsoever. By now, you should know better than to fall for it.

Toothpaste dries out pimples.

Toothpaste is meant for your teeth, not your skin. If you use it on your skin, you will gain nothing apart from probably a rash. And god forbid, if you have sensitive skin, you might even end up burning the area around the pimple. True, toothpaste is a drying agent, which might result in the clearing up of your pimples, but is it really worth the risk?

So, in my opinion, applying toothpaste on your pimple is an absolute skin care no-no, especially if you have sensitive skin. Grab that turmeric instead. Our grannies were wise. Some of those homemade remedies are really the best. I swear by turmeric for pimples.

If you don't like the idea of turmeric on your skin, you could always go for those over-the-counter-pimple medications. Any one containing salycilic acid or benzoyl peroxide should do. Use them in proper doses; don't overdo it and they'll clear up your pimples without drying out your skin.

Not applying lotion in upward strokes will cause wrinkles.

We've heard this one a zillion times. And most of us believe it. I used to, as well and I used to take so much care to not massage my skin in any kind of stroke but an upward stroke. But, luckily for us, this one is just a myth. It doesn't matter which way you massage your skin while applying lotion. It cannot possibly give you wrinkles. No, not even with daily repetition. The great thing about skin is, that it is elastic. Try it yourself, pull your cheek hard, then let it go and see how it bounces back. Yes, with time we lose this elasticity, but that has absolutely nothing to do with either upward or downward strokes. On the contrary, it has to do with age, and there is nothing you or I can do about that.

Make-up

Make-up is a tricky thing. If done well, it can make a plain Jane look like a diva. If messed up, it can make the most beautiful person on earth look like they've just been beamed down from some other universe. So you can see why it is so important to get it right. It doesn't matter much in day-to-day life. You can experiment and see what works for you and what doesn't.

But unfortunately, when it comes to beauty pageants, you have to remember, you are being judged every day, every minute, every second even. Those oh-so-friendly chaperones are not just there to take care of you. They are there to report back about you, what you did all day, how you did it, where you did it, when you did it, etc. These reports are then given to the judges who use this and their experience with you during the personal interview to decide who gets into the Top 10, or the Top 20 or 25, whatever the case might be. So, really you can't afford to let loose for a minute, even when it comes to make-up.

You must keep in mind that this is a beauty pageant. Your beauty is the main thing that is being judged. Your behaviour, oratory skills, talent, all come second. Your beauty comes first. Therefore, you must showcase it. Because it is not just the judges and chaperones who will be noticing you day and night. The whole world will. For the entire duration of your stay at the pageant, you will be in the public eye. You will be going in

Those chaperones are not just there to take care of you. They are there to report back about you, what you did all day, how you did it, where you did it, when you did it, etc.

for photo ops and press conferences, giving interviews, and be semi-stalked by the paparazzi all the time (semi-stalked because security is usually very tight at all the big pageants; no one gets to even talk to you without prior permission from the management). Bottom line—your pictures will be in the newspapers and your face on television quite a bit. And the judges will be watching you too, though it's not their job to do so. Their job is to judge you on the day of the personal interview and the day of the finale based on your performance and the reports given by your chaperones only. They are not supposed to take into account anything else. But that is merely a technical point. The judges, after all, are also human. They are not supposed to form any prior prejudices or biases, but it is not humanly possible to do so when your face is being shoved in their faces all the time by the local media. So what do we do about that? Well, we stay on our best behaviour and look good all the time, no matter whether its 10 am or 3 am. No judge is going to vote for a contestant who looks like she has just tumbled out of bed.

Before we start, I must state that I am not a professional make-up artist. I will just be sharing tips and pointers that I use myself, many of which I have learnt from various make-up artists I have worked with. In fact, there are two books on make-up that have taught me an incredible lot. The first is *Bobbi Brown Makeup Manual* by Bobbi Brown, and the second one is *Making Faces* by Kevin Aucoin. I will be referring to these two books throughout this section. Therefore, I recommend you either buy these books or borrow them from your local library. They will help you a lot.

Bobbi Brown Makeup Manual focuses on the technical aspects of make-up, on the science of it. It takes you through a step-by-step process of learning how to put on make-up. It is very useful as a basic guide. But once you have mastered that, you can move on to Kevin Aucoin's *Making Faces*. This is a book that I enjoyed a lot. It doesn't focus much on the 'how to' of make-up. Instead, it outlines different types of looks and how to replicate the same on your face. It's a book I use a lot.

But first, let us start with buying the right supplies. Without the right supplies, you can't produce proper results.

Stocking Up Your Make-up Kit

Know Your Face

The first step to good make-up is understanding your face. You need to figure out what type of skin you have, the shape of your jawline, your nose, your eyes, etc.

So step up to the mirror and have a really good look at yourself. Familiarise yourself with what you see, both good and bad. Whatever 'bad' there is, come to terms with it. Because like it or not, this is the face you are stuck with for the next sixty to eighty years. And believe it or not, somewhere deep down, you do believe you are beautiful, otherwise you would not have even considered participating in a beauty pageant. You just need to reinforce your confidence. And if covering your so-called flaws is your path to doing so, so be it. Learn by heart every detail of your face, because that is the only way you will be doing justice to it when you pick up your make-up brush.

The first step to good make-up is understanding your face.

Even to those of you who don't see any flaws in your face, I would say, look in the mirror once again. Everyone has flaws. It is but natural. I'm not trying to discourage you. I'm just trying to prepare you for the stress that you will inevitably face at a pageant. Because believe you me, during a pageant, someone or the other will point out a flaw in you. It could be a specialist making a purely clinical observation or a co-contestant trying to intimidate you. And at that time, you cannot doubt yourself. You need to remain strong.

For that, you need to be prepared. You cannot afford to be surprised at such a point in the contest. If someone points out a flaw in you, it needs to be old news so that you can take whatever required action (which you should have practiced a thousand times beforehand) against it quickly and efficiently if that nagging self-doubt creeps into your mind. The bottom line is, you need to keep your confidence up. That is why I say, know thy face.

During a pageant, someone or the other will point out a flaw in you. It could be a specialist making a purely clinical observation or a co-contestant trying to intimidate you. And at that time, you cannot doubt yourself... If someone points out a flaw in you, it needs to be old news... That is why I say, know thy face.

When I was a contestant at Miss India South, each contestant had a personalised meeting with a reputed skin specialist. This is standard procedure during pageants. The skin specialist closely observed my face and then said, in a very clinical manner, 'You have a classically beautiful face. The only thing wrong is that you have a tiny bump on your nose. It can hardly be seen, but it is there. But never mind, we can always fix it with a little bit of surgery, if you want, before you go on to any international pageants.'

I was shocked! Till that day, my nose had been a feature that I had been really proud of! I used to think I had a perfect nose. I had never seen that bump earlier, and god knows I spend enough time in front of the mirror. I went back to the room and leaned in towards the mirror. Strangely enough, for the first time in my life, I saw a crooked nose on my face. It freaked me out. I knew I didn't want a nose job. But I also knew I didn't want a crooked nose. No matter what my family and friends said otherwise, I was convinced that my nose ruined my looks. But the truth was, it didn't! I looked just the same as I did before I noticed this bump.

But understanding you face is not just to avoid or control your reaction to such incidents. A more important reason is that if you don't know your face, you will inevitably pick the wrong kind of make-up, be it a wrong type of foundation, a colour of eyeshadow that doesn't suit you or a mascara that does absolutely nothing for your beautiful eyelashes. That, in fact, can be disastrous. You need to pick the right make-up. But unless you know your face, there is no way you can do that.

The Perfect Foundation

Make-up foundation, also known as base, plays a very significant role. Without the right type and tone of foundation, an otherwise perfect application of make-up could look tragically amateurish. As Oprah puts it, 'Too much and you look like a clown. Too little and you look unpolished. Very tricky stuff, foundation.' This is why I asked you to know your face. You won't need to know every detail about your features in this section, just your skin, the colour and the degree of oiliness of your skin, to be precise.

The first question is: do you need cream, stick, liquid or powder? Well, the degree of oiliness of your skin will tell you. You do know how oily or not your skin is, right? If not, turn back a few pages to the section on skin and take that self-analysis test.

- **Dry skin** needs something that is a bit more moisturising than others. You can find this in either liquid or stick foundation. Both have a creamy consistency, which moisturises the skin. Alternatively, you could also go for a hydrating powder foundation, *hydrating* being the key word here. Normal powder foundations will only dry out your skin further. Hydrating powder foundations, on the other hand, are blended with ingredients that deliver moisture to the skin. Look for words like 'hydrating' or 'moisture-rich' when you buy your foundation.

- **Oily skin** requires either an oil-free liquid foundation or a powder foundation. For extra oily skin, I would recommend the powder foundation, since the powder will soak up any excess oil present on the skin giving a smooth matte look. Stay away from hydrating powder foundations as these tend to moisturise the skin and extra moisturising is something you do not need if you have oily skin. Look for words such as 'oil-free', 'oil control' or 'matte' when you go shopping for your foundation.

- **Combination skin** is something you will have to be careful about. Your best bet would be to use a powder foundation, which will give your skin an even matte finish. However, you will need to be careful since some parts of your face could be on the dryer side and might start to flake when they come in contact with a powder foundation. Therefore, moisturise those parts of your face before using it. Alternatively, if the degree of oiliness in the oily areas is not that high, you could use cream foundations instead.

- If you have **sensitive skin**, you should probably try mineral foundations. Mineral foundations suit all types of skin, but they especially suit sensitive skin.

Like everything else, these rules, again, are in no way set in concrete. Follow these guidelines but find your own rules. Get out there, try different products and figure out which one it is that really suits you. These guidelines only exist to help you get started. If there is a product you use that sits on your face like second skin, don't replace it just because it doesn't match the above classifications. If you have to change it, change it because it doesn't suit you. Then you can follow the guidelines given above to help you find one that is perfect for you.

If you have sensitive skin, you should probably try mineral foundations. Mineral foundations suit all types of skin, but they especially suit sensitive skin.

The perfect colour is also of utmost importance. Whenever you go shopping for foundation, keep in mind that the right shade of foundation looks invisible on your skin. If it gives an ashen look, it is too light. If it gives a brownish look, it is too dark. If it looks like it's a part of your skin, only better, then bingo! You have found the perfect shade for you.

In India, we have a cultural preference for lighter skin. This probably is not just a residue of our colonial past, but possibly developed because the so called 'lower classes', who work in the fields would inevitably have darker skin than the aristocracy who worked from the comforts of their homes. Today, that is not the scenario anymore, but we have learnt, wrongly, over time that lighter skin is more beautiful than darker skin, to such an extent that almost everyone in the country works towards owning lighter skin. This has given rise to a whole new branch in the cosmetics market because of which you have products like skin whitening creams and similar products being revered by most households.

We have learnt, wrongly, over time that lighter skin is more beautiful than darker skin, to such an extent that almost everyone in the country works towards owning lighter skin. This has given rise to a whole new branch in the cosmetics market because of which you have products like skin whitening creams and similar products being revered by most households.

I have seen countless girls go to the cosmetics store and ask for a foundation one shade lighter than their own complexion. In fact, a few months ago, I ran out of the foundation that I used to use. So I went to the store to replace it, only to find out that the brand had stopped manufacturing that particular line of foundations. So I was on the lookout again for a new foundation. The sales assistant sat me down in front of a mirror and painted a few shades across my jawline for me to check. One shade just disappeared perfectly into my skin. I told her that that is the shade I would like to buy. Immediately, she pointed to another shade which was slightly lighter than my skin tone and asked me if I would want that shade instead. I was taken aback. Here was a trained make-up assistant working at one of the most reputed make-up stores in the world and she was making such a basic but humungous mistake! I am relating this anecdote in order to tell you how ingrained this line of thought is in our minds.

Using lighter shades of foundation will not make you look fairer. Instead, it will make you look ashen. It will make your make-up look like a mask instead of an extension of your skin. Period.

First of all, I don't understand why you'd want fairer skin. Dark skin is just as beautiful as fair skin. Each skin tone has its own charm. But lets say you don't agree with me on this. Fair enough. That's your personal opinion. However, please do not opt for a lighter shade in a misguided attempt to make youself look better. It will not. Trust me, it will only make you look worse. But if you are worried that darker skin might affect your chances of winning, then I must tell you that that fear is utterly baseless. Look at the most visible beauty queens of India – Sushmita Sen, Diana Hayden, Priyanka Chopra. What do they all have in common? Wheatish to dark skin. Fairness creams might reign high, but luckily they seem to have no takers in the pageant industry.

When it comes to foundation, stick to your original skin tone. Here are some tips to help you choose the perfect foundation:

1. Go to a department store. Stores like Shoppers Stop or Lifestyle are usually the best, because you can find a wide variety of brands all under one roof. Sephora has opened shop in India now, so that is another option too.
2. Choose a brand to start with, because, believe me, this will be a long trip.
3. By now, you must have decided what type of foundation

you would ideally want—stick, cream, liquid or powder. But for a second opinion, you can ask an assistant there to analyse your skin and recommend a foundation. The assistants are usually trained in make-up and are quite knowledgeable.

4. Smear a streak of foundation along your jaw-line and check in the mirror to see if it fully disappears into your skin. Next, ask for a hand mirror and step outside to see if it looks just as natural in sunlight.
5. If it does, great! If it doesn't, check out another brand. If nothing comes as close to perfection as you would like, you can always buy two different shades and blend them yourself into the perfect shade. Ask the assistant there to help you choose these two shades. But don't just buy them because she says so. Test it out yourself and see if it is doable. Most of the time, the assistants are paid on commission, so they might try to pressurise you into buying a product. Don't get pressurised. Buy a product only when you feel that it is the right one for you.
6. Apart from your base foundation, buy one foundation, which is one shade darker. Not only will this help you with contouring, but also when you tan (especially in summer), you will have a feasible shade at hand.

Choosing Your Corrector/Concealer

Your concealer should ideally be a shade or two (definitely not more than two) lighter than your foundation. For Indian skin, stick to yellow-based concealers rather than pink-based since our skin tends to be more on the yellow side than the pink. However, some of you might need pink-based concealers. You will have to be the judge of that.

Step up to the mirror (under proper lighting) and observe whether your skin has more yellow undertones or more pink undertones. If you have more pink undertones, then go for a pink-based concealer. If you have more yellow undertones, then you can safely go for a yellow-based concealer.

Another way to decide is by analysing your skin type. Typically, skin types I-III will need pink-based concealers and skin types IV-VI will need yellow-based concealers.

In the previous paragraphs, I have used the words concealer and corrector rather synonymously. However, there is a difference between the two—a corrector brightens, while a concealer lightens.

A concealer is mainly used to hide the valleys or slight dark circles under the eyes. A corrector is much stronger stuff. It effectively hides strong discolouration under the eyes while at the same time giving a bright-eyed dewey look. It is the perfect pick-me-up.

Choosing Your Face Powder

This is a frequently ignored make-up accessory but one that is of most importance. Without using face powder to set your make-up, all your efforts will go to waste.

Choosing the right face powder is as crucial as choosing the right foundation. Most people slap on foundation, blush, eyeliner, eyeshadow, mascara and lipstick and think that their make-up is complete. That is incorrect. Immediately after application of foundation, you should brush on a thin layer of face powder so that your make-up can settle itself, thus preventing make-up lines, and keeping the face looking fresh.

Again, as with foundation, the right shade of face powder is one that disappears into the skin. For most people, it is mandatory for the powder to have yellow undertones in order to look natural. I think we can safely divide that into type I-III and type IV-VI. Type I-III might prefer a face powder to have pink undertones while type IV-VI might prefer it to have yellow undertones. So basically, stay away from white powder unless you have Type I skin. It is not for everybody. Instead, stick to a powder that matches your skin tone.

Also, contrary to popular belief, translucent powder is neither invisible, nor transparent. It is translucent and very much shows on your face. People often feel that since it's translucent powder, it shouldn't matter what colour it is. Well, that isn't the case. In fact, not only does translucent powder show up on your skin, it can also make it look ashen. So you might just want to stay away from it. It is not for everyone.

Contrary to popular belief, translucent powder is neither invisible, nor transparent. It is translucent and very much shows on your face... In fact, not only does translucent powder show up on your skin, it can also make it look ashen.

The texture of the face powder you use is also of extreme importance. I would recommend that you carry a pressed compact for touch-ups. Not only is it convenient, but it dispenses only small amounts on your skin giving a very natural look. My personal favourite is Chanel Poudre Universelle Compacte. I have used this for over six years now and have never had to question my loyalty to the brand.

Loose powder is much denser and facilitates more coverage. It's the ideal thing to use if you have blemishes or other marks that you would like to cover. However, the coverage it provides depends entirely on the application technique. It can vary from matte to sheer.

Those of you with extremely dry skin might not be happy using face powder. I can understand that. And truthfully, you really don't need it either. However, that being said, you should lightly dust the area around your eyes with some powder to set your concealer. The area under the eye is usually the one with the most amount of make-up and therefore it needs a light dusting of powder to settle it and prevent any make-up lines.

Choosing Your Blush

There are many different types of blushes available in the market. The most popular and easiest to apply is the powder blush. However, apart from this, you can also get cream blushes, gel blushes and cheek tints, cheek pencils and cream/powder blushes.

- **Powder Blush:** This is probably one of the easiest to use. It is simple to control the application and suits most skin types. It blends very easily and naturally into the skin. I would recommend you get at least one powder blush, even if your preference is for other types of blushes, mainly for the ease of application.

- **Gel Blush:** This gives the most sheer and natural sheen, but only when blended properly. It needs a certain amount of experience for a person to be able to apply it skilfully. However, once you have mastered that art, you will probably never go back to any other type of blush. It works best on smooth skin.

- **Cream Blush**: This, quite obviously, is blush in a cream format. Yes, I can hear claps all around for pointing out the obvious. Anyway, back to business. If you have dry skin, you might hesitate to use a powder blush despite its ease of application. In such a case, the best alternative is cream blush. It is not as easy to blend as powder blush, but that is just my opinion. You might feel differently.

- **Cream/Powder Blush**: The cream/powder blush is a cream blush that after application, goes on to dry as a long-lasting powder finish. It can be applied in the same manner as the cream blush. It works best on normal skin.

- **Cheek Pencils**: Frankly speaking, cheek pencils are not my cup of tea. They are not what I would use happily. However, it is ideal for dry skin as they are prepared with extra moisturisers and emollients in order to keep them soft and easy to blend with the skin. But if you have oily skin, it's best you stay away from cheek pencils.

- **Cheek Tints**: Also called 'cheek stains', these are very similar to gel blushes. They give a very sheer and stained look. They look awesome when applied properly, but unfortunately, they can be pretty difficult to apply. However, mastering that art is definitely worth it for the final look the cheek tints deliver. They are best suited for smooth skin.

That was the classification of blushes according to texture. Now it is time to classify them according to colour. Again, there would be only a few colours of blushes that suit your skin colour. Your job is to match that colour as accurately as is possible.

Once you have chosen your perfect formula or formulae, as the case might be, of blush, you need to choose your perfect colour. For a natural look (which, if you ask me, is the perfect look), you need to match the colour of your blush to the colour of your cheeks when they are flushed from the heat of exercise. Yes, I know that you would not want to go shopping right after your workout. You would want to shower, freshen up and then go by which time the flush from your cheeks is long gone. Well, worry not. Just pinch your cheeks and voila! Your perfect blush colour is on your cheeks.

So since you now know your perfect blush colour, you just need to match it to one from your favourite brand. If you can't try on your blush for whatever reason, just hold it up to your face right next to your cheek. After trying out a few shades, you will get to know which ones are your colour and which ones are not. As said before, the ones that match your natural flushed cheeks look most accurately are your colour.

Now, like all other things in make-up, you must be extremely careful when choosing the colour of your blush. A colour which is too light can make you look from dull to outright weird, while a colour which is too dark can make you look like a circus clown. So be careful while buying it.

Choosing Your Lipstick

Now we're getting to the fun part. With lipsticks, you don't need to stick to a single shade. You can experiment, go wild and have fun. Remember Rihanna's orange lipstick to match her orange hair?

'If I had to teach someone just one thing about lip colour, it would be this: Find a lipstick that looks good on your face when you are wearing absolutely no make-up.'
- Bobbi Brown

I'm not saying you should replicate that look, if you don't want to. I'm just saying lipstick and eyeshadow are where you can subtly throw caution to the wind.

However, that does not mean that there is no perfect shade of lipstick for each person. Luckily, all types of lipstick, whether matte or glossy, suit all types of skin, which means we don't need to bother about different textures, and that's a relief. But there are three colours of lipstick that I think every girl should have—nude, pink and red. Of course, there are many different shades of nude, pink and red and not every shade suits every skin colour. But these are the three basics. Beyond that, go wild! Hey, the world is your oyster!

When it comes to choosing the three basic shades, you need to be careful. The eternal question, as always: does this colour suit me? Bobbi Brown sums up the answer to that pretty well, 'If I had to teach someone just one thing about lip colour, it would be this: Find a lipstick that looks good on your face when you are wearing absolutely no make-up.' Trial and error, then, is what it is. After all, you never learn better than when you learn from experience.

But, there is a basic rule—the darker your skin colour, the darker the colours that'll suit you. For example, a fair person would be able to carry off a scarlet lipstick more or less effortlessly, but on dark skin, the same colour would look out of place. A dark-skinned person would be much better off with a darker maroonish colour of lipstick. Here is a guide to help you get started.

And while you are at it, buy the same shades of lip gloss and lip pencils as the lipsticks you buy. Remember always: nude, pink and red. You must have these in both lipsticks and lip gloss. Oh, and another thing – even though nude technically means skin colour, don't end up buying a lipstick of the same colour of your skin. It will look like you have no lips at all. Take it up a notch. Buy a shade that is slightly darker and brighter than your skin tone.

Choosing Your Eyeshadow

Again, I'd be naive to issue restrictions on the colour of the eyeshadow you use. Eyeshadow, just like lipstick is something to experiment with, to go wild with, to find your own personal statement with! But... but, but... everything within limits. Freedom does not mean anarchy, remember?

Whenever I go out, I see people wearing perfectly beautiful colours of eyeshadow, which unfortunately looks horrendous on them. I see women with dark complexion wearing bright pink eyeshadow just because their outfit is of the same colour. Then there are women with fair skin wearing red eyeshadow, not just because it matches the colour of their outfit but because they believe that since they are fair, they can carry off any colour. That is a misconception, I'm sorry to say.

The perfect base colour of eyeshadow for you is the same colour as your skin. But get one with a little shimmer in order to give yourself a slightly glam look.

The perfect base colour of eyeshadow for you is the same colour as your skin. But get one with a little shimmer in order to give yourself a slightly glam look. Remember, as with foundation, your perfect colour should disappear into your skin. But this is just your base colour. You need to pair your base colour with another colour to give your eyes proper shading. For this purpose, choose two other colours of eyeshadow, one which is slightly, just slightly lighter than your base colour, and one which is a shade or two darker than your base colour. The lighter shade of eyeshadow will make your eyes look bigger and give you a cheerful morning look, while the darker shade will give you a sultry look. Depending on your mood, you can decide which look to go for.

During the day time, you hould stick to the nude basic colours of eyeshadow. Keep the bright colours for evenings, and even then, never with an outfit of the same colour.

The next step is to match your eyeshadow to your outfit. Does it work? So if you are wearing an electric blue dress, does it mean you should wear electric blue eyeshadow? Absolutely not! In fact, during the day time, you should stay away from all colours of eyeshadow apart from the nude basic colours. Keep the bright colours for evenings, and even then, never with an outfit of the same colour. Instead, brighten up a sober monochrome outfit with a jazzy new colour of eyeshadow. Whichever colour you use, make sure it suits you. There is nothing more distasteful than a beautiful woman with a colour on her that does nothing for her.

Choosing Your Eyebrow Pencil

Choosing an eyebrow pencil is an essential part of make-up. Many of us miss out on this crucial equipment. You need not use it every time you sit down to apply make-up; use it only when you need it. But when you do need it (to cover up a few accidental bald patches in your eyebrows), you cannot, at any cost, go without it. So be wise in deciding when to use an eyebrow pencil.

When choosing, try on a variety of shades to find one that matches the natural colour of your eyebrows as accurately as possible. If that particular brand does not have the colour you require, just move on and sample other brands until the time you find your perfect colour. When it comes to any component of make-up, the one rule to follow is: never compromise.

Choosing Your Eyeliner

Most of us, when we talk of eyeliner, we mean the pencil kohl. But eyeliners are of many textures. They come in the forms of cream, pencil, powder, liquid, cake and gel liners:

- **Pencil kohl** is most commonly used. It is the easiest to apply. It has a creamy consistency that glides smoothly over skin. However, for smoky eyes, a pencil kohl would not be my first choice. With pencil kohl, you will also need frequent touch-ups since it has a tendency to smudge.

- **Cream eyeliner** has a creamy consistency, quite like pencil kohl. It also glides smoothly over skin just like pencil kohl and gives a similar look. However, a cream eyeliner is applied with a brush and therefore gives much more control on the thickness and intensity of application. The cream eyeliner too is prone to smudging.

- **Liquid eyeliner** is also very commonly used. If it is a dramatic and defined look you are going for, then this is the eyeliner to use. However, application can be a little tricky and it needs a little practice to master the skill and apply skilfully. The best thing about it, however, is that it does not smudge.

- **Powder eyeliner**, also known as shadow eyeliner, is my personal favourite when it comes to getting the smoky eyes look. Application can be a little tricky. It is, after all, in powder form and tends to spread all over the face. But with a little practice, it can be a delight to use.

It comes with a little angular brush (even if it doesn't, you can always buy one) which makes it easy to control the thickness and intensity of application. Fortunately, it does not smudge easily.

- **Cake eyeliner** is liquid eyeliner in a solid form. It is applied by moistening it with a wet brush which is then used to draw on the top of the eyelid. Many make-up artists I have met and worked with prefer cake eyeliner to liquid eyeliner because it is easier to control while giving the same dramatic defined look as a liquid eyeliner.

I think it is pretty useless to talk about eyeliner colours. We all know which colour an eyeliner usually is. Black! But you might also want to try other colours such as brown or grey for a softer day look. You could also try some of those new wild colours that are available today. That, however, should strictly, repeat, strictly be reserved for an evening out.

Choosing Your Mascara

Mascaras are of many types. Some are volume-enhancing, some are lengthening, some are curling. Most of the time you can distinguish from type to type by reading what it says on the label but it helps to know what each kind of wand means as well.

- Fat wands are usually thickening/volume-enhancing. Different brands call it by different names, but they are all ideally the same thing. They make your eyelashes look thicker than they actually are.
- Skinny wands usually prevent clumping.
- Curved wands curl your eyelashes (although you can curl your eyelashes just as easily with an eyelash curler).
- Wands with dense bristles lengthen your eyelashes.

You need to choose the shade of your mascara cautiously. Most of us Indians have black hair and black lashes, so it's not really a problem for us. We just need to make sure the mascara is black, and that's that. But if your lashes are not black, then you need to choose wisely. The shade that is yours is the shade that matches the colour of your lashes as precisely as possible. Additionally, you should also have transparent mascara in your make-up kit. It is perfect for the times when you would like your look to be soft and fresh.

It is also imperative that you invest in a waterproof mascara. During a pageant, you never know how your day might be. You might spend the day indoors, in a nice air-conditioned room. Or you might spend the day outdoors sweating it out in the sun. In such instances, a water-based mascara that runs down your face is not really helpful. You will really want a waterproof mascara at hand then.

Other Items You Should Have in Your Make-up Kit

- Tweezers
- Eyelash Curler
- Eyelash Brush
- Eyelash Comb
- Eyebrow Brush
- Nail File
- Nail polish in a shade of peach that suits you
- A complete set of make-up brushes; this includes a foundation brush, a blusher brush, a face brush, an eyebrow blender brush, an eye-shadow applicator brush, an eye-contour brush, a concealer brush, an eye shadow brush, eye smudge brush, eyeliner brushes (thin, flat and angular), and a lip brush
- A velvet powder puff
- Disposable sponges

Make-up Application

1. Start with a completely clean face. Apply a light moisturiser. It is the key to freshness. You might also

Use the [foundation] brush to evenly apply and spread the foundation on your face. Then pat it in using your fingers. The heat from your fingers helps to blend the foundation into the skin properly. In fact, you can use your fingers to pat it in even when you use a sponge.

want to use a light eye cream to make sure that the application of your concealer/corrector is smooth.

2. Now that you have found your perfect shade of concealer/corrector or both, use a brush (concealer brushes should ideally have bristles that are firm yet soft since the skin under your eyes tends to be very delicate and tapered towards the end) to apply it to the darkest and/or deepest areas of the under-eye area. Use your fingers to blend, the rule being: always pat, never rub. Use as and when necessary.

3. The next step is obviously the foundation. Decide what you'd want to apply your foundation with—a sponge or a brush.
   - A sponge absorbs most of the foundation giving your skin minimal coverage. This is good if it is a very natural and sheer look that you want. But you can also add on a few layers to give more coverage if you are more comfortable using a sponge. Dip the sponge in your foundation if you are using the cream/powder type, or tip a little onto your sponge if you are using a liquid foundation and pat it into your skin evenly. Never rub it in. Patting ensures that the foundation stays put for as long as possible.
   - A foundation brush is a flat brush with rounded bristles for a softer application. It offers extensive coverage. Use the brush to evenly apply and spread the foundation on your face and then pat it in using your fingers. The heat from your fingers helps to blend the foundation into the skin properly. In fact, you can use your fingers to pat it in even when you use a sponge. Just make sure your hands are clean. I find that brushes work best with liquid foundations.
4. Once you are done with your foundation, it is powder time. For powder, you need a large face brush. Dust the

powder evenly on your face. This is an important step since powder prevents your make-up from cracking and creasing. Alternatively, you can also use a velvet powder puff.

5. Blush should always be applied in a manner that looks natural. Use a brush, or your fingers (in case of gel, cream or tints) to apply the blush on the apple of your cheeks. Blend it upwards, towards your hairline and then downwards. This softens the colour, so that it looks like a natural flush. Before application, make sure you tap off some of the excess blush from your brush. It is better to start with light layers and then to add more as needed than to end up looking like a clown with red cheeks.
6. Next come your eyes, starting with your brows. I feel it is best to go to a salon and get your eyebrows shaped professionally. But if you decide to go ahead and do it yourself at home, remember—less is more. Start plucking any stray hairs outside the natural shape of your eyebrows. Once you are done with that, take an eyeliner and draw a thin line outlining the preferred shape of your eyebrows (or outlining the natural shape if you would like to retain the original shape). Pluck any hairs outside of the drawn line. Remember to pluck from above, below and between your brows. Erase the outline before starting your make-up. Next, use a light dusting of non-shimmer eye shadow which should be the colour of your brows to define it. Alternatively, you can also use a pencil. But take care that the strokes are soft and light enough to blend in with the brow. Also, the strokes should always be made in the natural direction that the hair grows in.
7. Apply an eye shadow in a neutral colour (refer to '**Choosing Your Eye Shadow**' on pg 81) starting from your lash line to your brow bone. Make sure it is applied evenly. Add a slightly darker colour to the lower lid all the way up to the crease of the eyelid. Blend, blend, blend. That is the mantra. If you'd like further

contouring, add a slightly darker colour to the fleshy part of the eyelid and blend well. This guide is only a basic how-to that outlines the method of application. You, of course, are free to experiment with colours as you wish (within the range that suit you, of course).

8. Having been brought up in India, you probably know enough about the application of eyeliner/kohl. We've all grown up with it. It was probably the first bit of make-up that we used. Even if you are not Indian, chances are you have more than enough experience with kohl, so I'm not going to explain how to apply it. However, there are a few things that I must point out. Most of us apply kohl only on the lower lash line. That is wrong. It makes the eye look unproportionate. The golden rule to remember is that the more kohl you have on your upper eyelid, the larger your eyes look. The more kohl you have on your lower eyelid, the smaller your eyes look. If it is an equal amount, it merely gives shape and definition to your eyes. However, even if you want to make your eyes look smaller, always apply a small amount on your upper eyelid to balance it off. Further, never forget to apply kohl on the inside of your eye, it lends continuity to the rest of your eye make-up. Kohl applied only outside the eye gives a very disjointed look. But just be careful not to poke your eyes out. And maintain good hygiene since the inside of your eye is quite susceptible to infections.

The golden rule to remember is that the more kohl you have on your upper eyelid, the larger your eyes look. The more kohl you have on your lower eyelid, the smaller your eyes look.

9 Mascara gives the final touch to your make-up. To apply mascara, hold the wand parallel to the ground with your eyes looking straight ahead. Brush the mascara in from the base of your lashes to the tips. Try rolling the wand while brushing in order to separate the lashes and avoid clumping. Apply up to two or three coats. If you feel the need to curl your eyelashes, do so before applying

mascara. Doing so afterwards can break the hairs. You might also want to try applying false lashes to give a more dramatic look. Choose a piece of false lashes, trim it to suit your lashes. Line the base with a thin layer of transparent eyelash glue (unless you are an expert, use the transparent variety to make your mistakes less visible: eyelash glue is also available in black), place the false eyelashes on your lash line and gently press into place. Do this before curling and applying mascara.

10. And finally we come to the lips. You must start with clean, smooth lips. Apply a thin layer of lip balm first so that the lipstick can just glide on. You can apply your lipstick directly from the tube or use a lip brush. You might want to stick to a lip brush for the darker colours since they need much more precise application. Once done with the lipstick, use a lip liner of the same colour to give your lips a definition that looks natural. Apply all along the edge of your lips. If you feel that there are any hard edges, use a brush to blend and thereby soften the effect. (Tip: filling in your lips with a lip liner before applying lipstick can make your lipstick last for a much longer time.) Top it off with a thin layer of clear or coloured gloss of the same shade (only if needed) to give the face a fresh, dewy look.

That outlines the basic application of make-up. It should do for daily wear, but for slightly more glam looks, you will have to experiment on your own to find out what suits you and what doesn't. But the basic rules to play by remain the same as above.

Make-up During the Pageant

Daytime

At your pageant, for your daytime look, I suggest you stick to a basic approach as the one given above. Yes, you need to look beautiful, but you also need to look like you. Under all that make-up, people should be able to look at you and recognise you. The approach given above will ensure that happens. Many a time, I have seen contestants who completely smother themselves with make-up. That doesn't work. Make-up is to be used judiciously. Less is way more. Look at the picture here. My skin looks radiant, my eyes sparkle, and I think I look pretty damn good! But I'm hardly wearing any make-up in that picture—just a little spot foundation, a light dusting of blusher, eyeliner, mascara and basic pink lip gloss. That is it. But it has turned out pretty well, hasn't it? Even if I do say so myself! That kind of a natural look is what you need to be aiming for during the daytime.

My daytime look

Evening

Always remember, for the evenings, especially during events, you should glam up a little. Don't make the same mistake I made when I went to meet the president of Suriname (meeting dignitaries is often a part and parcel of your pageant routine). Look at my face carefully. Does it match the outfit I am wearing? No. The outfit is simple yet glam but my make-up is not the same. It is plain old day make-up. I should have done up my eyes a little more. A slightly thicker and smudgier kohl blended with a copper-coloured eye shadow would have probably done the trick. I couldn't find any photo taken on that day, so I recreated it to the best of my ability. It serves the purpose. Basically, I'd advice you to go glam! But there are some crucial ingredients for going glam:

My evening look

- *Flawless skin*: You might need a foundation that offers extensive coverage while still giving the natural look. Over that, use a blush that is slightly brighter than the one that you normally use but take care to not go overboard. You could also consider using an illuminator all over your face or a pale dusting of shimmer on your cheeks.

Apply the blush slightly higher up on the contours of your face in order to emphasise your cheekbones. A little contouring (if you are good at it) will help.

- *Glam eyes*: Feel free to use darker colours (as long as they match your colour chart) to give your eyes a glamorous touch. Creamy and pearlescent eye shadows give your eyes a very velvety feel. And while you are at it, don't forget your kohl. Smoky eyes are classically glam.
- *Glam lips*: Use a shimmer gloss. Or for a more sophisticated look, use a matte finish dark lipstick. However, you must be careful to see that the colour on your eyes and the one on your lips do not clash. If you are going for ultra glam eyes, keep the lips simple and just use a neutral shade of shimmer gloss. If you are going for a dark lipstick, keep the eyes simple. It takes a very skilful person to do up both the eyes and lips glamorously in such a way that they don't clash. It also takes a very skilfull person to carry off that look. So if you are one of those who can, go ahead. But if you have even the tiniest of doubts, stay away from it until the time you are absolutely sure.
- *Shimmer*: I always add a light dusting of shimmer powder over my collar bones to slightly glam up my look. You could try it too.

Face Chart

Face charts are incredibly useful things. Whoever invented them, well, I could kiss him/her! A face chart is basically a blank template of a face on which the make-up artist recreates a look for future reference. It is usually made of a paper of a certain texture on which the artist can apply actual make-up products. An example of a blank face chart is given on the next page.

You can use this chart to map out different looks for yourself. Keep them handy. That way, you wont have to fret about what kind of make-up to wear every day during the pageant. Just pull out the right face chart and replicate that look. There is also an app available on the Apple Store that helps you create face charts on your iPad or iPhone. And I'm pretty sure you could find it on Android too. You could always download that. But I recommend you print out those face charts before you go to a pageant, because some pageants in India do not allow their contestants to use electronic or any kind of communication devices during the pageant.

Remember to take printouts of your face charts before you go to your pageant.

You should also visit a make-up artist and get a face chart done for day make-up. That way you will learn which shades are right for you and which ones are not, and how to apply them. Many make-up stores also provide this service. You could ask your local make-up store to know whether they provide this service or not. For readymade face charts to inspire a look for an occasion, Google is a good source.

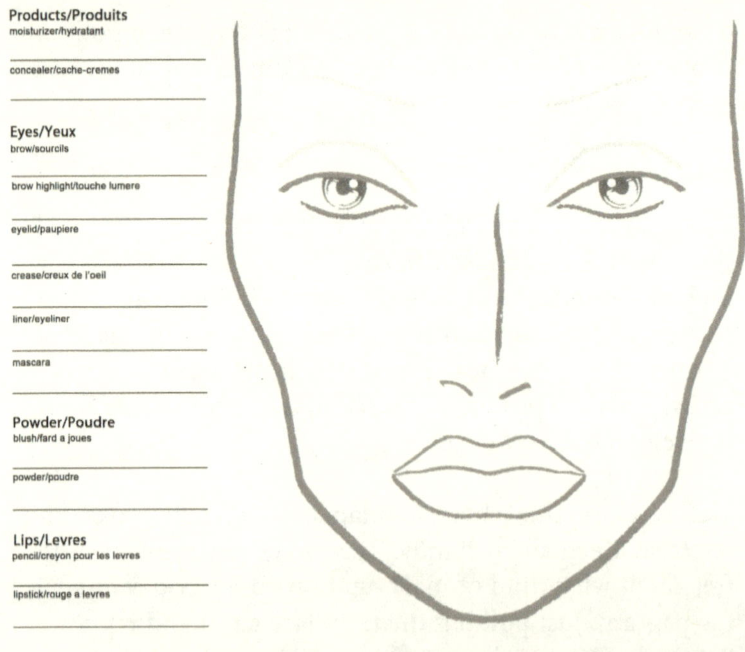

Face chart

Working with Make-Up and Hair Artists

At a pageant, you will most probably face a professional group of make-up and hair artists (MUAs for short) who are there only for one sole reason: to do your make-up (obviously) and more importantly, to make you look as good as you humanly can. That is their job. Many pageants prefer to have their contestants done up by professionals (and rightly so) before stepping out into the public eye. This is to ensure all the contestants have their make-up and hair done in such a way that it enhances their looks to the maximum. Please respect that sentiment while at a pageant. At all the pageants I have been in, I have seen contestants sneaking off to the washroom to 'repair' their professionally done make-up. While it is a very natural human instinct to think that 'I can do it better', please keep in mind that that is not always the case. You must remember that most of the time when you do this, you do not repair your make-up, you spoil it. Therefore, unless you are a professionally trained make-up artist or unless your skills are really up to the mark, it is best you refrain from doing so.

Many a times, it so happens that we look at ourselves in the mirror only to find that the make-up artist we trusted blindly has done, what we feel to be, a ghastly job on your face. But stage make-up is often like that. It is two-faced, literally. It looks horrible in real life but beautiful under the harsh lights of the stage. Let me give you an example. It was Talent Night at Miss India Worldwide. All thirty-five of us were to present our individual talent in front of a jury who would choose one among us to be awarded the sub-title of Miss Talent. My talent was kathak. I was looking forward to it, but then I took a look at my make-up. To my horror, it looked utterly garish, with green and yellow eye shadow and an exaggerated seventies-style eyeliner. At first glance, I was mortified. I couldn't imagine facing an audience looking like this. And I was just about to ask the make-up artist to take some of that colour off my face. But then, the head make-up artist came up to check the make-up and to my huge surprise, started gushing about how lovely I apparently looked. I didn't agree, but she was someone I trusted. So I decided to go along with it. And thank god I did, because on stage, it looked awesome.

The harsh stage lights do more than just light you up. The lights fall on your contours, highlighting your cheekbones and casting shadows around the eye and cheek area. That's just how light works. Even more so when light is made to concentrate on specific areas of your face. Stage make-up is designed to highlight and lowlight your contours in a specific manner. I am not sure if many make-up artists consciously understand and do this, but that is how they are trained. Usually, unless you have stage experience, you do not use make-up in the same way in your day-to-day life. Because, light in day-to-day life does not fall like that. It is much flatter. Stage light, on the other hand, is harsher. It creates more shadows. And stage make-up is designed to make the best of that light.

So what is garish off stage, usually ends up looking pretty good on stage.

What I am trying to say here is, trust the make-up artist. They're just trying to help you. They're not out to get you! No one is. And frankly, what will they really gain by making you look horrible? Think about it. Nothing. On the contrary, they will lose their name on such a huge platform. And that is something I am sure they do not want.

The only time when a make-up and hair artist can mess up your look is: (a) when they are incompetent and (b) they really are out to get you! Now what are the chances of either of these happening? Lets take (a). If the professionals are really so incompetent, chances are first that they wouldn't have made it to the pageant at all. But still, if you really feel that the artist is not up to the level that they should be, talk to the management, not the artist. The artist, if incompetent, will not be able to do any better than what they're doing, despite whatever pressure you put on them. So spare the artist. Instead, go to one of you chaperones and discuss your concerns with him/her.

What if it is (b)? What if the artist is really out to get you? Now again, chances are rare. Why would they? They are there to make a living, to do their job, so why would they want to mess it up? Exactly, they wouldn't. That is, unless you give them a reason to. If you keep criticising their work and throw a mini diva tantrum, you're basically asking for it. I know what you're thinking, 'I'm not throwing a tantrum! I'm just telling them I don't like what they are doing to my face. But they just don't listen!' Right? Okay then, let us discuss when you have a say in the matter and when you don't.

In national pageants, like Femina Miss India or I AM She–Miss Universe India, you never have a say. That is because, at these pageants, you don't really represent yourself as in yourself. You represent a potential Indian delegate to an international pageant. In such pageants, you have given yourself over to them. You are their responsibility.

As such, you will have next to no say officially about your 'look' for the day. However, that is only officially. Unofficially, you are a human, the artist is a human and humans have something called language which they use to communicate! If you really hate your look so much and if the make-up artist is competent enough, take them into your confidence. Most make-up and hair artists are sensitive to your opinions. They want you to like their work. So if you are unhappy, share your concerns with them. Don't just step up to them and say I don't like this, don't do it this way, do it that way. Don't tell them how to do their job. That is just plain rude. Rather, ask them politely if this is to be your look for the day and if they could give you some options. It would take a really hard-hearted person to send a contestant out in public when they feel ugly. If all fails, well, chin up, toss your fears away and out you march. You'll still dazzle the world anyway! You've got natural beauty after all, and nothing can hide that.

The golden rule is politeness. Arguing with the MUA is going to get you nowhere.

But in other pageants, especially international pageants, it depends on the occasion. Many pageants have fashion shows as part of their publicity package. It gives upcoming and established designers an opportunity to tie their names with a prestigious beauty pageant. Contestants of the pageants (obviously) are used as models for these fashion shows. During such occasions, you will be treated as a professional model, which means you have absolutely no say whatsoever on the outfit, on the hair or the make-up, officially or unofficially. So behave like a professional model and accept the look that has been decided for you. Remember, it doesn't matter whether you like your look or not. The objective is not for you to look pretty at all. The objective is for you to showcase the designer's vision. Nothing more, nothing less.

But there will be occasions like talent nights or the finale night when it is your vision that matters. On these occasions, you are the master. You get to decide your look. Find out with the make-up and hair artists when these occasions are and prepare your look in advance. On the day of the event, communicate the look you desire as clearly as possible to the artistes. Carrying pictures always helps. If it doesn't turn out as well as you wanted it to, communicate this to the artist. Listen to their opinions as well. If you are still not convinced, relay this to the artist as politely as you can and ask them to change/repair it.

The golden rule here is POLITENESS. Arguing with the MUA is going to get you nowhere. In fact, that can spell disaster for you. It doesn't sound very nice and nor is it fair, but the fact remains that you, having entrusted your face to the make-up artist in question, are at his/her mercy. It is up to them to send you out looking like an angel or looking like a circus clown. In fact, piss them off enough and I guarantee you will go out looking like a circus clown. So you need to stay on their good side. You won't believe the number of girls I've seen whining and whining on to the artist about how horrible they look. Please don't do that. Stay professional. If you have a problem, I repeat for the umpteenth time, communicate the problem to the artist in a polite manner.

Hair

Now we have our skin under control, we have our make-up under control, but what about hair? What do we do about hair? Hair is something that has always put me in a spot. As a teenager, I wanted curly hair and my hopes were dashed to the ground when my poker-straight hair just refused to curl. As a newcomer to Mumbai who had accepted that her hair would never be anything but straight, I was puzzled when the Mumbai humidity made it frizzy and brought waves into it that I never knew existed. As a tourist in Ladakh, I was perplexed and disappointed when my hair, that had always been able to take care of itself suddenly needed me now to desperately condition and hydrate it.

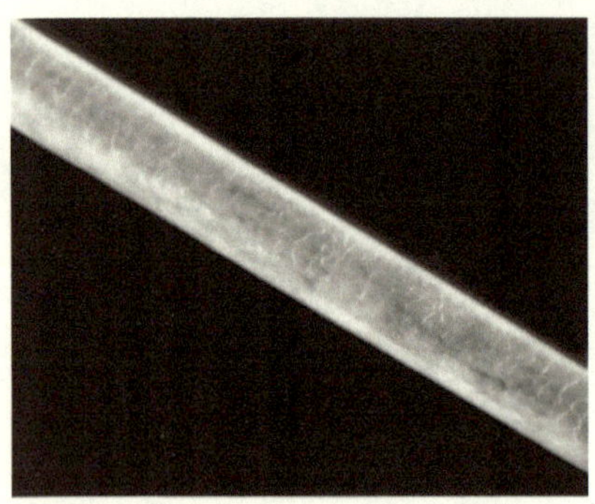

A strand of human hair at 200x magnification

Even today, whenever there is an event and I have to do my hair, the only thing I do is blow-dry it. Luckily, I have hair that looks presentable enough when simply blow-dried. But it would look way better if I had the patience to actually sit and style it. It's just laziness really, but since when did that become an excuse? You're right, it isn't.

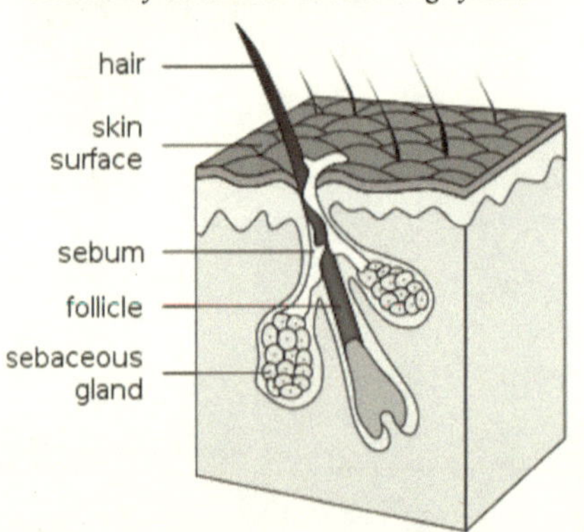

The structure of hair

What do we do about our hair? Well, as with skin, let's learn a little bit about the structure and biology of hair, so that we can learn to treat it right.

The Structure of Hair

According to Wikipedia, 'Hair is filamentous biomaterial, that grows from follicles found on the dermis.' I know, that sounds like Greek, at least to me! I prefer the *3 Idiots* style of explaining. Now, filamentous means 'a long chain of proteins' and biomaterial is anything that has to do with a biological system. Basically, hair is a structured chain of protein that grows from the follicles on our skin. We have hundreds of thousands of follicles on our head, which means, in turn, hundreds and thousands of hair (obviously). Each follicle produces numerous hairs during a lifetime. It is when those follicles get lazy and decide to just lounge about and do nothing that we start facing baldness. But that is nothing to worry about yet. As a twenty-something and especially as a girl, there's not much chance of that happening to you, not at the moment anyway. Now, excessive hair fall is a completely different matter and we will get to that in due course. For now, let's stick to the structure of hair.

It is when those follicles get lazy and decide to just lounge about and do nothing that we start facing baldness. But that is nothing to worry about yet. As a twenty-something and especially as a girl, there's not much chance of that happening to you, not at the moment anyway.

Hair is born, for lack of a better word, inside what is called the dermal papilla inside the follicle, or the bulb as it is popularly known. And as with most living things, new cells are constantly generated around it. But there is place for only so many cells in there. So the older cells, once dead, are displaced by the newer ones and are forced along the follicle towards the scalp. It is these dead cells that are compressed together to form a protein called keratin. So the hair we see growing out of our scalp is basically keratin, water and a certain binding agent that keeps the keratin and water together. Now you know why you hear so much about so and so hair colour or serum promising to deliver '25 percent pure keratin protein'. Whether it helps or not (and that we'll know in one of the forthcoming sections), it is definitely a great point to advertise on. Hair is basically keratin, so voila! Let's provide it with some more keratin!

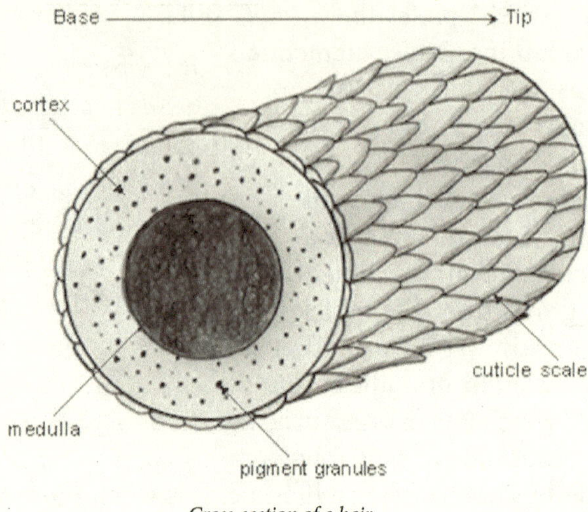

Cross-section of a hair

Hair shaft (the part we see growing out of our scalps) basically comprises three parts:

- Cuticle
- Cortex
- Medulla

The cuticle is the outermost part of the hair shaft. As shown in the illustration, it is formed out of overlapping cuticle scales, the thickness of which can vary. It can even be several layers thick. This is what they talk about in all those shampoo ads which promote themselves by showing how their brand, exclusively, can tame and smoothen runaway cuticles. However cheesy, the logic behind these ads is true. If the cuticle scales of your hair lie properly in order, your hair becomes smooth. It they refuse to behave and stick up from all sides, honey, you've got rough hair. It is these scales that make our hair flexible. Compare it to a silver chain. The more links you have in the chain and the smaller and closer set they are, the more flexible your chain is, right? If that chain is in fact a silver wire, with no links to speak of, would it be so flexible? Your cuticle scales are the links on the chain. They help your hair be flexible and to swish about. The healthier your cuticles, the lighter the movement. Cuticle scales are best off closed (just as the shampoo ads tell you), but sometimes, during hair treatments, you can open them up in order to let chemicals and other substances seep through.

The cortex is the main bulk of the hair. It consists of long fibres that twist together to form a rope-like structure. At the centre of the cortex lie the finest threads. These are three spring-like spiral keratin chains that have been bonded together. These chains are what give hair its ability to stretch. It would be pretty difficult for hairstylists to style hair into different hairdos without these chains. Hair would just break then. If you have hair that breaks easily, it is probably because your cortex is weak or a teeny bit malnourished. I'm no trichologist, but this is my diagnosis. Coming back to these three spring-like spiral chains—they are held together by three different kinds of bonds:

- Hydrogen
- Salt
- Di-sulphide or sulphur. The di-sulphide or sulphur bonds determine the shape of your hair—whether it's straight, wavy or curly. It is these bonds that are broken down when you have your hair treated in order to have the shape changed.

The cortex also determines the colour of your hair. It has within it two types of pigments:

- Melanin – the more melanin produced, the darker your hair/skin will be and the less melanin produced, the lighter. But in case, like me, you were sleeping throughout your biology classes in high school, you'll be

The cortex is the main bulk of the hair. It consists of long fibres that twist together to form a rope-like structure. These are three spring-like spiral keratin chains that have been bonded together. These chains are what give hair its ability to stretch.

interested to know that melanin only deals with brown and black. So what about blonde or red hair? That job belongs to:

- Pheomelanin – If you have hair that is blonde or red, note that it is your pheomelanin at work.

Hair can be classified under two completely different categories. The first is shape, or so we call it for lack of a better word (as in curly, straight, etc.). The second is the degree of oiliness (such as dry, oily, etc.).

You don't need to know this stuff. But if you're interested, knowing it will only help you. You will be able to understand your hair better, allowing you to treat and pamper it the best you can.

The medulla is the third and the innermost part of the hair shaft. The function of the medulla is not exactly clear to science yet. Apparently, in many types of hair, this layer is even absent.

Types of Hair

Hair can be classified under two completely different categories. The first is shape, or so we call it for lack of a better word (as in curly, straight, etc.). The second is the degree of oiliness (such as dry, oily, etc.). Lets deal with shape first.

The Different Types of Hair According to Shape

It is Andre Walker, a renowned Hollywood hair expert, who is credited with the classification of hair according to shape, in his book, *Andre Talks Hair!*. According to him, hair can be broadly classified into:

- Straight
- Wavy
- Curly
- Kinky

Each type of hair can be further divided into several subtypes.

Type 1

Straight hair is considered native to Asian and Caucasian people. It is said that when Homo Sapiens (that's us) moved out of the African continent and began to settle down up north, in Europe, they developed straight hair, as opposed to African curly or kinky hair in order to let some extra UV radiation into the skin, which is mandatory for the synthesis of Vitamin D. Straight hair can be prone to split ends, so make sure you visit your hairdresser once in two months for a trim. Straight hair can be further divided into three subtypes:

1a Straight Hair: This type of hair is usually very fine and thin. This is the type of hair that I have, so I'll tell you from personal experience as well that if you have this kind of hair and you plan to curl it, forget it! Not gonna happen! This kind of hair retains its shape no matter what. If you want curls, you'll have to spray it (with hair spray of course) so hard into place that even a tornado won't be able to displace a strand from your do. You know, I used to wonder at shoots why every hairstylist would insist on using such insane amounts of hair spray on me. Now after doing my research for this book, I know! Also, this kind of hair tends to be pretty oily, so you might want to wash it everyday in order to keep the excess oil at bay. While conditioning, take care to condition only the length of your hair. The roots have enough oil. But that's only on a very general basis and does not hold true for everyone. So you will have to be the judge of that. But the advantage is that the oiliness makes it hard to damage. You have inbuilt protective serum to

It is said that when Homo Sapiens (that's us) moved out of the African continent and began to settle down up north, in Europe, they developed straight hair, as opposed to African curly or kinky hair in order to let some extra UV radiation into the skin, which is mandatory for the synthesis of Vitamin D.

protect you from whatever damage that heat treatments like curling irons or blow-drying can cause. This, however, does not give you license to use curling irons or straighteners without applying protective serum first. Better safe than sorry, after all.

1b Straight Hair: This type has loads of volume and body. Like 1a, it is generally on the finer side and is quite smooth and shiny. Personally, this is the kind of hair that I would kill to have. It is easier to style and can hold a curl way better than 1a can, and still manage to take care of itself. For me, when it comes to straight hair, this type is the ultimate ideal.

1c Straight Hair: This kind of hair is generally quite coarse to touch. It is usually poker straight and can't hold a curl to save its life. But you know what the good part is? It is one of the strongest and most resilient types of hair. You'll have to try really hard to damage it. That is probably because this kind of hair is usually quite thick. While the two types of hair described above would ideally have five layers of cuticle scales, 1c has close to ten layers of cuticle scales. 1c is native to Asians.

Type 2

Wavy hair is caused by a moderate linking of the disulphide bonds in the hair protein. Remember I mentioned earlier that it is the linking of di-sulphide bonds that causes curly hair? Well, the more the amount of di-sulphide linking, the curlier your hair and the less the amount, the straighter. Wavy hair falls somewhere in between. Wavy hair is generally more prone to frizz, especially in tropical climates. Using some anti-frizz/humidity-protective styling products can help. Alternatively, try using

Wavy hair is caused by a moderate linking of the disulphide bonds in the hair protein... Well, the more the amount of di-sulphide linking, the curlier your hair and the less the amount, the straighter.

a blow-dryer with a diffuser attachment to avoid frizz. Wavy hair can be divided into three different subtypes.

2a Wavy Hair: This type of hair tends to be quite fine and thin, just like 1a, except, of course for the fact that 1a is straight and this is wavy. Like 1a, it sticks close to the head and doesn't have much volume. It also has quite a bit of sheen. And if this is the kind of hair you have, you are one lucky girl! This type of hair is said to be very agreeable to styling. It can easily hold any shape given to it without any fuss. And in our industry, that can only be a plus point, right?

2b Wavy Hair: Compared to 2a, 2b would be a little coarser to touch, although nowhere as near to the coarseness of 2c. It is also slightly curlier, or should we say, wavier, than 2a. Just like 2a, it tends to stick close to the head with limited bounce, even when layered. And it has a lovely sheen to it, when healthy. But apart from that how do you know if this is the kind of hair that you possess? Well, just look at your hair. Does it have near to no bounce (like 2a) and a nice sheen? Once you've extablished that, look out for the shape. Does it have a definitive 's' shape to it? If it does, you officially have 2b wavy hair. This type of hair is slightly more resistant to styling and has a tendency to frizz, so get that diffuser attachment.

2c Wavy Hair: Needless to say, this is the curliest, or rather, waviest and coarsest type of wavy hair. It tends to be on the borderline of curly vs wavy. As opposed to 2a and 2b, this type of hair actually consists of a few loose but actual curls. It is quite hard to style and cannot hold a shape. So you can expect a lot of hairspray coming your way. It is also quite prone to frizz. A gel-based styling product should help you handle that frizz.

Type 3

Type 3 tends to be curly. It usually has a definitive 'S' pattern to it, although it can also range from springy well-defined curves to corkscrew curls. You will find, if you have this kind of hair, that when wet, your hair will temporarily more or less straighten out, and then it will contract back into its original curly state once dry. This kind of hair is prone to frizz when exposed to humidity and has a lot of volume and body to it. It is probably not news to you that curly hair tends to get tangled more than its wavy and straight counterparts. For this reason, you must be careful to condition it regularly in order to minimise tangling. Brushing out tangled hair is not exactly what I would call fun! Curly hair can be divided into three subtypes:

3a Curly Hair: You must have noticed a pattern by now. 3a curly hair rests on the border of curly and wavy. These curls, like 2c wavy hair, are characterised by their signature loopy 'S' shaped curls. These curls tend to be springy, well-defined and big. You know those really thick curling rods? Well, 3a curly hair basically looks like it has been styled with one of those kind of curling irons. Not only are the curls big and loose, the texture of the hair is generally quite smooth and shiny, like both 1a and 2a. The best part about this kind of hair, however, is that it can be easily styled. So you're in the mood for straight hair? Not a problem. Your hair can hold the shape without the help, ok, maybe just a little of hair spray!

3b Curly Hair: 3b curls tend to be a little tighter than 3a curls. These well-defined copious curls range from bouncy ringlets to tight corkscrews. If you measure the circumference of these curls, you'll probably be surprised to find that it is rarely more than the circumference of an average-sized pencil. 3b curly hair is normally not that easy to style or straighten. It is not impossible, of course, it is very much possible! It's just that it's a chore. Plus it doesn't manage to retain its new shape that well without the help of a little hair spray. Also, like all kinds of curly hair, 3b curly hair is also quite prone to frizz when exposed to humidity. In order to avoid that, you might want to use gel-based and cream-based products. This rule, in fact, applies to all kinds of frizzy and/or curly hair.

3c Curly Hair: This is the last subtype when it comes to curly hair. As you have probably guessed, 3c curly hair is the curliest of all. This, in fact, lies right on the border of curly and kinky (African) hair. The kind of curls that this type of hair features are ultra-tight and fine corkscrew curls. They are usually packed together in such a manner that they create a lot of density and body in the hair. You will also find that each hair, if taken separately, is very fine and smooth in texture, thus differentiating it from kinky hair. But the downside to this kind of hair is that styling, or straightening it can be a chore. And I mean a real, real chore! One that will take ages. But it can be done. It takes time, yes, but can be done if you have enough patience.

Type 4

Now we come to the last and final type of hair, and that is kinky hair! For those of you who are not familiar with this term, kinky hair is, to put it simply, Afro-textured hair. This type of hair is ultra curly and frizzy and has a lot of volume and body to it. It's big, and when I say big, I mean big big! If you sit about counting it, you'll find that when it comes to the number of hairs, a person with kinky hair will have less hair than a person with straight hair, but since kinky, or rather, type 4 hair grows in a tiny spring-like helix shape, it occupies more space and therefore gives the impression of being denser than any other type of hair. It is generally quite coarse to touch and hard to style. In a recent, quite infamous incident, Andre Walker (who is credited with the classification of hair that we are discussing right now) got into trouble when he said and I quote, 'Kinky hair can have limited styling options. That's the only hair type I suggest altering.' People all over the world hated him for saying that. But you know what? Honestly speaking, he's not that far from the truth! Kinky hair is not for people who have limited periods of time at their disposal and that is really most of us. It takes effort and time to style. I'm not saying you should change it. No. In fact, I would be more than happy if you decide to go to a pageant with your kinky hair in its natural state. It gives an individualistic twist to your image and that can only be good. But you need to be prepared. Kinky hair, like curly hair, runs the risk of looking ungroomed and untidy if not meticulously cared for. If you feel you are up to the task, go for it. If not, maybe you should consider changing it. In the Indian subcontinent, however, it isn't very often that we come across kinky hair.

Like all other types of hair, kinky hair, or type 4 hair can also be categorised under four subtypes:

4a Kinky Hair: Following the pattern that this classification has followed till now quite predictably, 4a kinky hair is softer and finer than its 4b counterpart. Unfortunately, however, it is also much more fragile. It is tightly coiled (obviously, because without that coiling it would never have been classified as kinky) but the coiling is more on the spiral 'S' side than the helix side. This makes it easier to maintain on a day to day basis as it means that it does not tangle as much. Even if it does, detangling is easier because of the shape of the coil and its softness. One thing you need to remember though, is that 4a kinky hair looks much shorter than it actually is. You hair might actually be waist length but it curls so much that it ends up being only shoulder length. You must be careful to moisturise and seal this kind of hair religiously. Water, as always, is your best friend. Alternatively, shea tree butter is your next best friend. As soon as you step out of your shower, apply shea tree butter (in fact, it is best if you apply it as a leave-in conditioner), wrap your hair in a satin scarf and go to sleep. In the morning, rinse it out. And voila! Smooth, easy-to-manage kinky hair will be yours.

4b Kinky Hair: So you have 4b kinky hair. Right. But how do you identify it? Well, for one, it has a definite cottony texture to it. It's very dry, though not very coarse (thus leading to its telltale cottony texture. Also, this kind of hair does not curl in a spiral shape. It does so in a random helix shape, or in a 'Z'-shaped spiral. This type of hair is one of the driest, most delicate and one of the hardest to grow. It has 80 percent shrinkage, when it comes to hair growth. That means that the apparent length of your hair, i.e., what you see is only about 20 percent of its actual length. In effect, if your hair falls to your shoulder, you can be sure that this is only 1/5th of its length. In reality, if stretched out, your hair would reach your knees. Since it is the most delicate, it is also most susceptible to damage. That is why it should be treated with utmost care. Dermatologists say you should avoid heat styling. Well, that's simple to say, but in the fashion industry, it is not so easy to follow. So I would say, tweak that rule a little bit. Avoid heat styling where and when you can but at other times, just DO NOT, I repeat, DO NOT forget to apply protective serum beforehand. Also, immediately after the show or shoot, go home and give your hair a much-needed oil massage. Leave the oil overnight and rinse it out in the morning. I would recommend coconut oil, but maybe that's because that's what I'm used to. Experts say that kinky hair is better off with shea tree butter. The choice is yours to make. See what suits your hair the best and decide. But decide for sure. Your hair needs pampering!

4c Kinky Hair: This is obviously the coarsest and the kinkiest of kinky hair. You might think that is bad news. Well, you know what? It isn't! Really! Because of its coarseness, 4c kinky hair holds any style really well. And in the fashion industry, if that isn't good news, I don't know what is! But you know what they say – there is no such thing as a free meal. There is a downside to even this. It might be easy to style, but its also quite delicate, which means that excessive heat styling equals hair damage. But not to worry, the same rules that I mentioned for 4b kinky hair also apply to 4c. Style if you need to, but try and avoid heat styling where you can. I know it's not always possible, and that is where oiling and conditioning hair comes in. Did you know that the late Bollywood actress Sridevi never failed to wash her hair as soon as she got home to get rid of all the hair products that would inevitably be used to style her hair during shoots? And once it was reasonably dry, she would oil her hair, which was rinsed off in the morning right before her next shoot. That is the schedule you need to follow. Without fail. After washing, use a wide-toothed comb so as to detangle without breaking any hair.

I've always noticed that some people have the misconception that girls with type 4 hair cannot win a pageant. This is completely false. The case might have been true a few decades ago. But in today's politically correct age, such an argument has no meat to it. In fact, it didn't have any takers even in 1986. That was the year Halle Berry won Miss Ohio, complete with her Type 4 hair.

Throughout your journey, you will find people telling you that you have to be a certain 'type' to win a pageant – fair skin, straight hair, size zero, etc. They'll even tell you the colour of evening gowns that are most likely to help you win. Don't listen to them. Pageant history is full of 'anomalies'. In fact, every year is an anomaly. And that is because pageants are not looking for a type – they are looking for a person, a unique person who can represent their brand. The only thing that will make you win is you. So you just focus on that.

Types of Hair According to Degree of Oiliness

Clinically speaking, there is no such thing as dry hair, just as there is no such thing as dry skin (which we discussed earlier). That is because, as with skin, all kinds of hair contain some degree of oil. The level of oil present in hair might either be high or low, but it is always there. That is why I have classified it under the degree of oiliness, and not dryness.

Did you know that the late Bollywood actress Sridevi never failed to wash her hair as soon as she got home to get rid of all the products? Once it was reasonably dry, she would oil her hair, which was rinsed off in the morning right before her next shoot. That is the schedule you need to follow. Without fail, might I add.

Dry hair is basically nothing but hair that has a low degree of oiliness. This kind of hair, for various reasons, is unable to produce the amount of oil needed for it to maintain a smooth and manageable look. Examples of this kind of hair are basically all c types of hair – 1c, 2c, 3c and 4c.

Dry hair, as the name suggests, does not manage to produce as much oil as is needed for its maintenance. This could be due to many reasons, such as poor hair-care habits and constant styling without protection. Style all you want, but just don't forget to use protection.

Normal hair is hair that sports normal amounts of oil in it. It produces exactly as much oil as is needed. No more, no less. This kind of hair can be styled easily as it is neither too oily nor dry. Examples of this kind of hair are basically all b types of hair – 1b, 2b, 3b and 4b.

Dry hair, as the name suggests, does not manage to produce as much oil as is needed for its maintenace. This could be due to many reasons, such as poor hair-care habits and constant styling without protection. Style all you want, but just don't forget to use protection. Examples of this kind of hair are all 'a' types of hair – 1a, 2a, 3a and 4a.

What Kind of Hair Do You Have?

Now you know everything that there is to know about different kinds of hair. But what is really relevant to you is the information regarding your kind of hair. How do you find out? Figuring out whether it is straight, wavy, curly or kinky is easy enough. But is it a, b or c? Are your curls 'S' shaped or 'Z' shaped? And what the hell is the helix shape? (BTW, helix shape is just the official term for 'Z' shaped curls. Effectively, they are both one and the same.) For that, you need to ask (and answer) a few questions about your hair:

1. Is your hair straight, wavy, curly or kinky?

This should be easy enough to answer. Most of us have grown up knowing the shape of our hair. The straight, wavy and curly part, especially, is straight-forward enough. But if you are having trouble distinguishing between curly and kinky, let me clarify. Kinky hair is nothing but Afro-textured hair. If you are still having trouble recognising your type of hair, I have also given you some pictures along with the classification that you can refer to.

Now you know whether your hair is straight, wavy, curly or kinky. But is it a, b, or c? That comes next.

2. What is the texture of your hair? Is it fine, medium, normal, or coarse?

To find out pull out a strand from your hair. Yes, I know it hurts, but please do it, will you? Place it on a white piece of paper. Can you see it? If you can hardly manage to see it against the piece of paper, you have fine hair. That means you have Type a hair [it could be either 1 (straight), 2 (wavy), 3 (curly) or 4 (kinky)].

If you can easily see it without a problem, you have either medium or coarse hair. You need to put that strand of hair through another test now to find out which one it is. Pick up that strand of hair. Does it feel wiry between your fingers? If the answer is a no, then you have Type b hair [either 1 (straight), 2 (wavy), 3 (curly) or 4 (kinky)]. If the answer is a yes, then you have coarse hair, which means you have type c hair [either 1 (straight), 2 (wavy), 3 (curly) or 4 (kinky)].

In order to grow your hair to its optimum length, you need to know exactly how hair grows. Hair, as I've mentioned earlier, is made out of keratin, a protein.

Hair Growth

When I was at the I AM She–Miss Universe India, I met

a girl who was a chaperone. She was tiny, hardly over five feet tall and skinny. But she had hair that reached way beyond her hips. I've seen people with such long hair earlier as well. It's India, after all. Go to any small town and you'll see nothing but long hair! But this girl's hair was so well maintained — it was the best that I'd ever seen. It was type 1a hair — smooth and shiny, just like the kinds you see in a shampoo ad!

Ha ir usually grows in a cyclical phase. The three parts that form this phase are called anagen, catogen and telogen.Together, these three form the hair growth cycle

How many of us have craved for hair like that? I know I have. And I've always mourned the fact that my hair just refuses to grow beyond my waist. Yes, every person has their optimum hair length. For some it might be shoulder length, while for others it might be up to their knees. But for many of us, our hair never actually reaches that optimum length. We stay well below it and feel convinced that that is our optimum length, when it's not. In all probability, your optimum length is way longer than what you presume it to be, and only proper care and nourishment can help it reach there.

How Hair Grows

In order to grow your hair to its optimum length, you need to know exactly how hair grows. Hair, as I've mentioned earlier, is made out of keratin, a protein. It is these rope-like filaments that form keratin that provide strength and structure to the hair.

Hair usually grows in a cyclical phase. The three parts that form this phase are called anagen, catogen and telogen. Together, these three form the hair growth cycle.

The first part is the anagen phase, also known as the growth phase. It can last for up to eight years. However, this could vary according to genetics. During the anagen phase, hair grows at an approximate rate of 0.5 inches a month or 6 inches a year. That means that the longer your hair stays in the anagen phase, the longer and faster it will grow. For a person in his/her twenties, around 85 percent of their hair is in the anagen phase. Of course, along with age, this percentage goes down leading to hair loss.

The second part of the process is the catagen phase, also known as the transitional phase. Its purpose is mainly to allow the follicle to rest. It lasts for approximately two weeks, depending on your genes. During this phase, the follicle disintegrates slightly and shrinks, thus detaching from the papilla, thus (again) allowing it to rest and renew. This detachment from the papilla causes a complete shutting down of blood flow to the hair follicle. Because of that, the follicle shrinks further (told you, it's all a cycle!). Ultimately, over a span of two weeks, this follicle ends up shrinking to about 1/6th of its original size. This causes the hair shaft to be pushed upward towards the scalp.

The third part of the process is the telogen phase. This phase deals with, yes, you guessed it, hair fall. So far, the drastic shrinking of the hair follicle has led to the hair shaft being pushed upwards towards the scalp. As it inches upwards, it obviously reaches a point, where it has no other choice but to leave the scalp completely. This is what we know as hair fall. Right?

Wrong. That's what I thought too when I read about the catagen phase. This just seemed to be the obvious next step. But guess what? It isn't. What happens is that once the hair follicle shrinks to its smallest best and the hair shaft is (somewhat) pushed upwards, the follicle then decides that it needs a holiday. So it basically just lazes around doing nothing for a few months. This part could last between one to four months. During this time, understandably, those hair strands whose follicles are resting won't grow. After a rest of a few months, the follicle decides it has renewed itself enough to start work on a regular basis and the papilla once again starts multiplying cells within to create hair strands.

Now there is only so much room in one single follicle. So when the new hair starts to grow, it pushes out the old (which has now lost its root) and causes it to shed. This is nothing but hair fall.

A hair follicle needs constant blood fow, which helps it to function well and exercising acts as a stimulant. Blood carries important nutrients, which nourish the hair follicle so that your hair can grow in a healthy manner.

On a daily basis, it is normal to lose up to 100 strands of hair a day. It's only when it exceeds that amount (again, I'm talking about approximate numbers here, I don't expect you to go counting each and every hairs strand that falls out) that you need to worry. Until then, worry not! Hakuna matata!

Now that you know the technical side of hair growth, it's time to apply it in reality. How do you get your hair to grow at its optimum rate? The answer to that, my friend, lies in nutrition and proper hair care.

The two things that your hair needs most in order to grow well are exercise and nutrition

How Does Exercise Help?

Exercising stimulates blood flow. Remember reading just a few paragraphs earlier that in the catagen phase, as the hair follicle starts shrinking, the blood flow gets cut off and so the follicle starts shrinking even more? That's because a hair follicle needs constant blood flow, which helps it to function well and exercising acts as a stimulant. Blood carries important nutrients, which nourish the hair follicle so that your hair can grow in a healthy manner. The healthier your hair, the longer the anagen phase will last. The longer your anagen phase lasts, the longer your hair grows. Absence of these vital nutrients makes your hair brittle and easy to break — not exactly the recipe for healthy, long and strong hair.

So what are these vital nutrients that your hair needs? Why, that's Vitamin B mainly, Vitamin B3 to be precise. The nutrient that plays the biggest role in the production of keratin is Vitamin B3. What it all comes down to is that as long as your daily intake of Vitamin B3 is sufficient, your hair will grow as fast and as long as it is capable of. Beyond that depends on your genes. The recommended daily allowance for Vitamin B3 is 14 mg/day for women and 16 mg/day for men. The maximum that you are supposed to have, however, is 35 mg per day. Excessive doses of Vitamin B3 (unless recommended by your doctor) can lead to dermatological conditions such as skin flushing, itching, dryness and rashes including eczema. High doses could also, in rare cases, raise your blood sugar levels. Therefore, in case you are diabetic, I recommend consulting a doctor who can prescribe appropriate daily Vitamin B3 doses for you.

All that was theoretical. If only it was so easy! But it isn't. We live in an industrial age where pollution is a norm, a way of life. This pollution does a lot of harm to our health, so why on earth would it spare our hair? This is called weathering. So, what can you do to protect your hair from weathering? Well, you could always follow the following steps:

- Wash your hair regularly. The regularity of it depends on how oily your hair is. Dermatologists say ideally you should wash it every other day. That frequency is obviously for those with normal hair. I have oily hair, so I wash my hair every day to keep it from getting greasy. Washing it every other day would make my hair look like I have emptied a whole bottle of hair oil on my head. Those with dry hair might prefer a lower frequency, maybe once in two days, or once in three days. When we were kids, we only washed our hair once every Sunday, and it used to be fine. So it depends, but the key is to be regular. Don't let your hair get greasy. Greasiness attracts dirt and pollution to stick to the hair shaft.

- Condition your hair regularly. Whenever you shampoo, don't forget to condition your hair as well. In order to get rid of the dirt, shampoo strips your hair of any oil that might be there (as dirt particles stick to the oil layer). Now greasiness is bad, but your hair needs one thin layer of oil (called sebum) on top of it to keep it soft. Using a conditioner gives it that layer of oil. This is why our mothers and grandmothers used to apply oil to hair after washing. But we have an alternate solution—conditioner. So, use it.

- Oil your hair once a week. Not only does a hair massage make you feel relaxed, it also nourishes your hair. Dip your fingers in lukewarm oil and apply it on your hair. The trick is not to apply oil along the length of your hair; instead, apply it to your roots, where it can seep through to the hair follicle. Make sure you cover the entire surface of your scalp. Once your roots are done, you can apply some oil along the length of your hair. If you have fine hair (which tends to be oily), you can avoid this step as that oil will seep down anyway. For all other types of hair, this step is equally necessary. Ideally, you should leave it on for a few hours. Applying oil just before going to bed is a good idea as you can then wash it off in the morning. But if you forget and are pressed for time, you can run a wide-toothed comb through the oiled hair for fifteen to twenty minutes and then wash it off.

- When your hair is wet, use a wide-toothed comb. Hair tends to be delicate when wet and can break easily under the pressure that a hair brush yields. But don't make the mistake of waiting till your hair is dry. Water is a lubricant. It helps you detangle your hair much more easily than would be possible when hair is dry. The

Oil your hair once a week... Dip your fingers in lukewarm oil and apply it on your hair. The trick is not to apply oil along the length of your hair; instead, apply it to your roots, where it can seep through to the hair follicle. Make sure you cover the entire surface of your scalp.

chances of hair breakage and fall are much higher if you detangle it when dry.

- Brush your hair regularly. And by regularly, I don't mean the age-old adage of brushing your hair hundred strokes a day. I mean just what I said, regularly. Make sure your hair is detangled at all times. Not only does it look good, it will also prevent hair breakage. Plus, when you brush your hair, you massage your scalp leading to better blood circulation which means, as we all know now, longer and stronger hair.

- Exercise regularly. Now you have one more reason to head to the gym and work out. Exercise leads to better blood circulation, which, of course leads to longer and stronger hair.

- Eat a balanced, nutritious diet. Don't go deficient in Vitamin B3. You can find Vitamin B3 in food items such as chicken, tuna, eggs, tofu, soy, avacados, dates, tomatoes, most green leafy vegetables, carrots, nuts (yes, they are good for you, despite being high in calories), mushrooms and legumes.

Styling Your Hair for the Pageant

The thing about pageants is that you are always hard-pressed for time. At I AM She, we had to be at the gym by 5.30 am for our 6 am workout. After the workout, we were given about half an hour for two people to shower and get dressed. On top of that, we were expected to look drop-dead gorgeous. All pageants have similar schedules. So you, girl, have got to be on top of it all.

Make sure your hair is detangled at all times. Not only does it look good, it will also prevent hair breakage. Plus, when you brush your hair, you massage your scalp leading to better blood circulation which means, as we all know now, longer and stronger hair.

Now, when you have only fifteen minutes in the morning to get ready (since your roommate will take up the other fifteen minutes), you can't spend ages straightening your curly hair or curling your straight hair. No. You need to find a style that suits your original hair texture. Here are some tips on how to quickly style your hair:

Straight Hair

I have straight hair and what I have noticed about my hair is that the sides and the back don't matter much. It is the front, around my forehead that does. That has to be properly styled, the rest of it will all just fall into place. So, I suggest you blow-dry the front section of your hair. Blow-dry it straight. When blow-drying, do not hold the shaft of the dryer in one place. This will burn your hair rather than shape it. Keep moving it. Synchronise it with the movements of your hair brush. Remember, hot air moulds the shape of your hair and cold air sets it in place. So always follow up with cold air after shaping it with hot air. This is not the time for experiments. You won't have time to correct any mistakes. Blow-dry the front section straight and just off your face and voila! You're ready. The same applies for bangs as well. Keep those bangs straight and under control (use a light spritzing of hairspray if you need to) and the rest will fall into place.

Wavy Hair

So you have wavy hair? Cool, stick to it. Don't try to curl or straighten it (unless you are a pro who can do it in five minutes flat), there won't be enough time. Give yourself a beach look. Spritz some mousse and finger it through the length of your hair. Pick up a dryer with a diffuser attachment and blow-dry your hair. You don't need to dry it completely. And anyway, that'll simply take up too much time. Just remove the excessive dampness from your hair and let the rest air-dry to give it a very natural look.

Curly Hair

If you have curly hair, for god's sake, don't set about straightening it. First of all, why would you want to? Curly hair is so beautiful! Just let it be. Second, sweetie, you have fifteen minutes. Do you really think you'll be able to straighten it all in just fifteen minutes? I think not. For curly hair, remember, the number one rule is DO NOT brush your hair. That'll just make it frizzy. Instead, comb it with a wide-toothed comb. Finger some product like mousse into it to keep it from going frizzy and let it air-dry.

Kinky Hair

Kinky hair has been long known as inconvenient and one that requires high maintainance. Maybe it is. I wouldn't know, I don't have kinky hair. But what I do know is that I would like to help you keep your kinky hair as it is and avoid relaxing or straightening it out.

For kinky hair, all you need to do to style it is to comb in some leave-in conditioner right after shampooing. Use a wide-toothed comb. For type 4c and some instances of type 4b, leave the conditioner in. For all others, rinse it out but not entirely. Leave some in near the ends (that's why I suggested leave-in conditioner). Now let your hair air-dry. Don't blow-dry it. And don't touch it with your hands. Both these actions will only make it frizzy. Just let it be and let it air-dry.

Alternatively, for easier maintenance, what you could do is plait it all into tiny little braids or into cornrows. I personally prefer the little braids to cornrows as I feel they are more elegant. But the decision is yours. Who said a beauty queen can't have cornrows? But the only drawback with this is that the hair can get messy after a week or two and you might have to re-plait them. And doing that is near impossible during a pageant as the whole process takes some time. So while this is a viable option for short-term pageants, for longer ones, you might have to go for the former option.

Permanent Hair Treatments

A few centuries ago, if a woman wasn't happy with the shape of her hair, she had no option but to resign herself to it, simply because there was no way around it. But all that changed around a hundred and fifty years ago because of Marcel Grateau in 1872. He came up with a pair of specially manufactured tongs, which would be heated over a gas stove. The temperature would then be checked by pressing a piece of paper against the tongs. If the paper browned slightly, it meant that the temperature was correct and that the tongs could then be used to curl hair in a perm. This contraption was called the 'Marcel Tongs'. It was an early ancestor of what we today know as curling irons.

By 1930, permanent waving was an established ritual for modern middle-class women who would religiously visit their hairdresser every three months for a new perm as their roots grew out. And the trend was only to continue. In fact, the word perm itself comes from the word 'permanent'.

Like curling irons, Marcel tongs also produced an effect that was only temporary. And the damage caused to hair was also enormous. But that was only the beginning.

Soon enough, in 1906, a man named Karl Nessler came up with an electrical permanent waving machine. Others followed, made amends and changed Nessler's design a bit to make their own innovations. By 1930, permanent waving was an established ritual for modern middle-class women who would religiously visit their hairdresser every three months for a new perm as their roots grew out. And the trend was only to continue. In fact, the word perm itself comes from the word 'permanent'. Pretty obvious, huh?

But perms are not the only kind of hair treatments available in the market today. Nowadays, when we talk about permanent hair treatments, we mean hair relaxation and rebonding too. And we haven't even touched the subject of hair colour yet. Now, whether it is for an aesthetic purpose that you get a certain treatment done or for practical purposes, you ought to walk in with your eyes wide open. You need to know the pros and cons of the whole process. You need to know that these are chemical treatments, after all. They are not natural. You are, in effect, breaking down the natural structure of your hair. That means harmful side effects (like hair fall) are a given. If you understand well that there will be side effects, you can take action to minimise them. If you go there and get stuff done under the illusion that nothing will happen, then obviously you won't take any precautions and you will, therefore, be worse off.

I have had my hair permed and coloured and highlighted. I'm not going to be the pot that calls the kettle black. All I'm trying to do here is to give you a complete and true picture so that you weigh your pros and cons and make an informed decision.

Perm

The perms that I have mentioned till now, by Marcel and by Nessler, were essentially heat treatments. But those are not the techniques we use today. The ancestor of the technique that we commonly use today was developed in 1938, by a certain Arnold F. Willatt. He developed a technique called a cold wave, which did not require the use of machines and heat. Instead, he used ammonium thioglycolate on hair that was sectioned and wrapped around rods. This broke down the disulphide bonds in the hair. Next, hydrogen peroxide was applied to close the disulphide bridges which would have by then reformed themselves to the shape of the rods. The whole process took six to eight hours.

They [chemical treatments] are not natural. You are, in effect, breaking down the natural structure of your hair. That means harmful side effects (like hair fall) are a given. If you understand well that there will be side effects, you can take action to minimise them.

But that's history. Today, the perming technique is more or less similar to Arnold F. Willatt's method. The only difference is that today, we use sodium thioglycolate instead of ammonium thioglycolate at a pH of 8 to 9.5. Unlike the six to eight hours of waiting back then, today's process takes only fifteen to twenty minutes. And, we don't use hydrogen peroxide anymore. We use a neutraliser to bring the pH balance of our hair back to neutral. Also, many different types of rods are used to wrap hair around. Generally speaking, the smaller the rod, the tighter your curls will be.

Remember, a perm takes twenty-eight hours to completely relax. So don't worry too much about the results before the end of those twenty-eight hours. Save the worrying for later.

These classic alkaline perms are used for stronger, coarser hair generally, typically type 'c' hair. For finer, more delicate hair, acid perms are preferred. This method of perming was developed in the 1970s. For this glyceryl monothioglycolate is used instead of ammonia. This kind of perm takes a little more time but is much kinder to your hair. There is also a heat treatment involved in order to set the hair where the client is placed under a dryer (not the usual blow-dryers, but those hooded ones at the salon that look like space masks). Remember, a perm takes twenty-eight hours to completely relax. So don't worry too much about the results before the end of those twenty-eight hours. Save the worrying for later.

Hair Rebonding

Yes, even perms are all about rebonding the disulphide bonds in your hair. But that is just what this procedure is called. So while perm means waves and curls, rebonding means sleek and straight hair. Illogical nomenclature? Indeed!

So how exactly does hair rebonding work? Well, the process is more or less the same as it is for perming. First, hair is neatly divided into sections and a relaxant (usually an alkali like sodium thioglycolate or ammonium thioglycolate) is applied to each and every hair shaft, as is done for perms. The only difference is that hair is not wrapped around rods. Instead, a thin plastic board is used to keep hair poker straight. You have to wait for about half-an-hour while the disulphide bonds break.

Next, hair is steamed for forty minutes and then rinsed. It is then blow-dried and the dry hair is straightened once again with a straightening iron (preferably a ceramic one since that is less damaging to hair) in order to break any left over disulphide bonds that might have been left unbroken.

Once straightened, you must be careful to not wash your hair for at least three days as that will just reverse the effect created by rebonding. Also, avoid pinning up your hair or tying it up in a ponytail. It can get tiring but keep at it.

After this, hair is once again divided into sections and a neutraliser is applied to reset the disulphide bonds. The neutraliser is kept on for around thirty minutes and then rinsed off, thus giving you sleek, straight hair.

But once straightened, you must be careful to not wash your hair for at least three days as that will just reverse the effect created by rebonding. Also, avoid pinning up your hair or tying it up in a ponytail. It can get tiring but keep at it. It is only a matter of three days. And a messed-up procedure can look pretty terrible.

Relaxing

Hair relaxing is achieved through the use of relaxers. Relaxers can either be lye or non-lye. It is commonly assumed that non-lye relaxers are kinder to hair, but, unfortunately, that is not the case. Non-lye relaxers can be just as harsh as lye relaxers. The only reason relaxers are so popular today is because they are much more affordable than rebonding. But for me, that doesn't seem to be reason enough. If you are entering this industry, there will be a lot of wear and tear on your hair. So, it doesn't make sense for you to go through such a damaging process (especially since there is more potential damage coming your way) when there is a better option available. Trust me and go for rebonding instead. It's heavier on the pocket but it really is worth it!

Ever since the time of the Romans, we have constantly experimented with the colour of our hair. The ancient Greeks used to wash their hair with harsh soaps to redden and lighten their hair.

Hair Colour

If you have black or brown hair, it is because of the eumelanin present in your hair. If you have mainly red or blonde hair, it is due to the presence of phaeomelanin in your hair. But when have humans been happy and content with the colour of their hair? Ever since the time of the Romans, we have constantly experimented with the colour of our hair. The ancient Greeks used to wash their hair with harsh soaps to redden and lighten their hair. The Romans would rinse their hair with a dye made of walnuts and leeks to darken their hair. The Asians used to (and still do) redden their hair with henna. Today, we do all of the above, the only difference being that now we dye our hair with permanent and semi-permanent chemical dyes rather than soaps or other natural dyes. But what really happens when we dye our hair? How does the basic colour of our hair change?

Well, you know, that's just the thing—the basic colour of your hair never changes. If you've ever had your hair coloured, you'd have noticed that within a few weeks, your roots grow out and they are always the colour that your hair originally is, the colour that was genetically predetermined for you.

There are quite a few types of hair colour based on how permanent or not they are. These are:

- **Semi-permanent hair colour**: Being only semi-permanent, this doesn't last long. By the time you've had your twelfth hair wash, it'll have, in all probability, lost its lustre. These kind of hair colours contain tiny colour molecules that enter your hair through the cuticles and settle down in the cortex. However, they don't react with your natural hair colour pigments (which is what changes the colour of your hair permanently). If your hair colour says that it contains no ammonia and no peroxide, it is most probably a semi-permanent hair colour, or at least, you should hope so. Why? We'll get to that in the next section.

- **Demi-permanent hair colour**: This lasts longer, maybe upto twenty-four hair washes even. With demi-permanent hair colour, something called the pre-colour molecules enter the hair shaft through the cuticles to enter the cortex where they form medium- to large-sized hair colour molecules. The large size of the molecules makes it difficult for them to exit the hair shaft so easily, thus resulting in the hair holding on to the colour for a little longer.

- **Permanent hair colour**: This kind of hair colour will last as long as your hair does, although you will have to keep going in for root touch-ups every few months. But how do they work, really? To keep it simple, it's a two-step process. First the, bleach or hydrogen peroxide is applied to your hair to make it completely devoid of any colour. Now that it is a blank canvas, any colour can be applied to it. First, analine derivatives are inserted into the hair shaft. These analine derivatives are nothing but uncoloured dye molecules. Next, hydrogen peroxide is applied. This kickstarts the oxidation process, which makes the analine derivative molecules to blow up to three hundred times their original size so that they cannot just slip out of the hair shaft. Next, ammonia is used to raise the pH of the hair. Without raising the pH of the hair, the hair colour would not be able to penetrate into the cortex. It would just sit there in and around the hair shaft, which makes it easy to just wash out.

- **Gradual dyes:** These are rinse dyes (meaning you rinse your hair with them when you shampoo) that are applied over a period of time. Each time you shampoo, you apply it and gradually, over time, you will attain your desired hair colour. Unfortunately, these are best used for darkening your hair, not for lightening. Also, in order to maintain the colour, you will have to keep applying it every few days.

- **Temporary dyes**: These are perfect for a night out when you'd like to glam up your look. You just spray the dye onto your hair and voila! You have a different colour of hair. But don't touch your hair when you've dyed it such. That'll only make the colour run out, and believe you me… that is not a pretty sight. Most pageants have night-outs where you go to a night club and just let loose (of course, in all probability, the press will also be there so, letting loose, might just be a relative term over here). You could always use a temporary dye in a quirky colour to give yourself a streak of different colour or to give yourself a dip-dyed look for the night.

Ammonia vs Ammonia-free?

It's all the rage now, these ammonia-free hair colours. And we use them too, because we feel that just because ammonia isn't there in it anymore, it doesn't damage hair. Sometimes, we go as far as to convince ourselves that it is even organic! But guess what? It isn't. Prolonged exposure to ammonia can not only irritate your eyes and skin in what could be an allergic reaction, but also cause permanent damage to your cornea, skin and lungs. Of course, this is only with prolonged exposure and most hair dyes contain no more than one percent of ammonia. But the principal that most ad experts follow is: ammonia damages hair (which it of course does); so, if we come up with a product that is ammonia-free, sales will but obviously go up.

But sadly, that isn't how it works. If your hair dye isn't using ammonia, it is using alkanolomine. These do the same thing that ammonia does. They stink less and technically speaking, they are not ammonia; but that doesn't mean they are any less harmful. You will have to use hair colour at some point or the other in this industry, but you should know the pros and cons equally well.

A Few Hair-Colouring Techniques

Highlighting: We've all heard of highlighting. It is the most common technique used today. When you colour parts of your hair in a shade lighter than your natural shade you are effectively 'highlighting' them. When done properly, no one will even get to know that you have consciously highlighted your hair, it will look merely sun-kissed.

Lowlighting: Lowlighting is just the opposite of highlighting. When you colour parts of your hair in a shade darker than your natural one, it is called 'lowlighting'. It is a technique that gives results that are a lot more subtle than highlights.

Highlighted hair

Streaks: This type of colouring is not for the faint-hearted. It usually refers to a streak of colour (usually bold like red or purple) in your hair. It's perfect if you want to have a head-turning effect. Needless to say, it can neither be described as subtle nor natural.

Dip-dyeing: This is a relatively new trend. This, again, is not for the faint-hearted. Dip-dying would make your hair look like the ends

(and the ends only) have been dipped in a tub of dye. Again, this technique looks better with bolder colours.

Choosing the Right Hair Colour

You would have surely seen these people from time to time – they'd have platinum blonde hair with type 4 skin, or maybe blue-black hair with type 1 skin! Just doesn't go, does it? But you know what? These people truly believe that their hair colour suits them. And you know what else? That person could just as easily be you. Because we are all as capable of making mistakes as the person next to us. But in a pageant, you can't afford to. So here is a basic guide to help you choose the perfect hair colour for you:

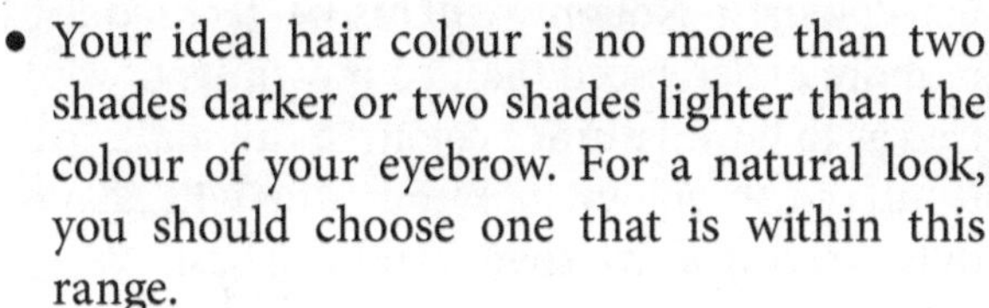

- Your ideal hair colour is no more than two shades darker or two shades lighter than the colour of your eyebrow. For a natural look, you should choose one that is within this range.

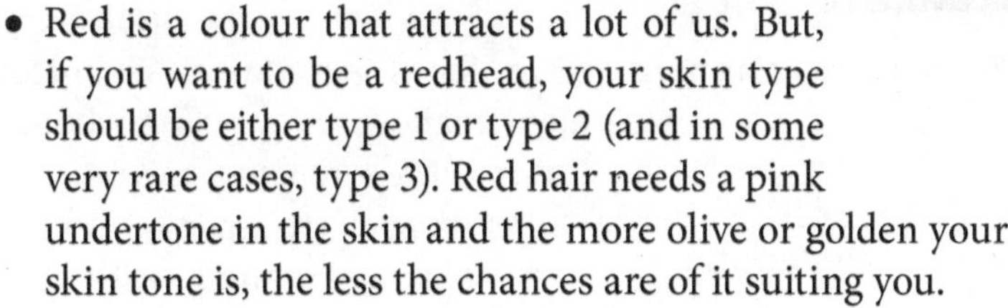

- Red is a colour that attracts a lot of us. But, if you want to be a redhead, your skin type should be either type 1 or type 2 (and in some very rare cases, type 3). Red hair needs a pink undertone in the skin and the more olive or golden your skin tone is, the less the chances are of it suiting you.
- If your hair is dull and damaged and you wish to colour it (which you should avoid, by the way, until your hair recovers), stick to a shade of brown. Dark hair is adept at reflecting light and is better at hiding any breakage or dullness than lighter-coloured hair.
- A basic guide is that the darker your skin colour, the darker your hair should be. Objectively speaking, you

can go for blonde hair even if you have brown skin, on the condition that it is a honey blonde or something of the type. But being from the Indian Subcontinent, I would advise you not to do so. On us, it just looks fake and well, 'wannabe', because such shades do not occur naturally among us. So stick to shades of brown.

- But if you're not from the Indian Subcontinent, have type 1 skin and want to have platinum blonde hair? Cool! Go for it. And while you are at it, ask your colourist to give it a golden base. Those almost white strands can actually look pure white in sunlight making you look like you're ageing prematurely.

- I know you get a lot of over-the-counter boxes of hair dye, but if you want my advise, stay away from those. Instead, shell out a little extra money and go to a professional colourist. Not only will his/her technique be better and more experienced than your own (you would be surprised as to how natural a colourist can make even the most outlandish colour look) but s/he will also be able to advise you on which shades suit you best.

A Word of Caution

If you are planning to go for a permanent chemical treatment, make sure you go to a reputed salon with a reputed hairdresser. With such treatments, you are playing around with the basic structure of your hair and a poorly performed treatment can result in breakage of the disulphide bonds. Yes, this is a part of all perm, rebonding and relaxing treatments. But a properly performed one will also reset the bonds to their new shape once done. And a poorly performed, careless one might fail to

If you are planning to go for a permanent chemical treatment, make sure you go to a reputed salon with a reputed hairdresser. With such treatments, you are playing around with the basic structure of your hair and a poorly performed treatment can result in breakage of the disulphide bonds.

reset them. This will inevitably lead to hair that is brittle and fragile. Even the simple act of combing might lead to excessive hair loss.

Don't listen to those people who say girls with short hair can't win pageants and pageants need long hair. That's rubbish.

But cheer up! This isn't permanent damage. It is the length of the hair that has been damaged, not the bulb. So the new hair that grows out will be healthy and strong. But the temporary hair loss can be quite depressing. In order to avoid that, I suggest getting a perm done about six months before you plan to enter your pageant, especially if you have never gotten one beforehand. That way, any mistakes can be set right and every three months, you can go to get your roots touched up in order to maintain the perm.

But if the treatment turns out disastrous and your once lustrous hair is now lifeless and dull, do not worry. You have six months. You can always grow back your hair. And worst come worst, you can grow your hair as much as it will grow in six months and have your hairdresser trim or even chop off the damaged ends. Don't listen to those people who say girls with short hair can't win pageants and pageants need long hair. That's rubbish. Ever heard of Armi Kuusela? She was Miss Universe 1952, the first woman ever to win the title and crown of Miss Universe. You must have read of her in chapter two, remember? Well, turn back to that page and check out her photograph. Do you see what I see? Yep, her hair is short.

Still not convinced? Well, here's another photograph for you.

Recognise her?

Flaviana Matata, Miss Tanzania 2007

She was Miss Tanzania 2007. She also made it to the Top Ten of Miss Universe in 2007, the same year that Riyo Mori from Japan won. She was my personal favourite, Miss Tanzania. And see that? She has a shaved head.

Whether it be Ariana Miyamoto (Miss Universe Japan 2015) or Kayla Martell (Miss Delaware 2011), the list of contestants with short hair is only growing longer and longer. Martell had been diagnosed with alopecia when she was ten, and at the time of her pageant she had no hair. Yet, she was placed in the Top Ten of the Miss America pageant. She didn't let alopecia stop her—so are you really going to let a little burnt hair stop you? I don't think so.

Caring for Treated Hair

Caring for treated hair is not very different from caring for untreated hair. You just need different products, ones that are sensitive enough to your chemically treated hair. Normal shampoos and conditioners won't do. Consult your hairdresser as to which products you should use for chemically treated hair. Given below are some basic tips:

- Wash your hair regularly but don't overdo it. Once in two days should be enough. Don't shampoo too rigorously. Keep it mild and gentle.
- It can be tempting to skip the conditioning part once in a while but for treated hair, that is a no-no. Whenever you shampoo, always condition. Without fail. Period.
- Use shampoos, conditioners and other products that have been specifically designed to be sensitive to treated hair. They might be a little expensive, but trust me, they're worth it. Consult your hairdresser to learn more about different brands.
- Chemically treated hair makes hair vulnerable to damage. And damaged ends never look good. So go for a trim once in a while to snip off those damaged ends.
- Once a week, use a deep-conditioning mask or massage

your scalp with oil to protect your tresses and keep them soft and healthy.

- You will not be able to completely avoid blow dryers, straighteners or curling tongs. Who knows that better than me? But you can make sure that whenever you go through heat treatment, you use some kind of a protective serum. Use one that is sensitive to chemically treated hair.

The sun doesn't just affect our skin. It affects our hair too. We've all seen sun-bleached hair. But chemically treated hair is more susceptible to sun damage than untreated hair.

- The sun doesn't just affect our skin. It affects our hair too. We've all seen sun-bleached hair. But chemically treated hair is more susceptible to sun damage than untreated hair. So make sure you invest in a sun block for your hair that protects you from both UVA and UVB rays.
- Lastly, remember that the word 'permanent' only applies to the length of your hair. That is the only part that has been treated. New hair that grows from the roots has not been exposed to this treatment yet. So if you have straightened your hair and you have originally curly hair, the new hair growing from your roots will be curly, not straight. The same goes for hair colour as well. So once in three months or six months or maybe even one-and-a-half months, depending on how fast your hair grows, go to your hairdresser to get a touch-up. Not getting a touch-up will just make your hair look shabby and uncared for.

Easy-to-do Hairstyles

When you're in the training period of a pageant, you don't have much time to get ready in the morning. Usually, you have to wake up at 5 or 6 a.m. for gym. It's usually an hour-and-a-half of gymming in the morning followed by breakfast. Now after this, the actual day begins, which comprises rehearsals, specialised training, photo shoots, press conferences and events. And for all of these, the pressure to look good is immense. And the actual time you'll have to get ready will be very little.

Usually, your chaperone will tell you after breakfast that you have half-an-hour to get ready. That might seem like enough time. But if you believe that, think again.

Keep in mind that you share your room with another girl who needs to get ready too. And you need to respect that. This is the girl you'll have to live with for the next one month to forty-five days. It would be helpful to get along with her. Pageants are stressful enough as they are without the added pressure of a roommate that you can't stand. So, in effect, that means you have only half-an-hour on a shared basis with your roommate. Actually, not even that! You need to be downstairs ten minutes early in order to avoid being late… so that is twenty minutes to shower, wash your hair, put on make-up and do your hair. You need to be peaceful and not panic.

So, under such circumstances, you can't spend ages in front of the mirror trying out various hairstyles that require a lot of effort. What you need are a few easy-to-do five-minute hairstyles that look chic but in reality require very less time and effort.

But first—the basics.

HAIRSTYLING 101

Hairstyle illustrations by: Anjali Sakleshpur

Braiding

I'm sure all of you know how to braid hair. We've all braided hair since we were kids, thanks to schools and their stringent rules. But since we are starting with the basics, why not start with the *very* basic. I don't necessarily recommend the school girl braid as a hairstyle for a pageant. That is a bit too, well, school-girlish. But the skill is useful to learn as many other hairstyles use this in their formation.

Step 1: Brush your hair to make sure it is smooth and free of any tangles.

Step 2: Pull all your hair back behind your shoulders. Divide your hair into three equal sections.

Step 3: Take the leftmost section and pull it over the middle section (so that the leftmost and the middle section exchange places).

Step 4: Take the rightmost section and pull that over the middle section too.

Step 5: Continue steps 3 and 4 until the desired braid length is reached and secure with an elastic.

Inverted Braid

This is very similar to the simple school-girl braid except for the fact that it is inverted. Personally, I find that this looks much more interesting that the normal braid.

Step 1: Brush your hair to make sure it is smooth and free of any tangles.

Step 2: Pull all your hair back behind your shoulders. Divide your hair into three equal sections.

Step 3: Take the rightmost section and pull it under (repeat: under, not over) the middle section.

Step 4: Take the leftmost section and pull that under the middle section too.

Step 5: Continue steps 3 and 4 until the desired braid length is achieved and secure with an elastic.

French Braid

A lot of you are probably familiar with the French braid. Personally, it is one of my favourites. It is easy to do and if rightly done, it doesn't rob you of any glamour either.

Step 1: Brush your hair to make sure that it is smooth and free of all tangles.

Step 2: Pull all your hair back behind your shoulders.

Step 3: Take a little chunk of hair from your crown area and braid it once.

Step 4: Add a few strands of hair from the right side of your scalp to the rightmost section and pull that over the middle section.

Step 5: Add a few strands of hair from the left side of your scalp to the leftmost section and pull that over the middle section.

Step 6: Continue steps 4 and 5, adding a little hair from the scalp into the braid each time, until the desired braid length is achieved and secure with an elastic.

Dutch Braid

The Dutch braid is very similar to the French braid. It is in fact an inverse of the French braid.

Step 1: Brush your hair to make sure that it is smooth and free of all tangles.

Step 2: Pull all your hair back behind your shoulders.

Step 3: Take a little chunk of hair from your crown area and braid it once.

Step 4: Add a few strands of hair from the right side of your scalp to the rightmost section and pull that under, rather than over the middle section.

Step 5: Add a few strands of hair from the left side of your scalp to the leftmost section and pull that under the middle section.

Step 6: Continue steps 4 and 5 adding a little hair from the scalp into the braid each time, until the desired braid length is achieved and secure with an elastic.

Four-Strand Braid

This braid looks simple like its three-strand counterpart but at the same time is much more chic. You can also try a French four-strand braid or a Dutch four-strand braid.

Step 1: Brush your hair to make sure it is smooth and free of all tangles.

Step 2: Pull all your hair back behind your shoulders and divide your hair into four sections. Let us name them 1, 2, 3 and 4 with 1 being the leftmost section and 4 being the rightmost section.

Step 3: Pull section 1 over section 2.

Step 4: Pull section 4 over section 1 making sure that the two outside sections are now inside crossing each other.

Step 5: Repeat steps 3 and 4 until the desired braid length is achieved and secure with an elastic.

Five-Strand Braid

This one is pretty hard to do by yourself but practice makes perfect. I remember my first few attempts at braiding my own hair with a three-strand braid when I was a kid. I failed miserably. It took me a good half-an-hour to manage a simple braid. And now? A mere five minutes. Also, you can try a French five-strand braid or a Dutch five-strand braid.

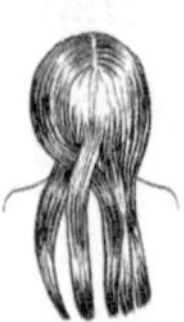

Step 1: Brush your hair to make sure it is smooth and free of all tangles.

Step 2: Pull all your hair back behind your shoulders and divide your hair into five sections. Let us name them 1, 2, 3, 4 and 5 with 1 being the leftmost section and 5 being the rightmost section.

Step 3: Pull section 1 over section 2 and then under section 3.

Step 4: Pull section 5 over section 4 and then under section 3.

Step 5: Repeat steps 3 and 4 until the desired braid length is achieved and secure with an elastic.

PONYTAIL HAIRSTYLES

Soft-Swept Ponytail

This, like the three-strand braid is a very simple hairstyle to do, even simpler, I should say. Also, it can look very chic when neatly done.

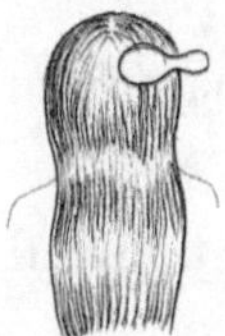

Step 1: Brush your hair to make sure it is smooth and free of all tangles.

Step 2: Brush all your hair back behind your shoulders and gather it in your hand at the desired height of the ponytail.

Step 3: Smoothen the top and the bottom parts of the scalp all around the ponytail with a hairbrush or comb.

Step 4: Secure with an elastic. If you want to look really polished, use one of those simple black elastics to fasten your hair, then take a lock of hair from the bottom of the ponytail, wrap it around the base (elastic-fastened area) and pin it into place using a couple of hairpins.

Bouffant High Ponytail

This particular hairstyle has been sweeping the red carpets lately. From Aishwarya Rai at Cannes to Kim Kardashian, the bouffant/pompadour with a high ponytail seems to be the favourite. And it's very easy to achieve.

Step 1: Brush your hair to make sure it is smooth and free of all tangles.

Step 2: Take a small triangular section of hair from the crown of your head and pin it up out of the way.

Step 3: Gather the rest of your hair into a high ponytail and secure with an elastic.

Step 4: Divide the triangular section at the crown of your head into three sections. Pin the two sections closest to your forehead out of the way.

Step 5: Backcomb the first section in order to add volume. The amount of backcombing depends on how high you want your bouffant. Also, if your hair is ultra soft like mine and does not respond to backcombing, use a little hairspray.

Step 6: Backcomb the second section. This section should receive the most amount of backcombing as it is this that will provide the majority of the volume.

Step 7: Backcomb the last section closest to your forehead just a little bit as this layer needs to be smooth.

Step 8: Sculpt your bouffant to the shape and size that you desire and pin it with hairpins near to the base of your ponytail in order to maintain a consistent look.

Step 9: Take the length of your bouffant, twist it lightly and wrap it neatly around the base of your ponytail. Secure with hairpins.

The Extra-Long Ponytail

This one is more of a trick than an actual hairstyle. It is perfect if you have medium-length hair and want to fake longer hair without all the added headache and expenses of hair extensions.

Step 1: Brush your hair to make sure that it is smooth and free of all tangles.

Step 2: Divide your hair into two sections horizontally; one large section covering the crown of your head to the back of your head and another smaller one from the back of your head to the nape of your neck.

Step 3: Gather the larger section and pin it up on the top of your head so that it is out of the way.

Step 4: Gather the smaller section into a neat ponytail just above the nape of your neck and secure with an elastic.

Step 5: Gather the larger section into a neat ponytail just a couple of inches directly above the lower ponytail camouflaging it.

Step 6: No step 6! Your hair is instantly longer by a couple of inches.

Topsy-Turvy Ponytail

This one is one of my personal favourites. It takes exactly two minutes and it looks so polished and classy. Because of how it looks, I also like to call it the waterfall ponytail.

Step 1: Brush your hair to make sure it is smooth and free of all tangles.

Step 2: Gather all your hair into a neat high ponytail smoothening out any bumps on the way.

Step 3: With your hand on the base of your ponytail holding it steady, loosen your ponytail just a bit.

Step 4: Part your hair above the ponytail carefully to create a space to pull your hair through.

Step 5: Pull your hair through the space created and tighten your ponytail. You can either pull it from under or from over. Both create equally interesting looks.

BRAIDED HAIRSTYLES

French Side-Swept Braid

This hairstyle is one that will keep your hair neat and tidy while at the same time, giving you a super casual side-braid look.

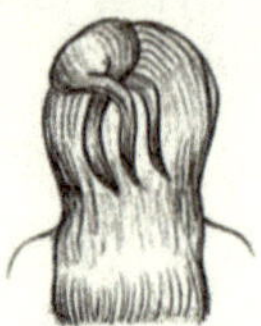

Step 1: Brush your hair to make sure it is smooth and free of all tangles.

Step 2: Take a small section of hair on one side near your forehead and start French-braiding it.

Step 2: Keep adding hair with each crossover. Say you started from the left side, add a few strands of hair from the hair line of your left side to the leftmost section and add a few strands of hair from the crown of your head to the rightmost section.

Step 3: Continue braiding this way until you are about two inches away from your neckline. At this point, continue the braid horizontally leading to the other side of your neck.

Step 4: Once you run out of hair to add to the braid, continue braiding your hair in a simple three-strand braid until you reach the desired braid length and secure with an elastic.

Dutch Side-Swept Braid

This hairstyle is very similar to the French side-swept braid, except for the fact that it is inside out. In order to achieve this hairstyle, you need to follow the exact same steps as listed above in the French side-swept braid with the exception that you braid your hair in the Dutch style this time rather than the French style.

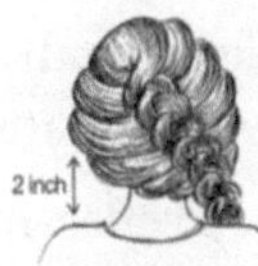

Step 1: Brush your hair to make sure it is smooth and free of all tangles.

Step 2: Take a small section of hair on one side near your forehead and start Dutch-braiding it.

Step 3: Keep adding hair with each crossover. Say you started from the left side, add a few strands of hair from the hair line of your left side to the leftmost section and add a few strands of hair from the crown of your head to the rightmost section.

Step 4: Continue braiding this way until you are about two inches away from your neckline. At this point, continue the braid horizontally leading to the other side of your neck.

Step 5: Once you run out of hair to add to the braid, continue braiding your hair in a simple three-strand braid until you reach the desired braid length and secure with an elastic.

Fishtail Braid

This one might be slightly difficult for beginner-level braiders but then… practice makes perfect! And it's worth it because the final look is awesome. You could do the braid down your back, swept to the side or do it French. Use your imagination.

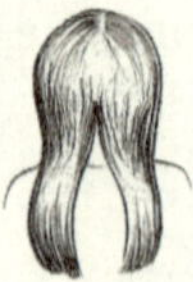

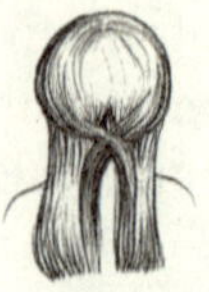
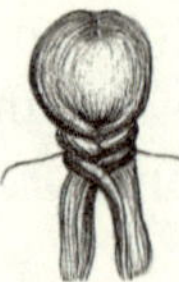

Step 1: Brush your hair to make sure it is smooth and free of all tangles.

Step 2: Divide your hair into two sections.

Step 3: Take a small strand of hair (the smaller the strand, the more intricate your braid will be) from the outermost part of the right section and pull it over to the left section.

Step 4: Take a small strand of hair from the outermost part of the left section and pull it over to the right section.

Step 5: Keep repeating Steps 3 and 4 until the desired braid length is achieved and secure with an elastic.

Braided Head Band

This is another look that has gained a lot of popularity lately, especially on the runway. And the best part about it is that it is extremely easy to do on your own hair as well.

Step 1: Brush your hair to make sure it is smooth and free of all tangles.

Step 2: Take a small half-inch section of hair from behind your left ear.

Step 3: Braid that section of hair in a simple three-strand braid all the way to the very end and secure with a simple black elastic.

Step 4: Take a small half-inch section of hair from behind your right ear.

Step 5: Braid this section of hair too in a simple three-strand braid all the way to the very end and secure with a simple black elastic.

Step 6: Bring this braid over your head to the other side and secure it in place with hairpins.

Step 7: Bring the other braid over your head to the other side as well and secure it in place with hairpins.

Take care to hide the hairpins either behind your ear (if your hair is long enough) or under the other braid.

Braided Brooch

I saw this hairstyle very recently on a friend of mine. I was intrigued. It looked so elaborate and intricate! But, as she told me how she actually got these results, my jaw dropped. It was so simple And the result? Outstanding!

Step 1: Brush your hair to make sure it is smooth and free of all tangles.

Step 2: Take a small one-inch section of hair from the opposite side of your parting. For example, if you part your hair on the left side, take this section from the right side of your head. But remember, it needs to be from the crown of your head, close to your parting.

Step 3: Braid this section in a simple three-strand braid all the way to the end and secure with a simple black elastic.

Step 4: Fold this braid up multiple times and pin it up with hairpins near to the roots. Take care to tuck the end of the braid under the 'brooch'.

Twisted Braid

This is a quirky hairstyle that gives a very youthful and bubbly look to the wearer. I recommend wearing this hairstyle during workouts at the gym. It will look cute and at the same time save your hair from tangles.

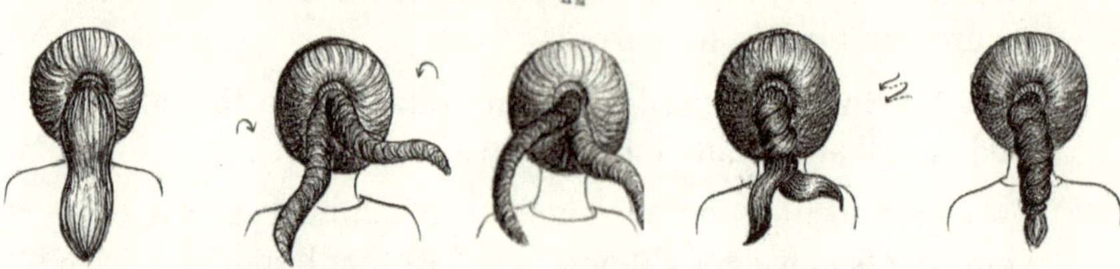

Step 1: Brush your hair to make sure it is smooth and free of all tangles.

Step 2: Gather your hair in a high ponytail and secure with an elastic.

Step 3: Divide the ponytail into two sections and twist both sections individually in the same direction.

Step 4: While ensuring that the twisted sections do not come undone, wrap one section around the other all along the length of the aforesaid section.

Step 5: Once the desired length of the 'braid' is achieved, secure with an elastic.

Alternatively, for a more casual non-workout look, you could do the same thing without tying your hair up in a ponytail first, just like you would do with a normal braid.

HALF UPDO

Bouffant

Step 1: Brush your hair to make sure it is smooth and free of all tangles.

Step 2: Take a triangular section of hair at the crown of your head and divide into three sections. Pin the two sections closest to your forehead out of the way.

Step 3: Backcomb the first section in order to add volume. The amount of backcombing depends on how high you want your bouffant. Also, if your hair is ultra soft like mine and does not respond to backcombing, use a little hairspray.

Step 4: Backcomb the second section. This section should receive the most amount of backcombing as it is this that will provide the lion's share of the volume.

Step 5: Backcomb the last section closest to your forehead just a little bit as this layer needs to be smooth.

Step 6: Sculpt your bouffant to the shape and size that you desire and pin it with hairpins.

Twisted Half Updo

The credit for this hairstyle should go to Kate Middleton's stylist. It is simple and elegant enough to be worn casually or on the red carpet.

Step 1: Brush your hair to make sure it is smooth and free of all tangles.

Step 2: Push all your hair behind your shoulders.

Step 3: Gather all the hair from the crown of your head and secure it at the back of your head with hairpins. You could do this as a bouffant if you wish.

Step 4: Gather all the hair from above your left ear and divide it into three sections.

Step 5: Holding these sections horizontally towards your right ear, twist them individually in a clockwise direction and secure all three sections together with a simple black elastic.

Step 6: Fluff the twists a little bit making them a slightly voluminous and secure them at the back of your head to the right side with hairpins.

Step 7: Repeat steps 5 and 6 on the right side as well taking care to twist these sections counter-clockwise.

Step 8: Secure these at the back of your head, a little to the left side with hairpins. While pinning it in place, tuck it slightly under the twists from the other side.

Smoothen the rest of your hair with a hairbrush if necessary and you are done!

Side-Swept Half Updo

This one is a quickie in the true sense of the word. It is especially for those days when you are running late but want to look amazing.

Step 1: Brush your hair to make sure it is smooth and free of all tangles.

Step 2: Gather all the hair from your crown and brush it upwards and sidewards to make it more voluminous.

Step 3: Twist it slightly and secure it at the side of your head with hairpins.

UPDOS

Basic Chopstick 1

The best thing about a chopstick hairstyle is that you really don't need anything... no hairspray, serum, gel, not even hairties. All you need is a chopstick. So you don't have a chopstick? No problem! A pencil will do... and so will a pen, for that matter.

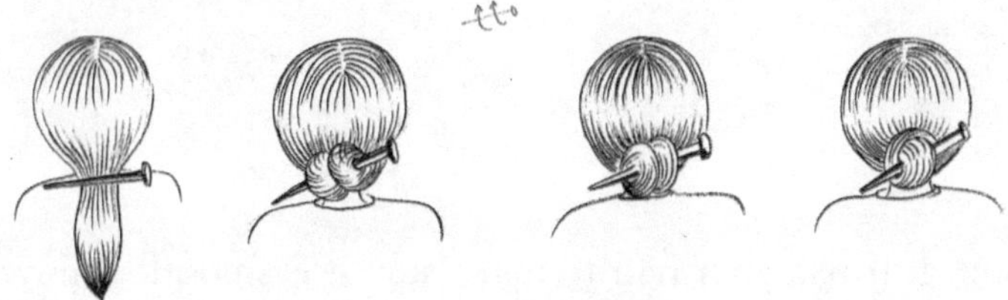

Step 1: Brush your hair to make sure it is smooth and free of all tangles.
Step 2: Gather your hair as if in a ponytail and hold the chopstick above the 'ponytail' horizontally.
Step 3: Wrap your hair around the chopstick once or twice depending on the length of your hair.
Step 4: Hold the chopstick firmly and twist it around 360 degrees all the while making sure with your other hand that the hair stays put.
Step 5: Push the chopstick downwards into your hair while making sure it scrapes your scalp.

Basic Chopstick 2

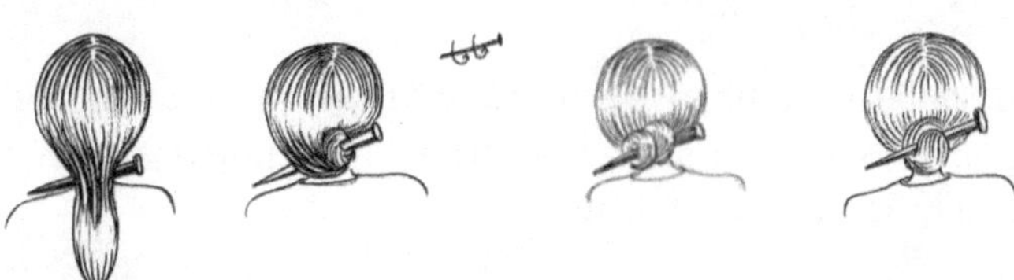

Step 1: Brush your hair to make sure it is smooth and free of all tangles.

Step 2: Gather your hair at the nape of your neck as if in a ponytail and hold the chopstick below your hair horizontally.

Step 3: Wrap your hair around the chopstick twice.

Step 4: Hold the chopstick firmly and twist it around 360 degrees all the while making sure with your other hand that the hair stays put.

Step 5: Push the chopstick upwards into your hair while making sure it scrapes your scalp.

Basic Chopstick 3

Step 1: Brush your hair to make sure it is smooth and free of all tangles.

Step 2: Gather your hair as if in a ponytail and twist it entirely.

Step 3: Wrap the twisted hair around the base of your ponytail in a circle.

Step 4: Push your chopstick upwards through the middle of the bun.

Step 5: As soon as the end of the chopstick pokes out of the top of your bun, invert the chopstick (so that the end that was facing upwards is now facing downwards) and push it down through the bun while making sure that it scrapes your scalp.

Braided Chopstick

This one would be my favourite when it comes to chopstick buns. It is just as simple as those mentioned above, but looks much more intricate.

Step 1: Brush your hair to make sure it is smooth and free of all tangles.

Step 2: Gather all your hair at the nape of your neck and braid the entire length in a three-strand braid.

Step 3: Wrap the braided hair around the base of your braid in a circle.

Step 4: Push your chopstick upwards through the middle of the braided bun.

Step 5: As soon as the end of the chopstick pokes out of the top of your braided bun, invert the chopstick (so that the end that was facing upwards is now facing downwards) and push it down through the bun while making sure that it scrapes your scalp.

Donut Bun

Personally speaking, I don't really like this particular hairstyle. It reminds of the Amar Chitra Katha depictions of rishi-munis! But, it is a hairstyle that is gaining popularity day by day. It has done rounds of probably every runway that exists on earth, so here it is! If you think you can carry it off without looking like a rishi-muni (especially in the Indian context; it wouldn't be so apparent in international pageants), here are the instructions:

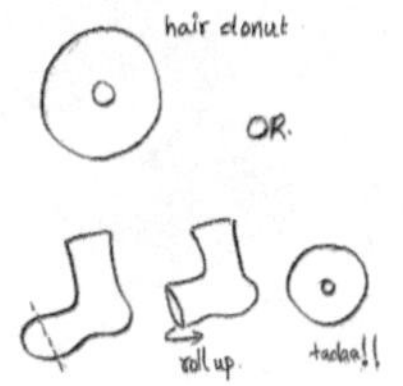

Step 1: Brush your hair to make sure it is smooth and free of all tangles.

Step 2: Gather your hair in a neat ponytail at the very top of your head and secure with an elastic. Smoothen out any bumps with a rat-tail comb.

Step 3: Now, for the actual donut part, you have a few options. You could buy a hair donut, or you could use what you already have. You could roll up a sock evenly and cut the tip of it or you could use one of those huge hair scrunchies. I always have a couple of them lying around when pageant time rolls by because I like to wear them during workouts. It adds an athletic feel. If you live in Mumbai, you could find them on Linking Road, Hill Road, Manish Market or pretty much anywhere that has stalls on the street. So you take this donut and pull your ponytail through it so that it rests all around the base of your ponytail.

Step 4: Spread your hair all around this donut and secure it with an elastic. You should have your preliminary bun by now.
Step 5: You will have some ends sticking out of the bun now. Twist them individually and secure them all around the base of the bun with hairpins.

The Knotted Updo

This is also one that I came across very recently. Trust me, it looks really exotic and beautiful if properly done.

Step 1: Brush your hair to make sure that it is smooth and free of any tangles.
Step 2: Using a rat-tail comb, take a small rectangular section of hair from the left side of your head near your hairline.

Step 3: Divide this section into two equal sections and knot it once.

Step 4: Like in a French braid, add two more sections from your unincorporated hair to the pre-existing sections and knot again taking care to move diagonally to the bottom of your right ear.

Step 5: Continue adding sections and knotting until you reach the bottom of your right ear. By this time, you should have incorporated all your hair into the knots.

Step 6: Continue knotting along the length of your hair until you reach the very end of your hair and secure with an elastic.

Step 7: Loop the knotted 'braid' (for lack of a better word) and wrap it in a loose yet tidy bun at the nape of your neck. Secure with hairpins and bobby pins as needed.

Teeth

When you smile, what is the most prominent part of your face that the judges and audience can see? Your twinkling eyes? Sure. But more importantly, your teeth. When you smile, your teeth are put on display. And frankly speaking, you will be spending a lot of your time smiling, displaying your teeth.

A couple of years ago, I was taking part in a certain pageant, in which there was this contestant (who I don't wish to name for various reasons). She was a beautiful woman, one of the most beautiful women I have ever seen. Despite being tall, she had a petite figure, which, paired with her huge almond-shaped eyes, gave her a very vulnerable, delicate, darling look. She was the first (and only, so far) woman who made me feel insecure about my looks. Adding to that, she spoke well and had the most beautiful mannerisms. It was like witnessing royalty. As I knew she would, she made it to the top five. But there, she took a beating. You know why? Because of her teeth. She had a beautiful mouth, but her teeth weren't properly formed. It was nothing serious, nothing that a few months in braces wouldn't have set right, but it cost her a crown.

I can give you many other reasons for having perfectly formed teeth, health reasons being at the top of that list. If you don't have properly aligned teeth, you will not be able to brush them that easily. Food particles that get stuck in between will remain stuck. Slowly, your teeth will turn yellow, and then brown. A few more years and you'll develop cavities and if you are lucky, you'll be able to

When you smile, your teeth are put on display. And frankly speaking, you will be spending a lot of your time smiling, displaying your teeth.

have them filled in, but if not, you'll have to have them pulled out and have new teeth constructed, which, by the way, you will have to take off every night before going to bed. Uh-uh… not something that anyone, let alone a potential beauty queen, would wish for. And no, despite what you think, I am not exaggerating in the least!

I want to stress on the point that bad teeth can cost you your crown.

But that is not the reason I am giving you. I want to stress on the point that bad teeth can cost you your crown. Throughout this chapter, I have tried to point out that there are no 'pageant types', that beauty is versatile, fluid. That you could have any kind of hair and skin and that has nothing to do with your beauty. But here, is where that advice falls apart. For teeth, there is a type. You could have big teeth or small teeth and that wouldn't matter. But if they are not properly aligned and if they are yellow, that will reduce your chances of winning drastically. You still have time; you still have a chance, so go to your dentist and get your teeth set right.

Eighty percent of the time on stage, you will be smiling. It is your teeth that will be on display. So take care of them. Please.

Let's start, as always, with structure.

Structure

What are teeth made of? Why, calcium, of course! Or if you want it in a technical manner, it is 'an organ with a cavity which consist(s) of dentine and enamel', (according to the FMA). Basically, a tooth is made out of the very

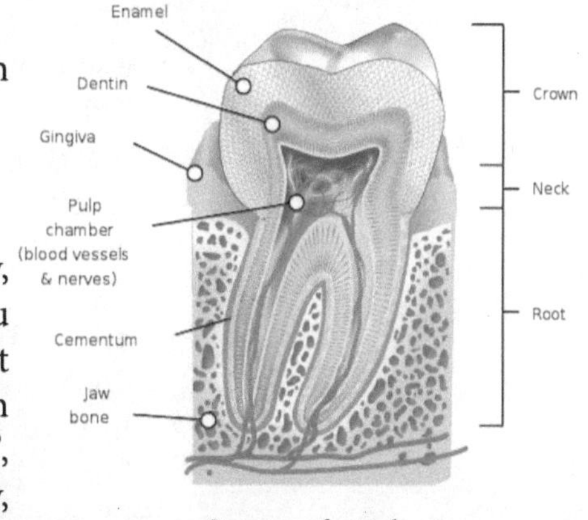

Structure of a tooth

same substance that a bone is. It is bone, in fact, probably the only bone in your body that you can see with your naked eye and touch. A tooth has five parts to it:

Remember the Golden Ratio? 1:1.61803? Well, it applies to your teeth as well.

1. **The Enamel:** This is the outermost (white) part of our tooth. This is where the calcium goes, in the form of calcium phosphate, which is a rock-hard mineral. The colour of your enamel could range from light yellow to grayish white. In fact, as it is translucent, the edges of it, where there is no dentine present under it, it could even appear slightly bluish.

2. **The Dentine:** Next comes the dentine. This is made up entirely of living cells. These cells secrete a hard mineral substance made of calcium and phosphate. It is a yellowish tissue that makes up the bulk of the tooth. It is softer than enamel, and therefore decays way more rapidly and can be subject to severe cavities if proper care is not taken. Despite these weaknesses, it takes on the role of a protector and supports the crown of the tooth.

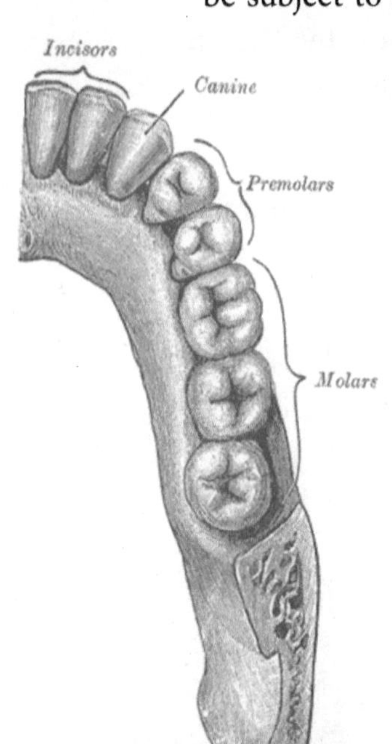

The Golden Ratio of teeth

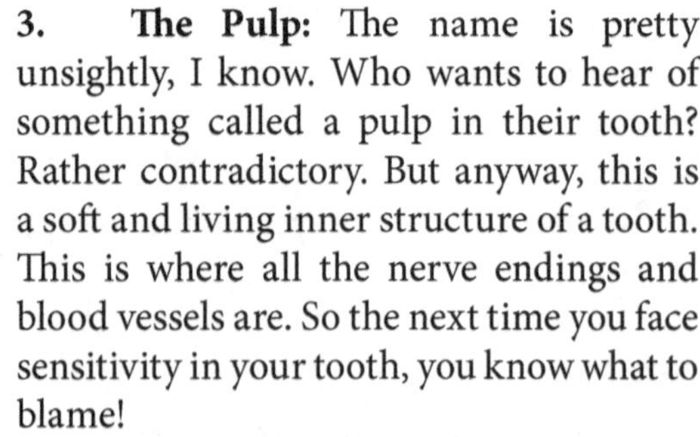
3. **The Pulp:** The name is pretty unsightly, I know. Who wants to hear of something called a pulp in their tooth? Rather contradictory. But anyway, this is a soft and living inner structure of a tooth. This is where all the nerve endings and blood vessels are. So the next time you face sensitivity in your tooth, you know what to blame!

4. **The Cementum:** Don't worry, you don't have some kind of concrete or mortar in your tooth. The cementum refers to a bone-like substance that covers the root of your tooth. It plays the same role that

cement does for building structures. It binds the root of your tooth firmly to your gums and your jawbone.

In total, we have thirty-two teeth (discounting wisdom teeth, which are four), which would all have 'erupted', as they say in dental terms, by the age of thirteen (most of us get it much sooner, in fact). These include eight incisors, four canines, eight premolars and eight molars.

So this is the structure of your tooth. This is what you need to take care of. Without fail, might I add, because you've only got one set to last you a lifetime and I don't think you want to go to your pageant sans a tooth, do you?

The Perfect Teeth

Yes, there is something called 'The Perfect Teeth.' You might never be able to find a perfect beauty, but perfect teeth, definitely. In fact, to understand the concept of a perfect set of teeth, we have to go back to the beginning of this chapter. We need to go back to the Golden Ratio.

Remember the Golden Ratio? 1:1.61803? Well, it applies to your teeth as well. Teeth are apparently considered to be perfectly aesthetically attractive when they are in the ratio of 1:1.61803. How exactly? Well, here is a picture of how they are ideally supposed to be in that ratio.

The ratio of your canines to your incisors is supposed to be 1:1.61803. That is when teeth are considered to be be aesthetically perfectly attractive. But you know what? I don't believe I have ever seen teeth that don't more or less fall into this category. Have you ever seen anyone whose canines are bigger than their incisors? I'm sure you have, they must exist. But somehow it doesn't stand out so much. One of the reasons is that teeth are structured in such an angle (as in the canines are slightly tilted backwards when compared to incisors) that whether or not they fall in the Golden Ratio, they definitely seem to. So when it comes to teeth, the Golden Ratio is not so much of a problem as alignment is. As long as teeth are properly aligned, they will look good. They will look perfect. For example, here are two pictures, (a) and (b). Which set of teeth look more attractive?

Which one is better? (a) or (b)? (a) is, right? Why? Well, for one, the teeth are all perfectly aligned. That makes them look much prettier than unaligned teeth. They are whiter, cleaner and shinier. Overall, they are very well-maintained teeth. That is the only reason they look so beautiful.

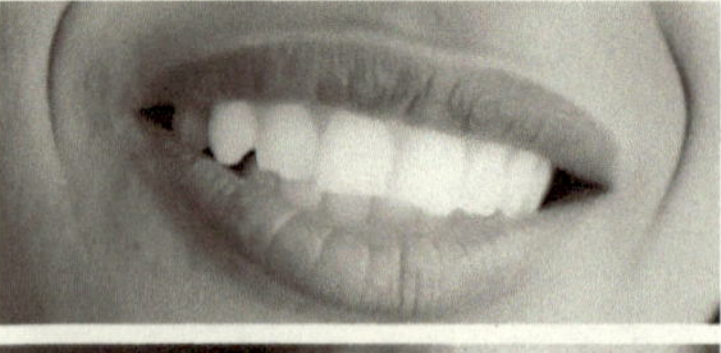

(a)

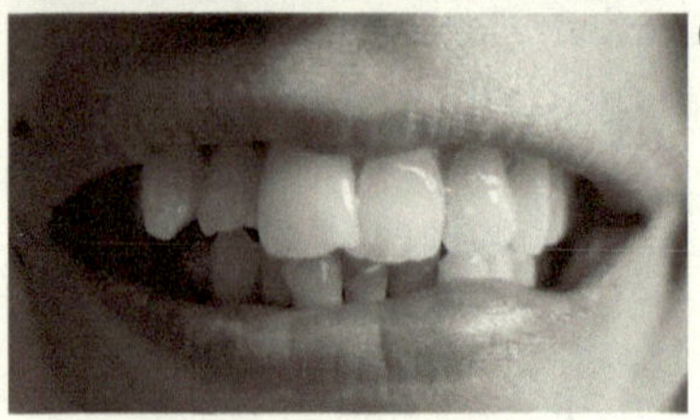

(b)

Top: Aligned teeth
Above: Unaligned teeth

And, really, it isn't difficult; all you need are braces. In fact, the earlier on in life you get those braces (and by earlier on, I mean a few years after your permanent teeth have grown), the better, because they will be more malleable then. And today, dental technology has progressed so far that you don't even need to get unsightly looking metal-wired braces made of stainless steel if that is what you are afraid of. These are the most inexpensive type of braces, but there are other types:

- **Clear Braces:** These are much less conspicuous that the traditional metal-wired braces and blend into your teeth much better. These use ceramic or plastic brackets to mould your teeth rather than the traditional metal brackets. Here is a pictorial example.

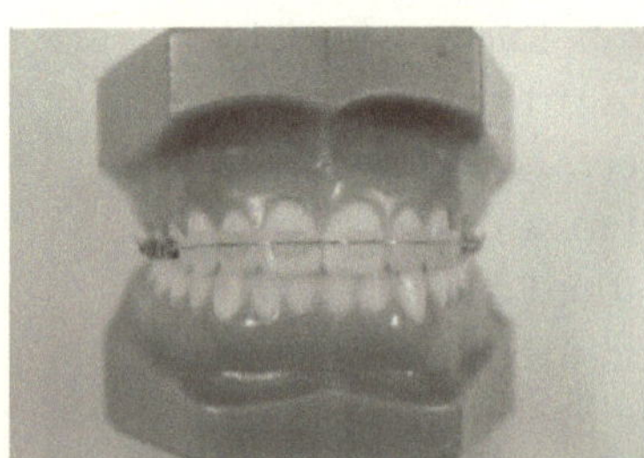

Clear braces

This picture shows transparent brackets with a metal wire. There are also braces made out of transparent elastic ties that are available today and are much less conspicuous.

- **Lingual Braces:** These are braces that are bonded to the back of your teeth, rather than the front, making it completely invisible to any onlooker. If I had to get braces, these would be the ones I would go for. Also, an added advantage is that if, for whatever reason, your dental treatment is not over by the time your pageant rolls around, you can keep your braces on. You need not have them removed because of your pageant. They will pull your teeth into shape, thus making them look beautiful and no onlooker would be able to make out that behind that gorgeous smile, lie a set of braces.

(a)

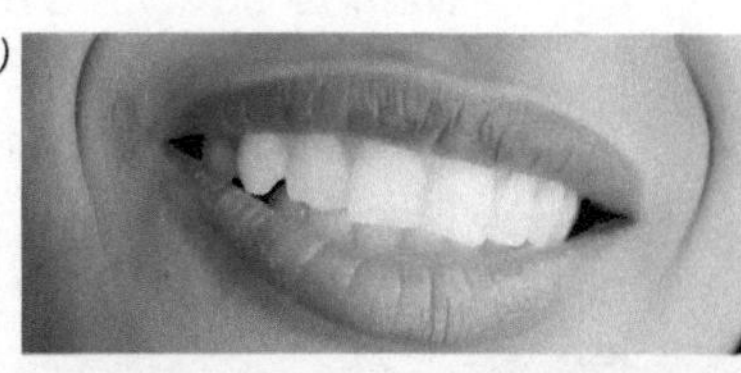

(b)

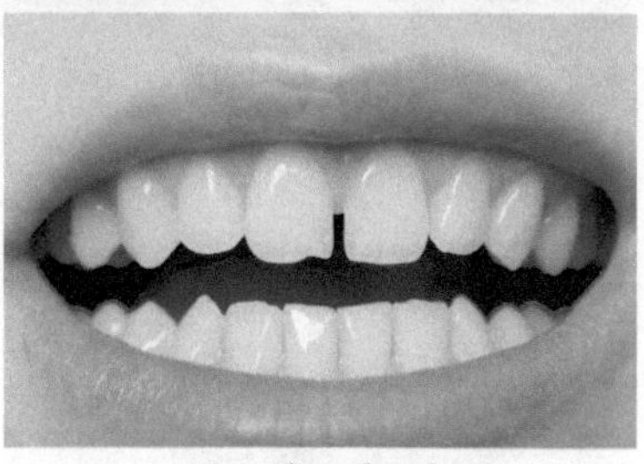

Top: Aligned teeth
Below: Gap teeth

Now, here are another set of pictures. You have to tell me which one you find more attractive.

The original colour of your teeth will be the same as the colour of the white of your eye.

So, (a) or (b)? That would be (a), don't you think so? Well, again, this is a fairly easy problem to fix. In fact, when you get braces, any gaps between your teeth will also automatically get fixed, in all probability. But if you don't need braces, if your teeth are all perfect except for this little gap between your teeth, what do you do? Well, you could get veneers.

When I was talking about this subject with my dentist, while researching for this book, I remember flinching when he said, 'veneers'. I have an aversion to anything that is not natural. Plus, I was worried about any side effects that it might have. But I needn't have worried. Veneers are perfectly safe. A veneer is nothing but a restorative material that is placed over your teeth. When done properly, it protects your teeth from external damage. It is only when it is done poorly that you might face problems. So there is really no reason to be scared of veneers. You might, in fact, want to be scared of a less than competent dentist instead!

Now, a third and last set of pictures.

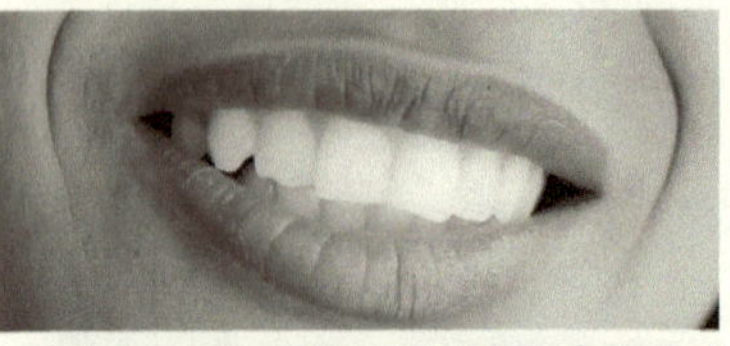

(a)

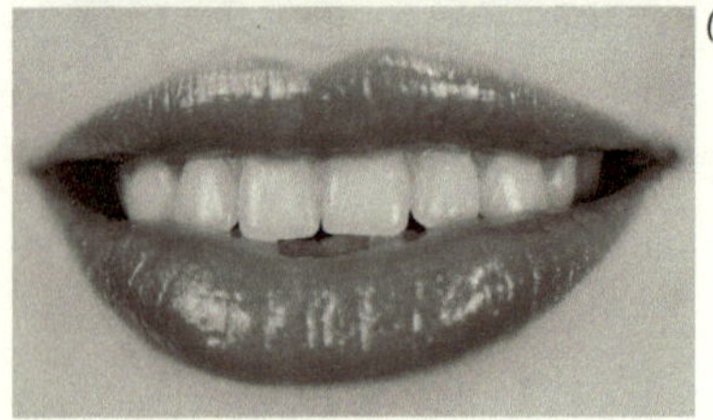

(b)

Top: White teeth
Below: Yellow teeth

Which set of teeth do you find more attractive? For me, it has to be (a). Yes, the set of teeth in picture (b) are perfectly aligned. But you know what is wrong? They are yellow. We all have an aversion to yellow teeth. Because in our minds, yellow teeth equal poor dental care. The less we brush our teeth, the more we ignore them, the more yellow they turn. Over time, they might even turn brown. So innately, we all have a preference for white teeth, because those signal properly cared for, healthy teeth.

Now, the first thing you must understand is that not everyone has pearly white teeth. The original colour of your teeth will be the same as the colour of the white of your eye. If your teeth are darker than the white of your eye, you need to work on them. First, visit your dentist for a cleaning and polishing and take it from there. Brush twice a day and don't forget to floss. Needless for me to say, you can't expect results within a week. So don't wait until there is only a month for your pageant. Start now. And when the pageant is around the corner, visit your dentist for another round of cleaning and polishing, just to be on the safer side.

But what if the colour of your teeth and the colour of the inside of your eye are both exactly the same, but you feel they are not white enough? Well, I'm afraid that is the whitest that your teeth can be naturally. Well done to you, in fact, for maintaining your teeth so well. The fact is that a child's teeth are much whiter than an adult's. That is not because of wear and tear (although that does play a part if the teeth in question are poorly cared for) but it is because of changes in the mineral structure of the tooth itself. It isn't something that is in your hands.

However, if you really feel you need your teeth to be pearly white, I suggest you visit your dentist for a whitening process. It is not something I recommend, but if it helps your confidence during the pageant, then so be it!

Teeth whitening is really nothing but a form of bleaching. Do-it-yourself whiteners that you use at home are nothing but carbomide peroxide, which reacts with water to form hydrogen peroxide. Procedures done at the dentist's clinic are basically the same, except that they use light energy to accelerate the bleaching process. Needless to say, this whole thing takes a toll on your teeth including potential chemical burns, pain, increased sensitivity and in some rare cases, an increased risk of tongue cancer.

So if you feel you need white teeth to boost your confidence, go for it. But don't make it a habit. One appointment around a week before your pageant starts should be both ideal and enough. Try not to keep repeating it. Weak teeth might not seem like a problem right now, but when you are fifty and your teeth are decaying, it will seem like a very bad idea! But, just once probably won't hurt, keeping in mind, of course, that the count stays at one. Not two, not three, but one!

The Pageant Smile

Ah! The famous Pageant Smile! We have all heard so much about this! What is this Pageant Smile? And why do we hear so much about it? Why is it such an integral part of a beauty pageant?

Well, you must have heard of the saying, 'Smiles are free, so give them away.' It's the same logic at work here. There is something about a smile that endears a person to us. Let's say you're out on a series of blind dates. You know absolutely nothing about these two guys. The dates that they have planned are also exactly the same (as though produced under lab conditions). The first guy you go out with is a grumpy, grouchy guy who probably wouldn't smile even if you offered him a million dollars. The second one is a sweet guy with a goofy grin who cracks you up with his sense of humour. Which guy do you think you would be more attracted to? The one with that goofy grin, don't you think?

It need not even be attraction. Let's take it out of the dating context. Let's say you are interviewing two people for a post. Two women have applied and have gotten through to the last phase of recruitment. They both have similar qualifications and work profiles. The first one comes in. She comes in and answers whatever you have to ask her flawlessly. She seems like the perfect professional for the job. Throughout the interview, she doesn't even give half a smile. But then the next woman comes in. She answers all your questions equally flawlessly. And to top it, she smiles graciously while shaking your hand and keeps that friendly look on her face throughout.

First, think of something that makes you happy. Connect with the audience. Establish eye contact with a member or members of the audience who will reciprocate your smile. And you will smile naturally…because you will feel like smiling now.

Which one would you hire?

Think about it.

It's exactly the same logic that works at pageants as well. A person with a smile is always endearing to others. And that fact is what you as a pageant contestant need to make use of.

You know, in my first pageant, that is one of the points in which I failed, I think. I didn't realise it at the time, but later, my friends and family told me that I had been trying so hard to keep that smile on my face that after a while it seemed frozen. It started to look unnatural. And of course it would. It wasn't a natural smile anymore, after the initial five minutes!

But how to keep it from looking unnatural? Smiling so hard and for so long has to be a strain on your facial muscles, right? Well, its simple. First, think of something that makes you happy. Connect with the audience. Establish eye contact with a member or members of the audience who will reciprocate your smile. And you will smile... because you will feel like smiling now. Trust me, I'm speaking from experience. During the finale of Miss India Worldwide, while walking down the ramp, someone from the audience called out to me, 'Child, you are beautiful!' I don't know who that was, but whoever it was, they helped me win the pageant. Because that one sentence helped me keep my smile on my face. Whenever I felt my smile faltering, I would think of this... and it would make me smile all over again. It still does.

Nails

Nails—it's so easy to forget them. They cover such a minuscule proportion of the entire body. It's so convenient to think, 'Oh, let it be! Who cares. No one will see them anyway.' I'm guilty of this line of thinking myself.

But the fact is, we notice nails all the time. And if you think we don't, you are just deluding yourself.

Consider the following, for example. When you pick up something, what's on display? Your fingernails. When you shake hands with someone, what's on display? Your fingernails. When you're just talking to someone, you're gesticulating and what's on display then? Yep, your fingernails.

Okay, so maybe I'm going a bit overboard. When it's day-to-day life, it really doesn't matter. Or does it?

Let's see, let's start with the purpose of fingernails.

Purpose of Fingernails

John Hawks, a biological anthropologist at the University of Wisconsin-Madison once famously said, 'We have fingernails because we are primates.'

Um… bravo! Gee, that sure explains it, doesn't it?

But wait, he clears it up. Quoting what he said, 'Most mammals have claws. They use them to grab onto things, to climb things, and to dig holes.' But fingernails differ from claws as they are broader and blunter. As *LiveScience* puts it, nails are, 'essentially flattened forms of claws.' And good luck trying to hunt, climb, tear or dig with them. Seriously!

So fingernails today don't really serve any utilitarian purpose. I did read some theory about how they provide support for the fingertips helping us feel things better, but since I wasn't able to make much sense of that theory, I'm not going to include it here. But even though they don't serve any utilitarian purpose and might be a mere leftover of our hunter-gatherer days, that doesn't mean they don't serve a purpose. Fingernails have actually developed into astute portraits of our current well-being. Meaning, if you are healthy, it will show on your fingernails and if you are not, that too will show on your fingernails. For example, if your body is just not getting enough nutrition, it will show on the colour of your fingernails.

Fingernails have actually developed into astute portraits of our current well-being.

Caring For Your Nails

The best way to care for your nails? Well, experts say, just trim them regularly and keep them clean. Really, that's all you need to do. Seems surprising when you consider all the rigmarole that we subject them to usually. But hey, don't worry, that stuff isn't detrimental either. It can only help.

If you look at my nails right now, they're nothing special. They're neatly trimmed and filed, with no nail polish on them. Because I like them like that, low maintenance. But then again, at a pageant, the rules change slightly. At a pageant it ceases to be a matter of just clean and well-kept nails. They need to be beautiful too. Time for some nail make-up.

Maniure-Pedicure

The easiest way to get your nails to look good and just radiate with health is to get a quick mani-pedi. Now, although you can easily give yourself a mani-pedi at home, I would still recommend going to a professional before your pageant. Why? Because a professional nail technician sees nails and does nails day in and day out. This is what they do for a living. They have much more experience than you can ever have (unless you're a nail technician yourself). Thus, you greatly reduce your chances of a misshapen nail or blotchy nail polish. Remember always—only your best foot forward will do at a pageant. And your nails are not excluded.

Did you know, ancient Egyptians used to grow out their nails and paint them? The richer colours were reserved for the aristocracy while the common man or woman, as the case might be, was only allowed to paint them in lighter colours.

Long vs. Short Nails

Long nails look so good, don't they? Did you know, ancient Egyptians used to grow out their nails and paint them? The richer colours were reserved for the aristocracy while the common man or woman, as the case might be, was only allowed to paint them in lighter colours. Long nails have been a symbol of status since the beginning of civilization, really.

Why?

Well, that's hard to answer. One theory suggests that since nails reflect our health so well, long nails have traditionally been considered beautiful because it takes a certain level of good health to grow them well. Another theory goes to say that since long nails are hard to manage, only those with ample leisure time on their hands could satisfactorily grow them, thus becoming a status symbol, much like fair skin.

Whatever the reason is, long nails are conventionally considered beautiful on women.

But how practical are they? Needless to say, long nails need a certain amount of regular care. And with your busy schedule at a pageant, will you be able to maintain them? Because trust me, there is absolutely no way you're getting any time off during a pageant to go get a manicure. No way.

So what do you do? I can't answer that question for you. The answer to that depends entirely on the basic make-up of your nails. Some people have sturdy nails, some have brittle nails. You know your nails best. So take that into account and make your decision. But whatever your decision is, make sure your nails are well-trimmed and properly filed. There is no excuse for shabby nails at a pageant.

However, on a more personal level, I would recommend growing your nails to a medium length for the pageant. Not only will it look elegant, it will also be easy enough to maintain. Nails grow brittle after a certain length because of lack of support. Think of it as a see-saw—both ends have to be in perfect balance. So growing them out a little bit would maintain that balance while also making them look very elegant.

As for shape, I would highly recommend getting your nails filed in a square shape. Oval nails are more brittle and thus more susceptible to damage. Now, this might seem like a tiny thing to you, but when you're running around, juggling photo-shoots, press conferences, rehearsals and events every day, it's really the last thing you want to worry about. And oh yes, carry a file with your everywhere! You never know when you might need it.

Paint the Town Red

Painting your nails is nothing new. As we just saw in the previous section, we have been doing that since the Pharaohs! But painting your nails comes with a cost. And that is chipped nailpolish. Nothing looks as shabby as chipped nail polish. And when you barely have time to tend to a chipped nail at a pageant, re-painting your nails is pretty much out of the question. So what's the solution around this predicament?

Stick to the nudes and the pale pinks. If they chip, chances are, no one will notice.

Stick to lighter colours.

Yes, I hear you. I love red nails too! There's just something about them, isn't there? But considering the circumstances, red nail polish really is not an option. Consider this, the darker the nail colour, the more apparent the chip. So, stick to the nudes and the pale pinks. If these chip, chances are no one will notice unless they subject your nail to very close observation, which they actually do at pageants! Well, in that case, just don't bother about it. They're going to find something wrong anyway!

Also, stay away from French manicures. I hear a lot of people advising pageant aspirants to get a French manicure before the pageant. Don't listen to them. A French manicure is definitely one of the most elegant styles we have, but also one of the most cumbersome. It's extremely high maintainence. And you do not need that headache right now. Not in the middle of all this.

Personally, I swear by clear nail polish. Looks elegant enough and is easy to handle. And if it chips, good luck finding the chip. Win-win!

Nutrition and Fitness

Recently, when I was at my Kathak class, some of us were standing around in a group discussing workouts, gyms and diets. Suddenly, one girl piped up and said, 'I hate gymming, ya! I can't stand it! That's why I decided to learn Kathak. That way I learn a new art form and get to work out, both at the same time.'

I immediately replied, 'I hate gymming too, that is one thing on earth I just CANNOT make myself do!'

Hearing that, she quickly turned to me and retorted, 'But you don't need to gym, ya! Just look at you.'

I was taken aback. And quickly, I did what she said, I looked at myself in the mirror. Sure, I was thinner and more toned than the next average girl, but did that really mean I didn't need to go to the gym or work out in any other way? Did it mean I was wasting my time with an hour of yoga every morning?

Being fit does not, I repeat, does not mean you don't need to work out.

No! It just meant I was fit. And being fit does not, I repeat, does not mean you don't need to work out. Maybe you won't put on any weight even if you don't work out. Maybe you're one of those girls I envy, who has a fantastic metabolism and can eat whatever you want without fear of putting on weight. Maybe. But none of these things mean you don't need to exercise. A basic level of fitness is something we should all strive for, regardless of whether or not we are pageant aspirants. And that basic level of fitness cannot be achieved without a proper exercise regime and a nutritious diet.

Many centuires ago, we were cavemen, and later on, farmers. Our lifestyle was such that our daily doses of exercise were taken care of. But today, it is not the same scenario. Today, we lead mostly sedentary lifestyles, sitting at a desk in the same position for extended hours. And the sad part of it is that we humans have not genetically evolved in the last 30,000 years to suit our modern lifestyles. Therefore, we need to make an extra effort to maintain the same levels of fitness that our ancestors used to have with absolutely no effort. I know, it's not fair! But c'est la vie!

But there's another side to the whole fitness game as well. If you're a size zero, that does not automatically mean you are fit. No! That just means you are thin. And being thin without being fit is as dangerous as being obese. We've all heard of bulimia, anorexia and anaemia. But what we don't know is that it is way more common that we think. A couple of years ago, I was taking part in Femina Miss India South. Frankly speaking, I didn't exactly have the perfect ten figure back then. Far from it. And all of us contestants were asked to have a medical test done. This is the norm in most pageants. Before they put you on an exercise and diet regime, they like to know your body composition. So I did. And to my shock and surprise, the medical test revealed that I was anaemic! I was really surprised. I hadn't expected that. I weighed just as much as I should for my height, and my body fat percentage was on the higher side, in fact. But what had happened was that in my stressful attempt at attaining a bikini figure in time for the pageant, I had gone on a crash diet. I had stopped having carbs completely (except for breakfast when I had watered down oats), stopped having dairy products (except for the milk that went into the watered down oats), and had tremendously cut down on the amount of food I was having. By the end of it, I had lost weight, yes. But I was also anaemic. My body just wasn't getting enough iron (the recommended daily allowance [RDA] is 18 mg per day).

The point to be noted here is that many of us in the fashion and pageant industry are thin. We are size zero, wear size 24 jeans and we feel, oh, so proud of ourselves. Why? There is absolutely nothing to be proud of in that. I'm sorry to break your bubble, but while you're strutting down the ramp in those six-inch heels, what if you fall? A normal person might just sprain their ankle, but you, darling, might fracture a bone. And that is something you really don't want, pageant or not. What is the use of that perfect ten figure if it isn't strong enough to support you throughout the duration of the pageant? It has happened earlier. Ana Carolina Reston, a Brazilian model died of anorexia nervosa. Luisel Ramos, an Uruguayan model died of an anorexia-induced heart failure during a fashion show. Isabelle Caro, a French model died of anorexia-induced immunodeficiency.

Ana Carolina Reston, a Brazilian model, died of anorexia nervosa. Luisel Ramos, an Uruguayan model died of an anorexia-induced heart failure during a fashion show. Isabelle Caro, a French model died of anorexia-induced immunodeficiency.

Trust me, you don't want to be the next one.

But maybe you don't care about any of that. Maybe you only care about winning the pageant, no matter at what cost, be it anorexia, bulimia or whatever. Fine. I respect that, totally. It's your body, it's your business, not mine. But you are a reader of my book, and it is my business whether you win that pageant or not. And tell you what? There is no way in hell you will, if you are ultra skinny. The judges of a beauty pageant are not all necessarily from a fashion background. They come from all walks of life. One might be a sportsperson, another a businessman/woman, a movie director, a politician and so on and so forth. And these people, like most of us, like women, not skeletons.

The Right Size for You; Size Zero or Above

Whenever I go online to any discussion forums, I see two schools of thought. The first thinks size zero is not to be encouraged. On one particular discussion forum, I even saw a woman exclaim that women who are naturally thin due to their metablosim should be forced to put on weight! The second thought that anything above size ten or twelve is not to be encouraged. Well, let me tell you something, it doesn't matter! Fitness cannot be determined by size, or even weight, to a large extent. The only things that are not to be encouraged are being overweight or underweight. Both are equally dangerous.

The trick to a great body doesn't lie in a size zero, nor does it lie in a size eight. No! It lies in the size that is right for you.

At Femina Miss India South, I remember a discussion that all of us had with Alesia Raut. Alesia Raut, as you probably know, is an Indian supermodel, and she was training us in ramp walking for the pageant. We were discussing sizes and figures. And Alesia said, 'Look at me, for example. I'm a (UK) size eight. And there's nothing I can do about that. I can never be size zero, because that's my bone structure. Nothing I can do about it unless I try and saw off my bones.'

Fitness cannot be determined by size or even weight. The only things that are not to be encouraged are being overweight or underweight.

She is right. All of us have different shapes and figures. We need to learn and respect that. Kareena Kapoor can be a size zero. She has a petite figure. She could probably even be double zero without looking too bad! But Deepika Padukone could never be that without looking and being undernourished. She has a 5'10" frame, broad shoulders and long legs. That's an athletic frame. She'll always be a couple of sizes bigger than a shorter, more petite woman. So you need to analyse your frame and see what size you can be. If your bone structure doesn't allow you to go beyond a certain size, respect that, because frankly, there's not much you can do about it, short of starving to death.

If you are planning to take part in a pageant, I think it is safe to assume that your height is a minimum of 5'6" (since most Indian pageants, with the exception of Miss India Worldwide, don't accept women who are shorter than 5'7"). Most pageant contestants that I have come across are around 5'8" (including me). 5'8" is considered short in the fashion industry (we're all borderline cases, in fact) but in real life, we are fairly tall women. And we tend to have figures corresponding to our heights. Makes sense, doesn't it? After all, our bones must be strong enough to support us, right? So, there are not many women I have seen who are tall and still have a size zero frame. And by a size zero frame, I mean a naturally size zero frame, not a malnourished underweight person. But, still, there are a few. At I AM She–Miss Universe India 2011, there was a fellow contestant who had such a frame. She wasn't malnourished, nor was she underweight. She was perfectly healthy. She was 5'7" tall and tinier than a size zero, in fact! If there was something called a triple zero, that would probably be her. At the same time, there was another girl, 5'10" tall (I think) and she had a pretty large athletic frame. The first time I saw her, I just noticed the width of her hip bones (which I had mistaken for fat) and I thought she could afford to lose a few kilos. But then, I saw her in a swimsuit. She didn't have an inch of extra fat on her. That was all bone and muscle.

There is no such thing as a perfect size. You could be size zero, or you could be size ten. And you can still win your crown.

In conclusion, the point to which all this rigmarole leads to is that there is no such thing as a perfect size. You could be size zero, you could be size ten, whichever! You can still win your crown. Uh-uh... not so fast! There's a catch here! Yup, no such thing called a free lunch right? The catch is you have to have a figure that you can show off in a bikini. It should be perfectly toned, no extra fat bulging out anywhere. Just losing weight isn't enough. That's just the first step. After losing weight, you have to gain some. Muscle weight, that is. And that's just what I'm going to help you do. I'm not going to chart out a diet for you or list out eight exercises to lose that tummy fat in eight days or anything like that. It would be unrealistic of me to do so. First of all, I don't know you personally, and it would be irresponsible on my part to list out one workout regime and expect it to suit everyone out there. Second, I'm not a trained nutritionist or a physical trainer. Only a trained nutritionist or physical trainer will be able to analyse how your body works and work on a diet and workout regime to suit it. Either them or you. No one knows your body better than you do, after all. What I'm going to do here is give you all the basics and you can use them to chart out a diet and workout regime for yourself!

Health

Being Overweight

What is it?

WebMD defines it as 'an excess proportion of total body fat. A person is considered overweight when his or her weight is 20 percent or more above normal weight.' It is a disease that must be treated on both a physical and mental level.

Who Suffers From It?

Generally, women and older people tend to be more prone to obesity than others. But that is just a generalisation, nothing more. If you let go and stop taking care of yourself, this generalisation goes right out of the window.

What Causes It?

There are many factors that contribute to obesity. Some of them are lifestyle, eating habits, the lack of physical activity, comfort eating, age, gender, illness, medication and your genes. Some are under our control and some are not. The factors we can control are:

- Our lifestyle and how much we eat on a daily basis.
- Physical activity. A lack of physical activities can obviously lead to obesity. Most of the obesity in the last twenty years is said to have been caused by this one factor.
- Psychological factors such as eating in response to negative emotions such as boredom, anger or sadness.

Factors we can partially control are:

- Age. As we age, our basal metabolic rate slows down. Of course, age is uncontrollable. But for most of us, leading a healthy lifestyle with proper eating habits will keep obesity at bay regardless of age.

- Gender. Women tend to be more prone to obesity than men. Again, we can't do anything about our gender, but, a healthy lifestyle with proper eating habits will keep obesity at bay, regardless of gender.

Factors that are more or less beyond our control are:

- Illness. This is common enough, but not as common as some people would have you believe. Some illnesses which cause disproportionate weight gain include hypothyroidism, depression, etc.
- Medication. Certain medications like steroids, anti-depressants and even some birth control pills can slow your metabolism down.
- Genes. Being overweight because it's in your genes is not as common but it's definitely possible.

Even if these factors seem to be out of our control, remember, a healthy lifestyle and proper dietary habits will keep you as fit as you can be.

What are the Dangers of Obesity?

There are quite a lot actually. Obesity can cause chronic depression, high cholesterol, hypertension, diabetes, cancer (yes!), sleep apnea (a condition that causes a person to temporarily stop breathing while sleeping), osteoarthritis, gall-bladder disease and gout.

I'm stopping here with the dangers of obesity and not expanding on it as most of you, my readers, are not really in danger of being obese. On the contrary, you are in danger of being underweight. So we'll concentrate more on that.

Being Underweight

What is it?

According to Wikipedia, being underweight 'refers to a

human who is considered to be under a healthy weight.' According to Mosby's Medical Dictionary, it refers to a 'body mass index of less than 18.5.'

What Causes It?

Well, more or less the same things as obesity, only in an opposite manner. There are factors we can control, those that we can't and some that we can partially control. The ones we can control are:

- Our lifestyle habits, how much we eat and how often.
- Psychological issues that lead to eating disorders like bulimia or anorexia nervosa. Yes, these are medical conditions and you will require medical help to cope with these, but then you'd be surprised by the power of the human mind!

Factors that are partially controllable to uncontrollable are:

- Genes. Sometimes you are just naturally thin.
- Illness. Don't you always end up losing weight when you fall ill? But don't be so happy about that lost weight, because along with it, you've also lost your health. Time to get back to that healthy, balanced diet now.

What are the Dangers of Being Underweight?

Again, as in obesity, quite a few, darling, quite a few! Some of the most common and well-known ones are obviously anorexia nervosa, bulimia and anaemia. These are in fact so prevalent that I will dedicate a whole section of this chapter to these three conditions. But they are not the only dangers. Far from it, really. A few of the issues you could face when underweight are:

- Lung problems. I've seen a lot of people avoid smoking because it can cause lung problems. That's great! But do you know that under-eating and not getting enough nutrients can also cause lung problems such as pneumonia, bronchitis and asthma? Isn't that just as dangerous?

- Brittle bones. A true story: When my dad was at University, his daily diet was a serving or two of aloo pakoras for breakfast, lunch and dinner. One day he was about to climb up some stairs when someone called out to him. He turned suddenly, lost his balance and fell. It wasn't a hard fall, but he broke a bone. You know why that happened? Calcium deficiency. It wasn't just my dad. The same thing happened to me a couple of years ago. I was at a cousin's wedding when my mom asked me to run over to my dad and get something from him as fast as I could. I hitched up my sari and ran in my six-inch stilettoes. While I was climbing down to the verandah, I slipped and fell. And boy! Did it hurt! I developed a temperature that night because of the pain. I was unable to sleep all night, in fact. That was the first time I had cried in a few years. I hadn't broken a bone, that was evident from the fact that I could still move my foot but the way it hurt, everyone, including me, thought it must be a hairline fracture. Luckily it wasn't. It was just a sprain. But it was a sprain that shouldn't have been there under ideal circumstances. It wasn't such a hard fall after all. I have suffered from calcium deficiency for a long time. Even today, during Kathak or when I'm walking extra fast in high heels, my knee just gives way and I fall to the ground in excruciating pain. That shouldn't happen to me, a girl in her mid-twenties. That shouldn't happen to you. That shouldn't happen to anyone. Especially during a pageant, you're vulnerable enough as it is.

- Arthritis. Need I say any further?

- Heart diseases and Type 2 Diabetes. A recent research has shown that people with a body mass index (BMI) of less than 18.5 are more prone to heart diseases and Type 2 Diabetes than people in the healthy range as they are more likely to have higher amounts of fat in their blood. So what do we do about it? No, we don't stop taking in fats, we start building up a healthy workout regime. One hour in the morning is more than enough.

- Breast cancer. Period.

- Infertility. Obviously, if you are underweight, your body will say, 'Hey, I'm sorry but you can't have any kids. I can't put two lives at risk.' It might not be a worry to you right now, and I don't expect it to be, but what about ten years later? Do you really know what you might or might not want ten years from now? Better to play it safe.

Eating Disorders

Eating disorders are way too common. 99 percent of the girls in the industry would have had a tryst with some kind of an eating disorder or the other at some point of time. It is important to be able to lose weight and tone up without succumbing to harmful practices that can eventually lead to an eating disorder. But before we can prevent it, we must know—what are eating disorders.

A misconception about eating disorders is that it only equals undereating. Nope. It equals both undereating and overeating.

Scarily enough, the average age around which the onset of anorexia is reported is about nineteen, twenty for bulimia, and twenty-five for binge-eating. This is the age range that most of us pageant aspirants are in! Scary, isn't it? Well, as the National Institute of Mental Health (NIMH) puts it, 'an eating disorder is an illness that causes serious disturbances to your everyday diet.' Basically, anything that stops us from eating as we should, and as we need, is an eating disorder. Of course, that 'anything' cannot be anything external; it has to come from your brain. But external factors like peer pressure do count. One misconception about eating disorders is that it equals undereating. That is wrong. It deals with both undereating and overeating. Either way, an eating disorder ensures we don't get the nutrients our body needs on a daily basis. At some point, this urge to eat less, or more, as the case might be, just spirals out of control.

But are eating disorders really that rampant here, you ask? In India, we barely hear of eating disroders. It's so widely spoken about in the West, but here… not so much. That doesn't mean it doesn't exist here. It just means that you don't hear about it. And if you ask me, that is even more dangerous. Because if you're going to keep it hidden, how are you going to ask for help? How will you be able to listen to someone else asking for help? Eating disorders are just as prevalent in India as anywhere else, especially in the beauty and fashion industry, where the pressure to look good at any cost is so high. Richa Chaddha confessed to bulimia nervosa. Elena Fernandes mentioned that eating disorders are taken as a quick fix. We might not have had anyone collapse on the ramp and die yet, but that does not mean that the danger does not lurk right there, behind the wings.

But you don't need to be part of that demographic. You have a choice. You can say no (and I hope you will). But in order to avoid it you must know what a certain type of eating disorder entails. You must understand the symptoms of the most common eating disorders so that you can immediately put a stop to it. If you don't know what the problem is, how can you expect to come up with a solution? So lets learn about different types of eating disorders.

According to the NIMH, three types of eating disorders are the most prevalent. I have already mentioned them in the previous paragraph, but let me expand a little more on them now.

Anorexia Nervosa

Why am I putting this one first? Because, it is the most popular. Sorry, bad choice of words. Because it is the one that has been popularised the most by local and international media. As I mentioned earlier, it wasn't long ago that a model, Luisel Ramos, dropped dead on her way from the ramp to the green room. Two other similar cases, those of Ana Caroline Reston and Isabelle Caro, also occupied the spotlight. The international media picked up on these cases, obviously. Prada, Versace, Armani along with Madrid and Milan fashion week took a stand and banned the participation of size zero models. Human rights groups, the media and the common man created a hype around it. Suddenly, size zero was the Big Bad Witch.

But in this commotion what we conveniently managed to forget is the common factor between these three unfortunate girls. No, it isn't size zero. It is an eating disorder called anorexia nervosa. While anorexia nervosa committed a crime, poor little size zero took the fall for it.

So forget size zero. That is not the point. The point is to avoid eating disorders like anorexia nervosa. So how do you recognise a case of anorexia nervosa? Well, it's simple. You just look out for a few symptoms like:

- The most obvious sign is emaciation, which is just another word for extreme thinness. We all have a limit to how thin we can be, and that is mainly decided by your bone structure (as we have already discussed). So look at yourself, do you look a little too thin? Are you nothing but skin and bones (additionally you could also get a DEXA scan done to know your fat percentage)? Muscle is good... skin and bones isn't. Recognise that.

- Next comes a refusal to accept that you are, in fact, thin and that you can get thinner. I know what you're thinking. You're thinking, 'But what's thin in normal day to day life isn't thin enough for the fashion world.' Well, forget all such parameters. Just dish out your latest photograph and observe yourself objectively, 'objectively' being the operative word here. If you look thin enough, rest assured, you are thin enough. It doesn't matter what is thin enough for the fashion world just now. But if you feel your eyes will cheat you, then check your BMI. The BMI isn't always an accurate way of measuring fitness as it doesn't differentiate between lean mass weight and fat weight, but it will give you an idea. If your BMI is less than 18.5, you are underweight. Time to get cautious.

- Along with a refusal to accept that you are thin and not fat, also comes an intense fear of putting on weight. Obviously, if you're not even convinced that you're thin, you will not want to put on any more. But this goes a little further than a simple want. It's a phobia.

- And all these symptoms listed above bring another friend along with them, and that is a distorted body image. Now everyone is telling you that you are thin, you don't need to lose weight anymore (I'm not talking about the neighbourhood aunties here, by the way) but you refuse to accept it. For a simple reason too. Whenever you look into a mirror, you just don't see a thin person there. You see a fat person and you feel disgusted by what you see. Sounds familiar? Well, that's what body image distortion is all about! Doesn't sound familiar? Good! Keep it that way! You're on the right track.

- But if you show all the symptoms that are listed above, you obviously restrict your eating as well. Right? Well, that's another symptom. People suffering from anorexia often ingest less that 800 calories a day. That is dangerous. You need a minimum of 1000-1200 calories a day. And that is just the minimum I'm talking about. I'll walk you through calculating how many calories you would ideally need in a day later on. So, if you are eating only one meal a day or have equally irregular eating habits, you could have anorexia nervosa.

Now, everyone is telling you that you are thin, but you refuse to accept it. Whenever you look into a mirror, you just don't see a thin person there. You see a fat person and you feel disgusted by what you see. Sounds familiar?

- Absent menstruation. But obvious, if you don't eat well, your body will not receive all the nutrients it needs. It will then decide it is not fit enough to build another life inside itself. And the consequence – no menstruation! I know periods are messy and cumbersome and that life would be truly wonderful without them. But paradoxically and unfortunately for us, if for whatever reason, Aunt Flow decides not to visit us, take that as an insult. Get offended, not relieved. Regular menstruation is a sign of good health.

- Other symptoms include excessive exercise, self-induced vomiting (like in bulimia nervosa), misuse of laxatives, diuretics, etc.

- There are a few other physical symptoms that develop over time. These include dry, brittle hair and nails, infertility, osteoporosis, yellowish dry skin, severe constipation, growth of fine hair called lanugo all over the body, anaemia, wasting away of the muscles (resulting in lost strength and stamina), low blood pressure, a drop in internal body temperature, structural and functional heart damage, lethargy, brain damage and multi-organ failure.

Bulimia is generally characterised by certain telltale behavioural patterns, particularly, binging and purging.

Bulimia Nervosa

Approximately 4 percent of women worldwide suffer from this condition called bulimia nervosa at least once in a lifetime. It might not seem like a lot to you, but we're talking about 4 percent from a population of 3,291,805,000 people. You do the math! 4/100 * 3,291,805,000 = 131,672,200 people! Almost 132 million people in the world have suffered from bulimia nervosa at least once in their lifetime! If that isn't alarming, I don't know what is.

But those statistics are not what I'm here to talk about. The point to note here is that you shouldn't be the one joining that group of 131,672,200 women. That's not where you want to be. You should belong to the rest of the 3,160,132,800 women who are healthy. Oh and by healthy, I don't mean it in the typical Indian way–'*Oh ji, aap toh bade healthy ho gaye ho*!' No. That's not what I'm talking about.

But first things first, let's learn a little bit about bulimia nervosa. The first step is, of course, to recognise it. Once you learn to recognise it, avoiding it becomes easy, peasy.

Bulimia is generally characterised by certain telltale behavioural patterns, particularly, binging and purging. If you are in a habit of overeating, and then vomiting it all out (voluntarily) because you feel so guilty you ate so much then chances are that you suffer from bulimia nervosa. However, there are also quite a few other symptoms related to bulimia that I'm going to list over here.

- A chronically inflamed and sore throat. When you throw up, you don't just throw up food that you ate. It's not like chewing the cud. As soon as the food reaches your stomach, it starts getting digested. And to help with the digestion, there are some gastric fluids present in the stomach. These fluids are acidic (now you know why they say an empty stomach induces acidity). So when you throw up, you also throw up the gastric juices. Being acidic, it burns your throat, which is not used to such acidity. Do it repeatedly, and well, there is only so much your poor throat can take.

- Your salivary glands in the neck and jaw area are swollen. Have you ever noticed, whenever you are about to puke (I mean, puke naturally like after a thrill ride), you automatically start salivating uncontrollably? Well, the same thing happens when you purge on demand. Obviously, your salivary glands can also only take so much.

- Your teeth start decaying. As mentioned earlier, when you puke, you also puke up your gastric juices which are acidic in nature. It turns out that your teeth don't like it either. This acid starts stripping the tooth of its enamel, and gradually turns it yellow, which is nothing but a sign of decay.

- Many people use their finger to puke. Others use laxatives. Your intestines can tolerate laxatives but they don't exactly like them. So when you abuse laxatives, your intestines protest in the form of irritation and in extreme cases, a burning sensation.

- You eat three times a day. You purge three times a day. That's a lot of fluid lost. You're bound to feel not only fatigued but also terribly dehydrated.

- Your levels of sodium, potassium and calcium can go awry. And this can cause a heart attack.

Why Am I Talking So Much About Eating Disorders?

I'm going to be blunt here, so please don't feel bad. If you, dear beauty pageant aspirant, are indeed binging and purging regularly, you need to get some help. By not eating properly and starving, you're just harming yourself both physically and mentally. And you want to win a pageant, don't you? Well, you can't do that in a weakend mental and physical state.

By pushing your body to such limits, you might lose weight, and maybe even quickly. But at what cost? At the cost of getting a heart attack? Or at the cost of a wheelchair because your bones won't be strong enough to support your meager weight? Is that what you are looking for? I really don't think so.

But the good news is, there is help readily available, as and when you need it. All you need to do is ask. There are trained professionals out there you can contact and they know how you feel. Some of them would have even been in your position once upon a time.

I have a mantra that I'd like you all to follow. When it comes to the question of eating, never say never. In fact, if you ask me what I had for dinner yesterday, I'm going to tell you that I had pizza! No, really! I did. But the point to note here is that the pizza isn't a habit (and I'm talking about fast food pizza here, not proper Italian pizza). A couple of years ago I was shooting for a project which went on till about midnight. I was hungry, tired and right next to the location where we were shooting was a pizzeria. So we all ordered pizza and ate it. FYI I'm a US size three or four.

So you must be wondering that if I'm supposed to eat, how the hell am I to lose weight? Aren't those two contradictory?

Well... not exactly. The opposite in fact. Let me explain.

Weight Loss

All of us have such a love-hate relationship with weight loss. You can't live without it... but you can't live with it either! It just drives you crazy. I get it! I've been there!

According to Wikipedia, weight loss is 'a reduction of the total body mass due to a mean loss of fluid, body fat or adipose tissue and/or lean mass, namely bone mineral deposits, muscle tendon and other connective tissue.'

Mean loss of body fat or adipose tissue (both of which mean the exact same thing, by the way) is fine. That's what we are aiming for. We don't want excessive body fat, do we? That's as should be. But then it gets slightly scary. Reduction of total body mass due to a mean loss of fluid? Something's very wrong there. 70 percent of our body is made up of fluid, aka water. Which means there is a lot of it to lose. Theoretically speaking, if you weigh a 100 kg today and you lose all of your water weight, you would weight just 30 kg tomorrow. Of course, in practical terms, that could never happen. Your body would never let you lose all that water weight. It would kill you before it would let you. Literally, I mean. You would die of dehydration. But I am just trying to make you understand the basic principles here.

When I was just starting out in the industry, I heard some very unhealthy advice. I was trying to lose weight back then and it wasn't going at the pace that I would have liked it to go. I had the Femina Miss India audition in a few days and I still had quite a bit of body fat to lose (of course, in those days, I didn't think of it in terms of body fat. I thought about it in terms of weight that had to be lost). I was a nervous wreck. And one friend came up to me and said, 'Don't worry. Just don't drink any water two days before the audition. Your body will shrivel up and you will look thinner. And if you feel thirsty, have a piece of orange, just one piece mind you, not any more.' Looking back now, I don't know what I'm more shocked at—her 'advice' or the fact that I tried my level best to follow it. Right after the audition, I caved in and started chugging down water like I'd never seen it before. She meant well, but she was misguided. Cutting down on water is not going to help you. It will only cause you to collapse due to dehydration, and at a pageant, you really don't want that to happen.

Weight loss is a very vague term. I would rather use the term 'fat loss'. Here we are talking about the loss of body fat and not about the loss of any lean muscle or water weight.

Now, look at the second part of the Wikipedia definition, 'or lean mass, namely bone mineral deposits, muscle tendon and other connective tissue.' In simple terms, this means loss of muscle, loss of protein, loss of calcium, loss of essential minerals. Isn't that scary? But the fact is more often than not, that is just what weight loss leads to.

Weight loss is a very vague term—one that I don't like to use. I would rather use the term 'fat loss'. Because it is specific. Here we are talking about the loss of body fat and not about the loss of any lean muscle or water weight. With fat loss, we know that we are approaching our ideal fitness level in the right manner, in the healthy manner.

So let us forget all about weight loss. That is not our goal. Who really cares whether you weigh 55 kg or 53 kg. Is that difference of two kilos really such a matter of life and death?

Of course it's not. How much you weigh matters, but only when lots of other things like BMI, body fat percentage and the levels of all essential nutrients and minerals present in your body are taken into consideration. Let's talk about fat loss and muscle build-up instead. But before that, let's understand some useful statistics and data that you can keep referring to throughout this chapter.

BMI

BMI stands for body mass index. It is a unit of measurement that helps in finding out whether your weight is in accordance with your height, whether you are in a healthy weight range or not. BMI is a very common measuring unit. Everyone uses it as though it is one of the Ten Commandments.

The fashion industry uses BMI as though it is the only unit of measurement on earth. But you know better. BMI will not tell you the whole truth, just a part of it.

But the fact is, it is not. BMI does not measure a person's body fat percentage. It just gives a general idea of how healthy you are; it is, however, the last word. So please don't take it as such. The fashion industry uses BMI as though it is the only unit of measurement on earth. But you know better. So take it with a pinch of salt. It is important to stay within the limits that your BMI sets; do not ignore that. But just remember, it will not tell you the whole truth, just a part of it. The rest of the truth lies elsewhere.

$$\text{BMI} = \frac{\text{mass (kg)}}{(\text{height (m)})^2}$$

$$\frac{\text{mass (lb)}}{(\text{height (in)})^2} \text{ X } 703$$

How do you measure your BMI?

Are You Within the Healthy Range?

Category	BMI range – kg/m2	BMI Prime	Mass (weight) of a 1.8-metre (5 ft 11 in) person with this BMI.
Very severely underweight	less than 15.0	less than 0.60	less than 48.6 kilograms (7.65 st; 107 lb)
Severely underweight	from 15.0 to 16.0	from 0.60 to 0.64	between 48.6 and 51.8 kilograms (7.65 and 8.16 st; 107 and 114 lb)
Underweight	from 16.0 to 18.5	from 0.64 to 0.74	between 51.8 and 59.9 kilograms (8.16 and 9.43 st; 114 and 132 lb)
Normal (healthy weight)	from 18.5 to 25	from 0.74 to 1.0	between 59.9 and 81.0 kilograms (9.43 and 12.76 st; 132 and 179 lb)
Overweight	from 25 to 30	from 1.0 to 1.2	between 81.0 and 97.2 kilograms (12.76 and 15.31 st; 179 and 214 lb)
Obese Class I (Moderately obese)	from 30 to 35	from 1.2 to 1.4	between 97.2 and 113.4 kilograms (15.31 and 17.86 st; 214 and 250 lb)
Obese Class II (Severely obese)	from 35 to 40	from 1.4 to 1.6	between 113.4 and 129.6 kilograms (17.86 and 20.41 st; 250 and 286 lb)
Obese Class III (Very severely obese)	over 40	over 1.6	over 129.6 kilograms (20.41 st; 286 lb)

Body Fat Percentage

Body fat percentage is just a measure of how much fat you have in your body. But if you ask me, it is a much more accurate way of measuring how healthy you are than the BMI.

See, an athlete has more muscle mass than a common person. And muscle is much heavier than fat. So an athlete and a common person might both have a BMI of say, 20. But does that mean they are both equally healthy? No! Because the common person has a large amount of fat that is contributing to the weight, which is not healthy whereas the athlete has a certain amount of muscle mass that is contributing to the weight, and that is healthy. BMI, under circumstances like what I described earlier, can be misleading. BFP (body fat percentage) on the other hand, does not mislead. Once you have measured your BFP, all you need to do is compare your results against the chart given below, and you'll know where exactly to stand. Easy, isn't it?

Description	Women	Men
Essential fat	10–13%	2–5%
Athletes	14–20%	6–13%
Fitness	21–24%	14–17%
Average	25–31%	18–24%
Obese	32%+	25%+

How to Measure BFP?

Now here's the hitch. Measuring BFP is complicated, cumbersome and expensive. In fact, the most accurate method of measuring BFP is the most impractical and maybe even the most expensive method of them all! Well, let me just chart out all the methods of having your BFP measured and you can decide which is best.

1. Underwater Weighing: Ah! This is my favourite. It is said to be the most accurate way of measuring BFP, but wait till you hear about it! The logic behind the methodology is something that I don't really understand, but let me try to explain. The density of body fat is much lower than the density of muscle mass. This is a fact. Now, take a person and dunk them under water. Okay, don't dunk them, that will give you an incorrect reading, just immerse them gently in water. Obviously some water will be displaced. Now the weight of the water displaced is used to calculate

the volume of the water displaced. But what does this have to do with body fat? Well, remember what I just told you about the density of body fat? This is where that comes into play. Body fat is less dense than muscle, but it is also less dense than water. Which automatically means that muscle is denser than water, which means it sinks. So now, the volume of water displaced basically equals the amount of muscle mass in your body. You do the math… and voila! Body Fat Percentage with an uncertainty of just +/-3.8percent. That's not bad!

The DXA sends electromagnetic rays, i.e., X-rays to penetrate the human body to determine the exact chemical composition of that particular human. That obviously would give us the exact percentage of fat that is present in the body. It is the most accurate way of measuring BFP.

2. Near-infrared interactance: Now this one is for all the tech junkies out there. All that is done here is that a beam of infra-red rays is, well, beamed into your bicep. And as it passes through the bicep, the pattern in which it travels is studied and that is then used to calculate your body fat percentage.

3. DXA: DXA stands for Dual Energy X-Ray Absorptiometry. Don't run away, guys, I'm still speaking English. Absorptiometry is a method of chemical analysis which is used to figure out what exactly the chemical composition of a substance, any substance, is. Now, we've always studied the human body under biology, but actually, what we are made up of are various chemicals. And fat is one such chemical. I won't go into the details, we're not here to analyse the chemical composition or formula of fat. The DXA sends electromagnetic rays, i.e., X-rays to penetrate the human body to determine the exact chemical composition of that particular human. That obviously would give us the exact percentage of fat that is present in the body. It is the most accurate way of

measuring BFP. But don't start jumping for joy yet, this method has more cons than pros. The pro obviously is the unrivalled accuracy. But the problem is it uses X-rays. Have you ever got an X-ray done? Have you noticed that the radiologist always stays out of the path of the rays and asks others to do the same? That is because repeated exposure to X-rays is dangerous and can cause cancer. So my advice would be to stay away from DXA unless of course it is unavoidable for whatever reason. The other con isn't such a big issue, but it's an issue nevertheless. DXA doesn't come cheap. It involves a lot of expensive machinery and highly skilled labour. One session of DXA can cost you anywhere from $150 to $500 depending on where you are getting it done. Now, considering the health risks involved, I would rrather spend that money on this gorgeous pair of Michael Kors boots I saw just the other day. And to think I came back empty-handed because I thought it's too expensive!

4. Body Average Density Measurement: Before DXA was developed, this was the most accurate method of measurement available to calculate a person's body fat percentage. It's a complicated procedure but I will try to explain it as simply as possible. First, you measure your body's average density (which is measured by dividing your total mass by total volume), and then a formula is used to convert that into body fat percentage. There are two formulae that can be used. One is the Brozek formula ($BF = (4.57/\rho - 4.142) \times 100$ where ρ stands for average density) and the other is the Siri formula ($BF = (4.95/\rho - 4.50) \times 100$), and no, it has nothing to do with voice recognition. Either formulae may be used for an accurate measurement. The logic behind this is more or less the same as in underwater weighing. As mentioned earlier, muscles, bones and fat—all have different densities. And fat has a lower density than muscle and bones. That is exactly what makes it possible to measure fat content.

5. Biometrical Impedance Analysis (BIA): Now this is

a pretty common method. You know those weighing machines which claim to measure your body fat percentage? Well, they use a diluted version of this same technology. What basically happens here is that a small electrical current is sent through the body through two or more electrodes. This electrical current faces some resistance while it passes through the body. Obviously. Try to push your hand through a pile of cotton. You will feel it pushing back, however slightly. The same applies to this electric current. But the point is that the amount of resistance that fat provides is different from that which muscle and bones provide. So, it is this difference that is used to measure how much fat there is in your body. Like any other method of calculation, this one too, has its pros and cons. The pro here is that it is quite affordable. But the con is that it is not the most accurate means of measurement. But pros and cons aside the fact is that it is the most practical way of measuring BFA. It might not be 100 percent accurate, but it is accurate enough.

6. Skinfold methods: Have you ever tried to pinch your waist to see how much fat you need to lose? I'm sure you have, I do it every day! Well, if you have, you are practicing a watered down version of the skinfold method. The skinfold method is one of the most popular for the one single reason that it is the easiest way of measuring BFA. All you need is a little tool that is known as the body fat caliper. You can find it easily on Amazon or in any health shop.

   The body fat caliper comes with a conversion table that tells you what BFP you have for a certain measurement. All you have to do is use this instrument to pinch your skin. Note that it has a measure on it that tells you how many inches of skin are pinched. Compare that to the conversion table and voila! You have an approximate measure of BFP. However, this is not my most favourite way. You know why? Because if you get too enthusiastic, the amount of skin pinched could easily include quite a bit of muscle, and that will definitely give you a wrong measurement. To me it seems there is just way too much room for error here.

7. Height and Circumference Method: This method is very popular with the US Navy, US Army and the US Marine Corps, and I just hope their testimony means it is an accurate measure, though I have my doubts. It is quite an easy way to measure BFP. All you need to do is measure yourself around the hips, waist and neck, compare your results with the help of a conversion table (which you can find anywhere on the internet) and get your BFP right away. I don't have any reason to be prejudiced against this method. My only reservation is that it seems too easy. There is, I am sure, a very good reason for the US armed forces to constantly use this method. So go ahead, try it and don't forget to tell me how it goes.

8. BMI: This is the method that surprised me the most. I don't know why I was surprised. After all the BMI and BFP are very closely related, even more closely than I originally thought, it turns out. It is said to be a pretty accurate measurement if you are in the healthy BMI range, that is. If you are obese, however, then it overestimates the amount of fat in your body. It is pretty simple to calculate. All you need is a calculator. Once you have your BMI, enter the following formula into your calculator: (1.20 × BMI) + (0.23 × Age) – (10.8 × Sex) – 5.4 (Sex is 1 for males and 0 for females). Try it! Go on. It's actually fun.

Have you ever tried to pinch your waist to see how much fat you need to lose? I am sure you have. All you now need is a little tool that is known as the body fat caliper.

So there we go. That's a lot of theory covered. Now comes the interesting part—applying the theory to practical life. That is time to start working out!

Sculpting a Perfect Ten

Now we're getting to the meat of it. All this theory comes down to just one thing: getting that perfect ten figure. And frankly, there is just one way to do it—work out and enjoy it! You know, I've tried every single form of working out that there is in the world… well almost. I've tried weight training, kickboxing, cardio, Pilates, strength training, yoga, dance, power yoga, swimming, sports and I can't remember what else!

Some people swear by yoga, some by circuit training, and some by Pilates. Everyone has their own opinion. And everyone is entitled to their own opinion too. Because it doesn't matter what sort of workout you do. What matters is how you do it, how regularly you do it and how much you enjoy it. I would, in fact, say that the how-much-you-enjoy-it factor is the most important of them all. Because if you enjoy your workout, you will do it regularly and you will definitely do it well. Working out does not have to be a daily torture! And trust me, I know.

It doesn't matter what sort of workout you do. What matters is how you do it, how regularly you do it and how much you enjoy it.

I was overweight as a teenager. I had always been a skinny child, but as soon as I turned thirteen, my hormones started acting up (the curse of puberty… as if an identity crisis wasn't enough!) and I immediately started putting on a lot of weight. Adding to that was my sedentary lifestyle. As a child, I had never been interested in going out and playing with other kids. I preferred sitting in my room with a copy of *Little Women* or *Anne of Green Gables.* But I had fantastic metabolism. I never put on weight! As I got into my teens, however, all that changed.

As a child, I had never been interested in going out and playing with other kids. I preferred sitting in my room with a copy of Little Women *or* Anne of Green Gables.

Within a year-and-half, by the age of fifteen, I was 67 kilograms. Yes, I was a baby elephant, literally. My mother was alarmed, obviously. My parents enrolled me in this neighbourhood gym for a trial period of a month. From day one, I knew I didn't want to go. My parents forced me, cajoled me and finally struck a deal with me that if I went for a month and I still hated it, I wouldn't have to go anymore. That sounded fine to me, since I had already decided that I hated gymming. And I still hate gymming.

A swimsuit has a talent—it enhances a person's physical flaws.

After a month, I called it quits and no force on earth could make me go back there again. Next, my parents tried to get me into swimming. It was something I was good at and enjoyed, more or less. So my mom told me that as soon as I got back from school every day, it would be one hour of swimming for me. All hell broke loose. Every single day, my mom and I would fight. I went swimming half of the time, but never without a screaming match with my mom first. I resented having to go swimming every day. That's strange, actually, since I've always enjoyed swimming. I think my reluctance was more to do with my swimsuit. A swimsuit has a talent—it enhances a person's physical flaws (more on this later) and I didn't exactly have the figure of a Victoria's Secret model. To this day, in fact, whenever I put on a swimsuit, never mind if it is for a pageant or just a swim at my gym, I feel fat. Some residues last long, I guess.

Finally, I settled upon a routine with my mother. Our TV room became my exercise room. I would lock myself in this room, switch on the TV, select MTV or Channel V and start. First I would jog. There was no treadmill. Somehow, I have never liked treadmills so much. They are useful, no doubt, but I've never gelled with them. Instead, I would jog from one end of the room to another for half-an-hour to forty-five minutes. Once I was done jogging, I would dish out old issues of *Seventeen* (that I used to read religiously back then), create a workout routine based on the exercises given there and top it up with a little bit of yoga and I was done. I would do this every day. And by the end of the year, I had lost almost ten kilograms. Not a meager achievement.

I can't tell you what your perfect workout regime should be. But I can tell you this:

- It must be regular. Doing it one day and then forgetting about it for the next two weeks is not going to help. It's only going to make things worse, because you will feel that since you are working out, you have the license to eat whatever you want. But, in fact, you haven't really worked out. It was just one odd day when you did. See the logic?
- Deriving from the first point, just because you are working out regularly does not give you the freedom to binge. Eating right and eating healthy is only half of the battle.
- In order to see results, you will need to work out at least three or four times a week, preferably every day. Once upon a time, we had to hunt for our food, which ensured that we got our workout before the reward. Maybe it would help to keep the same logic in mind.
- You should preferably work out in the morning, on a near empty stomach. Not only will this aid your digestion, but hey, you're getting it out of the way. Then you're free to enjoy the rest of your day.

Nutrition

So now you have your ideal workout regime. Yayy! But just working out will not get you anywhere. Workouts work only when supplemented with a proper diet. Without that, it doesn't matter how much you work out at the gym. You really cannot have one without the other.

Food and Pageants

Food and pageants don't really get along, sadly. And that is a problem. At most national pageants, your diet is strictly controlled by their resident dietician. At international pageants, that is not so, but you will most likely be accompanied by a dietician who will pick what you will eat from that scrumptious buffet.

I remember, at I AM She, we had to adhere to a very strict diet. We would get one dosa with chutney (with no coconut) for breakfast, and a tiny portion of veggies and dal for lunch and dinner. If you were one of the thinner girls, you'd get a roti or two, otherwise none of that either. We weren't even allowed fruits except for half an apple before our workout. I actually remember trying to smuggle back some fruits into my room from the breakfast buffet. I wasn't very successful. And my fruits were confiscated. That should be warning enough for any drug cartel looking to hire me. I can't even smuggle two oranges up six floors! But to our luck, someone forgot to remove the tea and coffee supplies in our hotel room. Dude, we pigged out on sugary tea (while hidden in our rooms between sessions) and dairy creamer sachets, both of which were illegal substances (with respect to the pageant, at least)!

A few years before that, at a prominent pageant in India (that I was not part of), the standard lunch was one tiny piece of smoked salmon. I think I heard of a record number of girls fainting that year. The next year, when I participated, however, we got lucky. We got dal, veggies and bajre ki roti. But that was only thanks to those girls fainting the previous year.

Truth be told, the biggest pageants don't care a hoot about your health. What matters to them is how you look. And if you don't meet their standards, you will be put on a very taxing diet and maybe an extra hour at the gym. And at least fifty percent of the girls they choose don't meet their standards.

So it's up to you to take care of your health. But here is the problem. How do you do that? Here you are at a pageant.

You have to follow their schedule, which often means you're on your feet twelve to fourteen hours a day. You have to eat what they give you. They are pretty good at detecting smugglers (seriously, they should go professional on that). And you are not allowed to bring any food from home.

What do you do? While you are at the pageant, there's nothing you can do. But while you're preparing for your pageant, you'll need to take care of your body so well that it will be able to take care of you when you need it the most – when you're hungry and sleep deprived during that one month of the pageant. And you can accomplish this partly by eating right, and giving your body the nutrients it needs. So let's figure out how to do that.

Diet Versus Balanced Diet

It's sad to see how many of us have a completely distorted view of what a diet is. If someone says they're going on a diet, we shoot them pitying looks and cry, 'But you don't need to go on a diet! You're fine as you are!'

Umm... no. I beg to differ. Technically speaking, you shouldn't have to go on a diet. You are always on a diet, from the moment you are born till the day you die; always, constantly on a diet. Confused?

Let me explain.

A diet is what you eat. So unless you are a yogi living high up in the Himalayas existing solely on the thin mountain air, darling, you are on a diet. If you eat McDonald's all day long, that is your diet. If you eat a flimsy excuse of a salad every day, that is your diet. But this is where differentiation comes into play. A diet is not always healthy; the fact is, most of us are on a very unhealthy diet!

So what we should be aiming for is a balanced diet, where the body gets exactly what it requires. But before I start on a healthy, balanced diet, let's deal with the naysayers first.

Say No To Fads

The naysayers have a point, you know! Most of the diets that we hear of from popular media channels are not healthy. They are fad diets, whether it's the Atkins or the Orange Juice diet. And fad diets are not healthy.

See, the thing with fad diets is that they work. They totally work. They're supposed to get you to lose weight and they do. But at what cost? Is that a cost that's really worth it?

See, the thing with fad diets is that they work. They totally work. They are supposed to get you to lose weight and they do. But at what cost?

Let's look at some of the most popular diet fads:

1. The Tapeworm Diet: The tapeworm diet is when you willingly, voluntarily introduce tapeworms into your body. Why? So that whatever you eat, they can gobble up, robbing your body of its nutrients so that you can grow thin. Do I really need to explain why this is bad? Tapeworms are parasites, period! And those nutrients that they're gobbling up? Well, those are the nutrients you need in order to live! This is dangerous stuff.

2. The Master Cleanser Diet: Oh, I could write pages and pages about this! Where do I even start? The Master Cleanser Diet is a variation of the Fruit Juice Diet, which I believe was very popular among some Bollywood starlets a little less than ten years ago. Really, it was all the newspapers wrote about! Such irresponsible journalism. But the original Master Cleanser Diet consists of surviving on a mixture of water, lemon juice, maple syrup and cayenne pepper. Nothing else. No carbs, no proteins, nothing. Sure, with this, you'll lose some water weight, but you'll also lose muscle mass as the body will increasingly start to use up its stored protein in order to provide you with some much-needed energy, and that is not good. There is a reason proteins are called the building blocks of your body.

3. The Grapefruit Diet: This is like the father of all fad

diets. Or rather, the grandfather of it all! Hey, it's more than eighty years old! It first found its footing among the youngsters of the 1920s. In the Grapefruit Diet, all you eat is a grapefruit. Yep, just that. Grapefuit for breakfast, grapefruit for lunch, grapefruit for dinner. Now you will lose weight in this because it's an extremely low calorie diet, restricting your calorie intake to less than 800 calories a day, which, by the way, is dangerously low. And also, keep in mind that you're not getting any other nutrients here. Those should really be all the red flags you need to stay away.

4. Cookie Diet: Don't rejoice just yet. This diet does not give you the permission to gorge on those yummy chocolate chip cookies all day long. Quite the contrary. The Cookie Diet offers pre-packaged cookies from brands like Dr Siegal, etc. Now these pre-packaged cookies are all you eat! The whole day. The primary problem with this diet is that it depends on extreme calorie deprivation. With this Cookie Diet, you are getting a maximum of 800-1000 calories per day! That is just not enough to sustain you. That's starvation. And you must agree with me here, starvation is not good.

5. The Five-Bite Diet: The Five-Bite Diet is when you take only five bites of whatever meal you choose. And the rest, you ask? Well that will go to all the overflowing trashfills in the world. Two problems with this. First, depending on what meal you have chosen, you could either starve yourself or just plain go over to the unhealthy side. I can fit one gulab jamun in my mouth as one bite. So are you giving me leeway to stuff myself with five gulab jamuns for every meal? On the other hand, if you do choose a balanced diet, five bites is just not enough to sustain you (unless, of course, you take inhumanly large bites). This diet relies on calorie deprivation. And that, as we already know, is really not a good idea. Now the second problem: you've eaten five bites of that sandwich. What about the rest? You're just going to throw it away? Hold on a second, what exactly was that about not wasting food that we learnt as kids?

There's a good way to get fit and there's a bad way to get fit. And the best part is, your body will tell you if you're on the right track or the wrong one. All you need to do is listen to it. If you give your body all that it needs, trust me, not only will you feel good but you'll also have so much more energy to go about your daily life. Now that can only be a win-win situation, right?

What is a Balanced Diet?

There's a good way to get fit and there's a bad way to get fit. And the best part is, your body will tell you if you're on the right track or the wrong one.

Simply put, a balanced diet is a diet that provides your body with all the nutrients it needs. It is the ideal diet. It is the holy grail of diets! So let's look at all the ingredients that go into making the perfect balanced diet.

PROTEINS

Proteins, as we learnt in high school, are the building blocks of the body. Chemically speaking, they are nothing but large molecules of amino acids bonded together. But they are very important for our body's functioning. The presence of proteins is critical for our organs, our body structure, the regulation of our cells and our muscles to function. Be it our muscles, skin, organs or cells, they all contain significant amounts of protein. In fact, upto 20 percent of our body weight could be protein.

Types

There are different types of amino acids. I won't go into all that right now since it's really not relevant and if I may say so, quite boring to list. But if you are really curious, the world wide web is at your service.

Purpose

Primarily, proteins help to build and/or replace tissue, hair (the Keratin that you see advertised on all those shampoo bottles is nothing but a type of protein), skin, muscles, etc. But in their free time (these guys don't know how to chill), they go around making antibodies for our immune system, hormones (now you know whom to blame for those mood swings), enzymes and also help in muscle contraction and movement. So just the simple fact that you're reading this book right now, you owe to your proteins.

Whenever you ingest any kind of protein, that protein sets about building your body. But, if you starve, that is, if you provide your body with way less energy than it needs, it will start digging into your protein reserves, i.e., your muscles. And that, for obvious reasons, is something you do not want.

How it Works

Technically, one gram of protein carries in it 4 Kcals of energy. But energy production is not its primary purpose. Whenever you ingest any kind of protein, that protein sets about building your body. But, if you starve, that is, if you provide your body with way less energy than it needs, it will start digging into your protein reserves, i.e., your muscles. And that, for obvious reasons, is something you do not want.

Now, an important point. We are often told by our gym trainers and other peers to ingest copious amounts of protein drinks. This might or might not be useful, depending on how much muscle-building activity you are really doing per day. But any extra protein ingested is not stored in your body. Protein does not work the way fat or carbohydrates do. Your body will only absorb as much protein as it needs, regardless of how much you feed it. The rest, it will expel along with your other waste.

Sources of Protein: Pulses, eggs, soy products, dairy, meat, fish, seeds and nuts.

Protein Deficiency

Protein Deficiency is not pretty. As mentioned above, one thing it will definitely lead to is muscle shrinkage and wasting. But that's not it. Among other things, it can lead to growth issues (if you're still at a growing age), diarrhoea, anaemia and a weak immune system.

CARBOHYDRATES

Carbohydrates are the primary source of energy for your body. You wake up in the morning, brush your teeth, make yourself coffee and breakfast, eat that breakfast... Well, carbohydrates give you the energy to do all that. This book that you're reading, carbohydrates give you the energy to do that. Chemically speaking, they are exactly what its nomenclature suggests. They are hydrates of carbon.

Types

Carbohydrates can be divided into two main types:

- Simple: Simple carbs are also called simple sugars. As the name itself suggests, simple carbohydrates have a simple molecular structure made up of only one or two sugar molecules. Since the structure of these carbs is relatively simpler, it is also easier and quicker for the body to break them down, i.e., digest. Thus, they're really good sources of quick energy. The simplest form of simple carbs is glucose. Now that makes sense, doesn't it? So apart from glucose drinks and glucose drips, what are the other sources of simple carbs? Well, anything that's easy for the body to digest, i.e, dairy, fruit, etc.
- Complex: Complex carbs have more of a complicated molecular structure and thus are a little more time-consuming when it comes to your body breaking them down. But that's not a bad thing, that's a good thing! It takes longer for the body to break down complex carbs. Which also means that it will not only keep you feeling satisfied for longer but will also provide you with more energy for longer. Try it. Can you survive solely on fruits? I think not!

Purpose

I think we have already established the need for carbohydrates. But let me expand a little more, mainly because the fad nowadays is to go on low-carb diets. Nothing wrong with that! But when the low-carb diet becomes extremely low carb or no carb, something's really wrong. The idea behind low-carb diets is that if you do not provide the body with the carbs it requires for its day-to-day work, it will dig into its reserved fat storage. Thus you burn fat. But the caveat here is that while your entire body can run on stored fat, your brain cannot. Your brain needs carbs. That's why right after you workout, you must always eat some simple carbs. Just to quickly give your brain sufficient energy to function. In fact, if you feel that your workout is going to be strenuous and long, you should also eat something with simple carbs in it right before you work out. Apparently, the human brain can use upto 25 percent of the entire body's energy budget and up to 60 percent of blood glucose. That's quite a bit. And there is no substitute! In fact, recent research suggests that carbs might be the very reason we have big, intelligent brains.

The caveat here is that while your entire body can run on stored fat, your brain cannot. Your brain needs carbs.

How it Works

Well, we know the basics already. You eat something that contains carbs, simple or complex. Your stomach, with its gastric acid, breaks it down into its most elementary forms. Now this broken-down carb is ready to be absorbed. It travels down your small intestine where small finger-like projections called villi absorb the carbohydrates into the bloodstream to give you energy. But the body will only absorb as much as it needs. No more. So what happens to the extra carbs? Well, unlike proteins, your body will not simply throw them away. It will still absorb them, but in the form of glycogen. This glycogen is not fat, technically, at least, not yet. It is stored in your liver and your muscles, waiting to be converted back into energy to energise your body. But unfortunately, the liver really does not have a lot of room. So if this glycogen is not spent immediately and the body produces another batch of glycogen (because you have ingested more carbs than you need), the old glycogen loses its home and takes shelter in your body as adipose tissue, aka, fat.

So what do we learn from this? Not too much, not too less. Everything in moderation.

Sources: The sources are different for simple carbohydrates and complex carbohydrates. Simple carbs can be found in fruits, refined sugar, dairy, etc., while complex carbs can mainly be found in any type of cereal. However, do make sure that it is whole grain, since refining it can deprive it of fibre content, making it much simpler in structure.

FATS

The big bad guys of the nutrition world! We can just imagine them in their Italian suits, hair slicked back with gel, whispering, 'I'll make him an offer he can't refuse.'

Right?

Wrong.

You know the one kid in primary school that everyone makes fun of and everyone avoids? That's our poor fat. It's not really bad for you! It's just misunderstood. Yes, too much can be, well, too much. Too much of anything is bad. But fat, taken in reasonable amounts, is actually good for you. That's why, it is one of the three macronutrients, the other two being: carbohydrates and proteins. It is essential.

Types of Fats

Fats can be divided into two main types:

- Healthy Fats: These are good for you. Since they are unsaturated, they are usually liquid at room temperature, and in limited amounts, they are essential. They can be divided into two types:

1. Mono-Unsaturated Fats: These are usually found in avocado, nuts and a few other plant oils like canola or olive (now you know why olive oil is supposed to be good). Taken in the right amounts, it can help to reduce your bad cholesterol.
2. Poly-Unsaturated Fats: You like eating seafood? Well, poly-unsaturated fats are mainly found in seafood. They are also found in vegetable oils like safflower, sunflower, soybean, etc. Just like its twin, mono, poly is also good at reducing your levels of bad cholesterol. Poly-unsaturated fats can be further divided into two types:

Fat, taken in reasonable amounts, is actually good for you. That's why it is one of the three macronutrients, the other two being: carbohydrates and proteins. It is essential.

- Omega 3 Fatty Acids: Found primarily in seafood, but also in some nuts and plant oils like canola, Omega 3 Fats are essential for you.
- Omega 6 Fatty Acids: Omega 6 fatty acids can be found in vegetable oils like safflower, sunflower, soybean, etc.

- Unhealthy Fats: Unhealthy fats are mainly of two types:

1. Saturated Fats: One easy way to identify saturated fat is that it would be solid at room temperature, like butter, cheese, etc. Now saturated fats are listed under unhealthy fats. And yes, compared to unsaturated fats, they are indeed unhealthy. But what we often forget is that these sources of saturated fats also have other nutrients in them. Butter, for example, is a good source of Vitamin A. Cheese is an excellent source of calcium and protein. So it's probably time we took our blinders off. Eating a

slice of cheese a day is not going to harm you. In fact, it will probably do you a lot of good! But as I always say, everything in moderation.

2. Trans Fats: But all that *gyaan* really holds true only for saturated fats. Not for trans fats, though. These guys are bad! Trans fats 'happen' when a process called hydrogenation takes place. What it basically does is increase the shelf life of the fat and also make it much harder at room temperature. Now an important baking lesson; the harder your fat, the crispier your cookies. So all those butter cookies, or chocolate chip cookies, or pies, etc., that we love... trans fats, trans fats, trans fats. But why are trans fat bad for you? Because they raise your cholesterol. Cholesterol is the little guy who creates a blockage in your arteries causing severe heart problems. I'm sure you don't want that!

Purpose

Fats provide you with energy. One gram of fat contains 9 Kcals of energy. And also depending on the type of fat, as we saw earlier, it can help in lowering your levels of bad cholesterol too. But energy is something you can get from carbs also. And isn't the whole point of lowering the intake of carbs, to burn fat? So why take fat?

Well, I used to be of the same opinion once upon a time. But did you know that there are certain nutrients, e.g., Vitamin A that can only be absorbed by fat? I'll get into the details of how that works in the Vitamins section. But if it wasn't for fat, you wouldn't be able to absorb some essential nutrients. You must take in a minimal amount of fat every day in order to fortify your body with nutrients.

What we often forget is that these sources of saturated fats also have other nutrients in them. Butter, for example, is a good source of Vitamin A. Cheese is an excellent source of calcium and protein.

Sources: Well, different types of fats have different sources. So let's deal with this type wise.

- Mono-unsaturated Fats: Olive oil, canola oil, peanut oil, avocados, nuts and seeds
- Omega 6 Fatty Acids: safflower oil, sesame oil, sunflower oil, various nuts and seeds
- Omega 3 Fatty Acids: Seafood, canola oil, soybean oil, flax seeds and walnuts
- Saturated Fats: Meat, dairy, butter, lard, coconut oil, palm oil, palm kernel oil and cocoa butter
- Trans Fats: Any processed snack, fast food or ready-to-eat meals.

VITAMINS

Vitamins are a little hard to generalise. But overall, they are substances that sustain your body and help it grow and function. Specifically, however, each vitamin has a different function.

Types

Vitamins, like most other things we have looked at, can be primarily divided into two types:

- Fat Soluble: This constitutes for most of the vitamins. Fat soluble simply means that the body requires fatty acids in order to absorb this kind of vitamin. If fatty acids are not found (because you have been avoiding them like the plague), then these vitamins are thrown out of your body. Fat soluble vitamins are of four kinds:

1. Vitamin A: Vitamin A helps in your vision, bone growth, reproduction, cell functions and immune system. It's somewhat like an all-rounder. However, you'll be missing out on this if your fat intake is zero. Vitamin A is also an antioxidant. But where do you find it? Well, in any colourful fruit or vegetable (like carrots, like our mothers told us). Dairy products are also a good source of Vitamin A.

2. Vitamin D: Vitamin D is extremely crucial. It helps your body absorb calcium. And calcium, as we all know, is imperative for bone growth. Now it is a common misunderstanding that Vitamin D can only be sourced from the sun. Two natural sources of Vitamin D are the sun and your diet (although the sun still remains the primary source). Alternatively, thanks to advances in medical science, Vitamin D can also be sourced from supplements. However, I would still recommend getting out into the sun and obtaining it naturally. Also, keep a keen eye on the Vitamin D levels in your body. Thanks to our modern lifestyle, which shields us from the sun, it is one of the most common deficiencies today. Keep in mind, a Vitamin D deficiency can lead to loss of bone density, broken bones and osteoporosis on the milder side and rickets and osteomalacia on the severe side.

If fatty acids are not found in required quantity in the body (because you have been avoiding them like the plague), then these vitamins (Vitamins A, D, E and K) are thrown out of your body.

3. Vitamin E: Vitamin E is an antioxidant. It boosts your immune system and your metabolic processes. A deficiency would obviously mean a lower quality of your immune system, and really, who wants that?
4. Vitamin K: Now Vitamin K is one important but underrated dude. It helps in building proteins for healthier bones and tissues. And when it's not doing that, it also makes proteins for blood clotting. What that comes to is, if you don't have enough Vitamin K in your body, a tiny scratch on your arm may mean a never-ending stream of blood. Do not ignore this guy! One word of caution: if, for some reason, you take blood thinners, you should consult your doctor and be careful about how much Vitamin K you take everyday. Because remember what we just said about clotting?

- Water Soluble

1. Vitamin B: Oh this one is a never-ending saga! There are eight types of B vitamins, namely: B1 (thiamin), B2 (riboflavin), B3 (niacin), B5 (panthothenic acid), B6, B7 (biotin), B12 and folic acid. To quote the US National Library of Medicine, 'These vitamins help the process your body uses to get or make energy from the food you eat.' They are also crucial in the formation of red blood cells.
2. Vitamin C: Remember every time you had a cold in your childhood and your mom would give you a Vitamin C tablet? That's because Vitamin C helps in healing. It is an antioxidant and extremely important for your bones, skin and connective tissues. Plus, it also helps your body absorb iron. This guy is a true multi-tasker. But if you don't take in enough Vitamin C, it can lead to scurvy. And trust me, that's not pretty. Just remember, however, Vitamin C cannot be produced in your body. It has to be ingested via your diet or supplements. And as always, getting vitamins through your diet will guarantee better absorption.

Vitamin C helps in healing. It is an antioxidant and extremely important for your bones, skin and connective tissues. Plus, it also helps your body absorb iron. This guy is a true multi-tasker

Purpose

Vitamins come in all shapes and sizes. It is difficult to group them together and say, this, is their collective purpose. No. Each vitamin comes with its own individual set of uses.

Sources:

- Vitamin A: Colourful fruits and vegetables like carrots, dark leafy greens, lettuce, etc. Animal sources include cod liver oil and liver.
- Vitamin B: Many cereals, breads, green leafy vegetables, beans and peas are good sources of Vitamin B. Animal sources include fish, poultry, meat, eggs and dairy products.

- Vitamin C: Vitamin C primarily comes from a variety of fruits and vegetables, including citrus fruits, red and green capsicum, tomatoes, broccoli and green leafy vegetables.
- Vitamin D: Most commonly, Vitamin D is produced in your body when exposed to sunlight. But other sources include egg yolks, saltwater fish and liver. So if you are vegetarian, sorry, but the sun it is for you.
- Vitamin E: You can find it in vegetable oils, margarine, nuts, seeds and green leafy vegetables. Green leafy veggies seem to have everything. I guess our mothers were right!
- Vitamin K: You can get your Vitamin K primarily from green vegetables. There are certain bacteria in your intestine that produce it too.

MINERALS

Phew! Where do I even start? Like vitamins, minerals are also all over the place. But if I must group them, let's just say they are inorganic substances that the human body requires in small amounts for various functions. What functions? Well, we're just getting to that, but we'll be brief. If I go into detail about each one, not only will you get bored but this book will also cross a few thousand pages. And you thought *War and Peace* was extensive!

Types

Minerals are of many types. Those needed by the body are:

- Calcium: One of the most important and most abundant minerals in the human body, calcium is extremely important in the development and maintainence of healthy bones and teeth. This one must not be ignored.
- Phosphorous: Like calcium, phosphorous also helps in the development and maintainence of healthy bones and teeth.
- Magnesium: This mineral is hard to get along without, since it is needed for the activation of various enzymes

in our body. It is also needed for maintaining muscle and nerve function.

- Potassium: Now, potassium is the one that keeps the body water content and electrolyte balance in your body.
- Sodium: Just like potassium, sodium too maintains the body water content and electrolyte balance. It also plays a huge role in the absorbtion of water. Yes, that's right! Water.
- Iron: You must have heard of haemoglobin. Well, iron is the guy behind the formation of haemoglobin. This is one important dude. Not to be ignored! At all!
- Zinc: This mineral is overall crucial in the functioning of your metabolism, immune system and the health of your skin. It also plays a major part in wound healing.
- Iodine: Have you ever heard of the thyroid? Well, the thyroid is a gland that produces hormones, which regulate your metabolic rate and also your physical and mental development. And iodine is a major component of that.
- Fluoride: Yes, we've seen this name on the cover of most toothpastes. Fluoride helps in the mineralisation of bones and teeth.
- Copper: No, not the metal. This copper is a major part of many enzymes and also helps in the production of red and white blood cells.
- Selenium: This mineral is a part of some important antioxidant enzymes.
- Manganese: This is necessary for bone formation and energy metabolism.

Sources: As with every other nutrient, let's deal with this type wise:

- Calcium: Can be found primarily in milk, cheese and any other dairy product that comes to your mind. To a much lower extent, it can also be found in green leafy vegetables (broccoli, cabbage, etc.), soy products and fish (sardines, salmon and whitebait).
- Phosphorous: Abundant in red meat, dairy products, fish, poultry and cereals.

- Magnesium: This is the mineral in chlorophyll. So you find it primarily in green leafy vegetables and also in nuts, fish, meat and dairy products.
- Sodium: Salt would be the main source of sodium. But be careful with this one. Too much sodium can lead to a high blood pressure.
- Potassium: Most fruits, especially bananas, contain potassium. But vegetables, meat, nuts, seeds, pulses and milk are also good sources.
- Iron: Liver, red meat, pulses, nuts, eggs, dry fruits, poultry, fish, whole grains and dark leafy veggies are good sources of iron.
- Zinc: This mineral is most readily absorbed into the body from meat. But vegetarians, do not fret; for you can also find zinc in milk, cheese, wholegrain cereal, nuts and pulses.
- Iodine: The richest source of iodine is seafood, though it is also available in milk to some extent.
- Flouride: We don't really need, oh-so-much of fluoride. But sources include tea, fish and toothpaste.
- Copper: Cereals and nuts are good sources of copper, along with shellfish.
- Selenium: You can find this one in cereals, fish, meat and eggs.
- Manganese: Surprisingly, tea is a rich source. But if you don't like tea, you can also depend on vegetables, cereals and nuts.

WATER

Technically speaking, water is not a nutrient, so I will not put it through the whole how-many-types and how-it-works rigmarole. But water is essential for the smooth functioning of the human body.

Because of our modern lifestyle, or our fascination with fad diets that propagate the loss of water weight, we just don't seem to take in as much water as we need.

The human body contains anywhere between 55 to 78 percent water. On a day-today basis, water intake must be, on a broader scale, anywhere between one to seven litres. But, as I say, that is a very broad scale. In fact, most experts agree that a minimum intake of two litres of water is a must, a non-bargainable must. Mind you, however, that it is a minimum, not a maximum. And it might not be your ideal. The ideal amount is whatever your body tells you. If you are thirsty, you must drink. It's as simple as that. Drink as much as you need to quench your thirst. And don't worry too much about taking in too much water. Yes, too much water can also cause major issues, but if you have healthy kidneys, your body will not let you drink too much water. However, we are at a major risk of drinking a bit too less.

Because of our modern lifestyle, or our fascination with fad diets that propagate the loss of water weight, we just don't seem to take in as much water as we need.

If you do not provide your body with enough water to maintain proper hydration, you are putting your body at a risk of dehydration. Dehydration simply means water deprivation. And what it can lead to is even scarier, i.e., swelling of the brain, seizures, kidney failure and finally into a coma or even death.

That's why I say, drink up!

METABOLISM

Metabolism is a great thing. And the more you use it, the more it works. But what exactly is metabolism?

According to Wikipedia, 'Metabolism is the set of life -sustaining chemical transformations within the cells of a living organism.' Metabolism is, at the very basic level, the rate at which your body burns your calories. All of us are born with a basal metabolism rate. But you know what the best thing is? Metabolism isn't one fixed rigid thing. It is flexible. You can train it to a large extent.

Let's compare it to your car battery. If you keep your car running, it automatically charges the battery. And just letting your car sit idle depletes the battery. Your metabolism is like that. No worries, it's not going to die on you anytime soon. But the more you use it, the more it will charge itself up. And the more you keep it idle, the more it will just deplete itself.

The most common mistake we all make while trying to lose weight is that we stop eating. We eat just the bare minimum using the logic that starvation = weight loss. But that is really counterproductive.

The most common mistake we all make while trying to lose weight is that we stop eating. We eat just the bare minimum using the logic that starvation = weight loss. But that is really counterproductive.

First of all, if you starve yourself, you're not getting enough nutrients.

But did you know it can also harm your metabolism?

When you don't eat regularly your body goes into survival mode. It panics (and probably deduces that you're in the middle of some sort of famine or drought) and starts saving up every bit of energy you get. So you might be taking in just as many carbs as you need per day, but your body, instead of spending it, will start hoarding it. Just like when we heard that Maggi was going to be banned and we started stocking up for the apocalypse. Now hoarding in this sense would mean fat accumulation. Your body is basically saving up for a rainy day. But that doesn't really help, does it?

Instead, what you can do is reassure your body that there is no famine or drought around the corner. For that, you eat at regular intervals, preferably every two-and-a-half to three hours. This reassures your body there is a lot more to where that food came from and so it will spend without saving for a rainy day. The only thing that it will save, in this case, is anything that it gets in excess.

How to Formulate the Best Diet For You

Now that's a tough question. Each body is different. We can try and generalise as much as we want, but it will never ever fit neatly into those little square boxes.

The best diet for you depends on a lot of things, including your basal metabolism rate (which can only be determined through trial and error) and your purpose. Your purpose should not always be losing weight. You need to look at your body objectively and decide what you need. Sometimes it's losing weight. Sometimes it is toning up. Sometimes it is just plain maintenance.

The best diet for you depends on a lot of things, including your basal metabolism rate and your purpose. Your purpose should not always be losing weight. You need to look at your body objectively and decide what you need. Sometimes it's to losing weight. Sometimes it is toning up. Sometimes it is just plain maintenance.

Now each purpose will need to have a different diet, specifically tailored to it. And the best judge of that specificity is you and your nutritionist/ dietician.

I can only provide you with the tools to understand your body better. But to use those tools for the betterment of your body is entirely up to you.

I can, however, offer some nuggets of wisdom.

Things to remember when going on a diet:

- Take care while reducing carbs: Your body needs a certain amount of calories a day. The idea behind reducing carbs is to force the body to dig into its fat storage in order to produce those calories. But in that we often forget that the brain cannot function on fat produced calories. It needs fresh carbs! In fact, if you are ingesting just as many carbs as you need, up to 60 percent of it might be monopolised by your brain. So keep that in mind when reducing carbs. Reducing carbs is imperative for effective weight loss, but it is a delicate balance to achieve.

- Breakfast/Lunch/Dinner: You might have heard of the saying, 'Eat breakfast like a king, lunch like a prince and dinner like a pauper.' Well, that's one of the ten commandments of eating well. When you wake up in the morning, your body hasn't had anything to eat in eight hours! Eight hours is a lot. It needs energy now. It needs glucose. And that's why breakfast is the most important meal of the day. And that's also why you should save most of your carbs for breakfast. But at night, keep your dinner light.
- Timings of meals: The human body likes order and discipline. It likes to know what to expect. Feeding it regularly at a set time every day gives it the reassurance that food is plentiful and it does not need to hoard. But if you eat irregularly, it gets the (wrong) message that you are caught in some godforsaken famine and every bit of food that enters the system must be preserved for future use. You and I know, that is not true and we're just being a little disorganised. But the body doesn't know that. And how are you going to make it understand? By getting a little organised. The body doesn't work on your terms. You work on its terms.
- Keep snacking: As we've already discussed, the human body lives in utter anxiety of being caught in a famine (talk about having an anxiety disorder, eh!). The longer the gap between two meals, the more it will convince itself that it is starving. And then it starts hoarding. So feed it regularly in limited quantities and it will reprogramme itself to actually ulitise the energy it is getting rather than hoard it.

Nuts are basically embryos. They carry the ingredients for new life within them. Thus, they are highly nutritious.

- Nuts: Your very own friendly neighbourhood superfood, almost complete food. I really respect nuts! You know why? Because those little things have everything in them!

They are some sort of a superfood. Think about it. Nuts are basically embryos. They carry the ingredients for new life within them. Thus, they are highly nutritious. They should definitely be an integral part of your diet, just for their nutrition content. But be careful. Nuts are also high in calories. So, as I always say, everything in moderation.

- The importance of milk in the vegetarian diet: For vegetarians, dairy products become the single most important source of calcium. As we have seen already, calcium is what helps your bones grow strong. Non-vegetarians can get their calcium from meat too. But vegetarians? Well, your best option is dairy products. And even in dairy products, milk has the highest calcium content. So if you're charting out your diet, make sure milk is an integral part of it. A glass of milk a day really does keep the broken bones away.
- Listen to your body: You might not know what you need, but your body most definitely does. Keep an open mind, and listen to the feedback that your body is giving you about your new diet. For example, if you keep blacking out once in a while (and by blacking out, I don't mean full on fainting, though that is dangerous too. I'm referring to dizziness), then you are really not giving your body enough carbs. You must up your carb intake. There are tiny signs that your body will give you. Listen to it. Use the feedback to provide it with what it needs.

SAMPLE DIET

This is the diet I usually follow as it works best for me. But by no means is this a diet that works best universally. I have spelt out this diet here just to provide an example. And that is all it is—an example. But please do not follow it blindly without taking into account the needs of your own body. Stop and think for a moment. What is it that your body requires?

5.00 a.m.	Wake up
5.10 a.m.	Five almonds, five cashews, ten raisins (35+40+20 = 95 Kcals)

5.30 a.m.	Yoga
6.30 a.m.	One cup of herbal tea and breakfast: muesli (200 Kcals) /oatmeal (150 Kcals) /egg: (150 Kcals) parantha (250 Kcals) /dosa (150 Kcals) / idli (190 Kcals) (altogether 180 Kcals)
8.00 a.m.	Kathak class
10.30 a.m.	One cup of low fat yoghurt (100 Kcals) /one banana (200 Kcals) /one slice of cheese (31 Kcals) (altogether 181 Kcals approximately)
12.00 p.m.	One cup of coffee (you feel like it)/ one glass of milk
1.00 p.m.	One cup sabzi, one cup dal and two rotis (250 Kcals approximately)
3.30 p.m.	One or two fruits (150 Kcals approximately)
6.00 p.m.	A tiny handful of peanuts and one pinch of flax seeds/ one bowl of clear soup/ salad altogether (50 Kcals)
6.30 p.m.	Yoga
7.30 p.m.	One cup of sabzi, one cup of dal and one roti (approximately 200 Kcals)
9.30 p.m.	Bedtime
TOTAL:	1,200 Kcals (approximately)

Catwalk

The catwalk is one of the most integral parts of a pageant. And why shouldn't it be? It is what forms the first impression of you as a contestant in the judges' mind. And you know what they say about first impressions! They are the last impressions.

But why the catwalk, you ask? How does the catwalk help form a first impression? Shouldn't it be the way you look, the way you present yourself, the way you dress? Well, those count too (especially the way you dress, don't listen to those who say you don't need a good wardrobe to win a pageant, you do; more on that later, but imagine this:

There is a room with the judges sitting around a table. You walk in and settle yourself into a chair facing them, all ready for your preliminary interview. Repeat, you walk into the room, walk being the operative word here. Because those five seconds help the judges form their first opinion of you. And you need that opinion to be favourable.

There is a room with the judges sitting around a table. You walk in and settle yourself into a chair facing them, all ready for your preliminary interview. Repeat, you walk into the room, walk being the operative word here. Because those five seconds help the judges form their first opinion of you. And you need that opinion to be favourable.

Moving further, let's say it is the day of the finale. Around ninety of you (if it is an international pageant; around thirty if it is a national one) are required to parade on stage. It is the grand opening. Thousands of people are eagerly waiting for all of you to walk on to stage. They want to be able to see you in person and create an opinion of you and your chances of winning. The catch—there are ninety of you, all in similar if not identical costumes. And what you are doing is walking from one end of the stage to the other. You don't get to speak, you don't get to introduce yourself. All you get is thirty seconds to walk from one part of the stage to another. A thousand people would be forming an opinion of you in those thirty seconds—their first impression of you. You might think, 'This is just the audience, let them think what they want. The judges have already met me, they have spoken to me and they have decided on their top ten or twenty or sixteen or whatever it is.' Let us call it top ten for convenience's sake. So the judges have already decided on their top ten. So why do you need to impress the audience?

You do need to impress the audience. You, as a pageant contestant are a public figure. And the public's love is what sustains you.

But that's exactly the point! You do need to impress the audience. You, as a pageant contestant are a public figure. And the public's love is what sustains you. And if you win the pageant, you need it even more in order to have a successful reign and be remembered long after you have crowned your successor (otherwise how will you make use of that platform?). Even if you don't win, the fact that you are popular with the public will make it easier for you to pursue whatever career it is that you have chosen. In such a case, you want them to think, 'Oh, why didn't X win? She deserved it so much more!'

Plus… yes, there is yet another reason. Let's say you are in the top ten (lucky you). But for whatever reason, the judges don't want to promote you into the top five. What happens now? Well, if the audience loves you and is cheering you wholeheartedly, the judges might just be convinced to change their mind. They are, after all, human. If someone keeps repeatedly whispering in your ear that a certain person is perfect, sooner or later, you are bound to believe it. More so if it's an auditorium full of people chanting your name. That is what mob mentality is all about. We, as humans, are tempted to believe in something that the majority believes in. If the majority believes that you should be the winner, well then, the judges might just be persuaded to believe the same thing too.

And those are not the only reasons. There is one other reason that should make you extra careful. In fact, this is probably the most important reason! The judges will be looking at you as you walk across the room or across the stage because they have been instructed to do so. If they are mainly from outside the industry, you might be able to get away with a few mistakes. After all, if they are not fashion insiders, what do they really know about a catwalk (unless they also happen to be fashion enthusiasts)? But that is something you cannot gamble on. More often than not, you will not know who the judges are until you walk into the room, by which time it is too late. So stay prepared, stay alert, stay ready.

So What is the Pageant Catwalk?

The thing is, I don't know you. I don't know what you have done till now. Maybe you are an upcoming model who has been continuously walking the ramp for the last few years. Or maybe you are a fresh high school graduate who is looking to break into this industry (yes, you need to break in… it doesn't exactly open its doors wide and welcome you with arms wide open).

But whatever you are, you need to learn the pageant walk from scratch. Just because you have been a model doesn't mean you know the walk. The walk you know is what I call the fashion walk. The pageant walk is very different from the fashion walk.

In fact, unfortunately, if you are a model, it is actually harder for you. Because you are used to a certain kind of walk when you walk on the ramp, and you will find yourself unconsciously slipping into that over and over again while walking the ramp for a pageant. Most pageant coaches or ramp choreographers that I know encourage contestants to unlearn the fashion walk and learn the pageant walk instead.

Well, the fashion walk is rather stylised. It's actually quite a lot like a McDonald's burger. It is standardised. Wherever you go, it's the same.

I don't encourage that. This pageant will be with you for a few months or a year at most if you win it. But beyond that, you can't really make a career out of it. So don't unlearn your fashion walk. Our mind isn't a DVD that, once completely filled with data, needs to be erased in order to write on it again. Nope. Our mind is more like a notebook. So you have filled one page completely? Doesn't matter, turn over and you will have a new page to write on. And the old information isn't lost. It's still there for you to use whenever you need to. All you need to do is turn over a few pages.

What really is the difference between the pageant walk and the fashion walk?

Well, the fashion walk is rather stylised. It's actually quite a lot like a McDonald's burger. It is standardised. Wherever you go, it's the same. Whichever model is walking the walk, it is the same. Otherwise, the emphasis will end up being on the model, not the clothes. The fashion walk's only purpose is to present the clothes of the designer to the audience. It is to sell the clothes. A good fashion model does not draw attention to herself but to the clothes. Just like the McDonald's burger. It doesn't matter how it is dressed up or how good or bad the ingredients are. We buy it for the taste.

That is what matters.

So what does a fashion walk look like? Well, as I said, it is highly stylised and artificial. Have you ever seen anyone walk on the streets like they do on Fashion TV without looking ridiculous? Nope, I thought not. It has a lot of oomph to it. There is a lot of hip-swaying and arm-swinging, which look beautiful on the ramp, but would look ridiculous in real life.

Also, it is very cold. As I mentioned before, a good fashion model draws the audience's attention to the dress, not to herself. For this reason, it is imperative to keep emotions and facial expressions in check. There are usually no smiles, no narrowed eyes, nothing! Unless, of course, the designer decides to add facial expressions because they help showcase his/her clothes better.

The pageant walk is completely different. For one, the objective of walking the pageant walk as opposed to the fashion walk is completely different. While walking the pageant walk, your objective is to sell yourself, your personality, unlike in the fashion walk where it is to sell the clothes that you are wearing. For this reason mainly, the pageant walk is generally less stylised and more realistic, which basically means minimal hips and arms swaying. It also has a lot less oomph (unless, of course, you are someone with a lot of oomph in your personality).

So let's go through the pageant walk step-by-step:

POSTURE

Now, whichever walk you are attempting, posture is of utmost importance. Most of the things that we find physically attractive are in fact physically attractive to us only because they may have a health benefit. We like a slimmer and well -toned look as compared to an anorexic or overweight look. We like clear skin better than acne-ridden skin. Similarly we like a straight posture when compared to a slouch. I might be wrong, but I believe that it is nature's way of ensuring that we stay healthy. Look around yourself. We tell ourselves that it doesn't matter what size or shape the person is, everyone is beautiful. But look beyond what we say as a society to be politically correct. Ask yourself. What do you find more beautiful? A straight spine? Or a slouch? The straight spine, right? I thought so. And guess which is considered more beautiful by the human eye? Yep, you're right—the straight spine.

We like clear skin better than acne-ridden skin. Similarly we like a straight posture when compared to a slouch! I might be wrong, but I believe that it is nature's way of ensuring that we stay healthy.

I don't want to lecture much. I have done that a lot already. I'm sure you feel like you're back in school with all the biology, chemistry and mathematical formulae that this book is filled with (and there is still political science and philosophy to come—in the Q & A section… just warning ya!). Even I do! Maths and science never interested me as a kid, and they definitely don't now. But obtaining the perfect posture has a lot to do with understanding the structure of your spine. So I guess it's back to biology!

The Structure of Your Spine

Beauty may be subjective. Beauty may be in the eye of the beholder. But there is also one more thing that beauty is. And that is, it is natural. To my eye, you can never have beauty if it is not natural. And that is just one of the many reasons why I am so opposed to plastic surgery and botox. So yes, a straight spine indicates beauty. But why? Well, the logic that works for our face and hair applies here too. Because a straight spine is a healthy spine. An imperfect posture might indicate that you have a deformed spine, which is unhealthy, and thus, un-beautiful, if I may invent that word.

Standing up straight and having a good posture is something that should come to us naturally. Correction, it does come to us naturally. Have you ever seen a toddler sitting upright? Have you noticed how straight his spine is when he sits up? You could measure it against a ruler, that's how straight it is. Toddlers don't learn this like they learn language. No, it's a natural instinct. As their muscles develop enough to be able to support their weight, they start sitting up, and they sit up straight. So why do they sit up straight? Well, it's because when you sit up straight, you are causing less tension and stress to your muscles, and thus exerting less pressure on them. It's just energy effective. In other words, it's biologically the easiest way to sit, especially if you want to sit long. Why is it biologically the easiest way to sit? Because that's how the spine is constructed.

When viewed from the side, the spine should make an 'S' curve, but when viewed from the front, it should be absolutely straight. Any posture apart from the aforesaid one is a wrong posture and harmful.

Let's refresh our Class 9 biology lessons to recover that lost knowledge. Don't fret, I'll make it short.

As we have all studied, the spine is divided into twenty-six bones—seven cervical bones, twelve thoracic bones, five lumbar bones, one sacral and one coccygeal bone.

When viewed from the side, the spine should make an 'S' curve, but when viewed from the front, it should be absolutely straight. Any posture apart from the aforesaid one is a wrong posture and harmful.

Think of the spine as a tower made with lego cubes. If you put the cubes on top of each other in a lopsided manner, what's going to happen? Well, it's going to collapse. But if you place the cubes exactly on top of each other, making sure that you maintain the centre of gravity, you have a well balanced cube tower which is going to last much longer than the lopsided one. We do this pretty well as toddlers. So where along the road exactly do we forget this important bit of knowledge?

Good Posture

Okay, so now let us imagine a beautiful person standing right in front of you. How are they standing? Standing up straight, right? But what does standing up straight mean? Let us list it point by point:

- Their shoulders would be straight, not pushed back or slouched forward.
- Their head would be held high.
- Their chin would be parallel to the ground, not tilted upward nor downward.
- There would be a slight natural curve in the small of their back. It wouldn't be flat and nor would it be excessively curved.
- The pelvis would be in a neutral position. It would neither be tilted forward nor backward.

All in all, the perfect posture is when your body is perfectly balanced, when none of your muscles are overworking to maintain that posture and most importantly, when your centre of gravity is centralised.

The centre of gravity is the point around which the weight of the whole body is centralised or balanced.

In the human body, the centre of gravity lies in our pelvis. And we humans have always known this. Look at yoga, for example. Among all the chakras, the *Muladhara Chakra* is said to be the seat of human instinct, security and survival—

All in all, the perfect posture is when your body is perfectly balanced, when none of your muscles are overworking to maintain that posture and most importantly, when your centre of gravity is centralised.

things that can only be done properly if the centre of gravity is centralised. If a caveman hunter was unable to stand up straight, what were the chances of him being able to jump out of the way of a tiger lunging at him?! Pretty slim, eh? And where exactly is this *Muladhara Chakra*? Bang on the pelvis.

So the aim of proper posture is to make sure our body is aligned properly over the centre of gravity, so that we can actually manage to walk in a straight line. No one ever won a pageant by walking in a zig-zag manner.

But then, the question arises, how exactly do you know if your posture is correct? Very simple. All you need is a wall and, of course, yourself. Stand up against the wall. First, we are going to do a small exercise we used to do in drama class back in high school to relax our spine.

- Bend forwards from the waist and let your upper body just hang downwards. Your arms should be hanging from your shoulder and your head should be down. Stay in that posture for a few seconds until you feel the blood gushing to your head.
- Now slowly, start rolling up. Don't come up with your spine straight. Rather, let's put it this way. You should feel as though each spinal bone is being straightened one by one. At the end, when all that is left is your head that hanging down, roll that up extra slowly so that you don't feel dizzy.
- Now step back against the wall.
- Bring your feet together making sure that the heel of your foot is about two to three inches away from the wall.
- Make sure your hips are rested against the wall.
- Now straighten your spine. Imagine you have a thread coming out of the top of your head and someone is pulling you upwards with that.
- By the time you are done with straightening your spine, your shoulder blades should also be resting against the wall.

- Now it's time for your head. The back of your head should be resting against the wall, in the same line as your hips and shoulder blades. But don't just tilt your head up to do that. No. Tilt your neck back so that it is straight while making sure that your chin remains parallel to the floor.
- Now check your feet one last time. Both feet should be parallel to each other. Knees should be straight but not locked.
- Get a friend to check your posture to see whether it is indeed correct or not, as your won't be able to see yourself.
- Lastly, make sure you stick to this posture.

No one ever won a crown by slouching.

Sticking to this posture is going to be hard. You have acclimatised your body to a wrong posture and now it is going to resist the right posture. You will feel uncomfortable. You will feel like a robot, walking like a robot. But in the end, your body will thank you for fewer muscular and joint problems. You will thank yourself for it when you have the crown on your head and the sash across your shoulders. Trust me on that. No one ever won a crown by slouching.

Sitting Posture

Remember your mom calling out to you while you were doing homework: 'Sit up straight! Don't slouch!' Well, she was right. You know, our generation suffers from a collective disease of slouching. That's because we lead such inert lifestyles.

Imagine a usual boring day at office. You sit in your chair, shift around to find a comfortable position and settle down to work. You start typing on your computer and slowly start to lean back. Simultaneously, you start moving your neck forward so that you can still see your computer screen.

Half-an-hour later, you sit back up, but then what happens? You start sliding back down again after another half-an-hour.

Or it might be this scenario. It's a stressful day at work. You have a deadline coming up tomorrow and you have a truckload of work to finish off before the end of the day because it's your dad's birthday today and you know you won't be able to work post 6 p.m. Stress makes us more alert and that reflects in your body posture. You sit forward in your chair, muscles all tensed up and leaning towards the computer screen. What makes you think you won't end up with hunched shoulders?

There are two very common mistakes that we make with our posture while sitting:

1. We sit back, far too back (I plead guilty to this one right now) thus tilting our pelvis backwards and actually sitting on our coccyx which is not made to withstand our entire body weight.

2. We sit up way too erect in an attempt to sit up straight, and end up tilting our pelvis backwards. In this posture, we end up sitting on the joint of our thighs and our hips, which is not so bad, as the thighs are strong enough. But it is not so good for your lower back. This posture creates an extreme curve in the lower back (like in Kyphosis Lordosis) which is not good. You know why it isn't. We have discussed that already.

In a survey done by researchers Dolan and Green in 2006, the subjects of the study were asked to slouch while sitting for three seconds. Once the three seconds were up, the same subjects were asked to find a neutral position (i.e., sit up in a proper posture). They did this easily enough.

Next, they were asked to slouch in their seats again, but this time for three hundred seconds. Once the three hundred seconds were up, the subjects were once again asked to find a neutral position. But this time, it was much harder for them to do so!

Moral of the story: The more you slouch, the harder it will be for you to get back to a normal, or rather proper posture. So quit slacking and sit up straight right now.

The more you slouch, the harder it will be for you to get back to a normal, or rather proper posture. So quit slacking and sit up straight right now.

But what, is a proper sitting posture? To discover that, we are going to do something very similar to what we did with standing.

- First, sit down in a straight-backed chair, not one of those fancy cushiony so-called ergonomic swivel chairs. I am talking about an old fashioned straight back wooden chair (or maybe not a wooden chair) with four feet flat on the ground.
- Scoot all the way to the back of the chair until your tailbone, i.e., coccyx, hits the back of the chair. Now sit back until you feel your shoulder bones against the back of the chair.
- Place your feet flat on the ground, bending your knees at a ninety degree angle. (You will not sit like this during pageant training or on stage, this is just a neutral position.)
- Memorise this posture as it will be the principle upon which you will build later.

Walking Posture

Walking is divided into two parts:

The Swinging Phase (I know, unfortunate terminology):
So what is it that you do while you walk? You lift one leg off the ground, put it in front of the other and lift another leg off the ground and put that one in front of the first. That's how you walk, right? Right, so the swinging phase is basically when one foot is already in front of the other and

you push your body off the ground and swing it forward, using the foot as the propeller.

Sounds easy enough.

The Stance Phase: I really don't know why they call it a phase, since neither of these are actually phases. They both occur simultaneously. The stance phase occurs at the exact same moment that the swinging phase does. What it refers to is when one foot stays on the ground in order to support the body and its entire weight while the other swings forward initiating the next step.

However easy this sounds, there are a few things to take care of while walking:

- How you place your foot: There are basically three points on the foot that take our entire weight and project them onto the floor on which we are standing; the ball of our big toe, the ball of our little toe and the heel of our foot.
- The weight of the body is to be distributed evenly between these three areas, I repeat, evenly! When you walk, again it is these very areas that you use. First, in the swinging phase, you put the heel of the swinging foot on the ground and then go through a rolling motion to arrive at the ball of your foot.
- Secondly, in the swinging phase, when you are putting the foot down to enter the stance phase, your knee should be straight. Not locked, never locked. But straight.
- Thirdly, your legs move parallel to each other, not towards each other nor away from each other.

Walking in Pageants

As mentioned before, walking is easy-peasy. We've all been doing that. But the pageant walk is a slightly different ball game. It's not the runway walk, but it's not the usual day-to-day walk either. It is a careful combination, a delicate amalgam of the best of both walks. It is stylised yet casual. It is artificial yet natural. It is put-on yet innate.

The purpose of the pageant walk is to project your beauty. It is to declare that you, and no one but you, are the most beautiful woman on earth.

The pageant walk is not merely artistic. It is also very technical. In fact, it is all technical at first. The artistic part of it, the dancer's gait, is yet another add-on that comes later once the technicalities have been mastered.

The purpose of the pageant walk is to project your beauty. It is to declare that you, and no one but you,are the most beautiful woman on earth.

So what exactly are these technicalities of the pageant walk? Let's begin step-by-step, and by that I mean literally footstep by footstep.

There are two techniques I personally like that can give you the desired style of walk. I'm sure there are many more out there. Unlike other fields, the behind-the-stage workings of the pageant industry are not shared with others. There is no formal training. Nothing has been standardised. The pageant industry today is what the acting industry was two hundred years ago.

But of the few techniques that I am aware of, these two are the simplest and they work the best. I have included the two techniques over here because no two people are the same. Different techniques work on different people. Like in acting, you actually have to know the person personally before you can teach them how to walk, since no two strengths and no two weaknesses are the same. But here, that is not possible. Hence, the two different techniques. You be the judge as to which one would work on you the best.

The Straight Line Technique

- Take a piece of chalk and draw a straight line on the

floor. If that is not possible, take a long piece of ribbon, lay it out on the ground in a straight line and secure it with some cellophane tape.

- Relax your spine in the manner described in the posture section.
- Shake your limbs out to loosen your muscles (and no, this is not optional).
- Take a deep breath. This serves three purposes. One, it will fill your lungs with oxygen and thus relax you. Two, it will relax your muscles due to which, automatically, you will stand up straighter. Three, when you take a deep breath, you will automatically tuck your tummy in.
- Now you're all set to start walking.
- Place one foot exactly in front of the other following the line you have drawn on the ground. Keep repeating slowly until you gain enough confidence and balance to be able to do it inconspicuously. Don't worry about your hips swinging. If you place one foot right in front of the other, your hips will automatically swing. Swinging them further will only make it look fake and artificial, to say the very least.

The Serpentine Technique

This is a technique that I'm stealing from former Miss Venezuela turned pageant coach Rita Verreos. I, in fact, have to credit my walk to her. When I was training for pageantry, my coach taught me how to walk by showing me a YouTube clip of this technique.

That said, I would recommend this technique only if you are having trouble learning the walk using the basic technique. Why is that? Well, absolutely no offence to Ms Verreos, but this technique requires you to do an exaggerated walk first and then bring that down to a more modest version. It actually

Do it like Rita Verreos did. And like my film-making teacher always said, 'Get them to perform at 200 percent first and then bring down to 100 percent.'

reminds me of what my filmmaking teacher used to say when it came to directing actors—get them to perform at 200 percent first, then bring it down to a 100 percent. And the thing is, doing that actually works. But only if the actor is having trouble grasping the character, or in this case, if the model is having trouble grasping the basics of the walk.

So let's get to the nitty-gritties of the serpentine walk now:

- The basic preparation part of it is just the same as the straight line technique. However, instead of drawing a straight line across the floor, what I would like you to do is draw a wavy serpentine line and then one line through it.
- Relax your spine in the manner described in the posture section.
- Shake your limbs out to loosen your muscles.
- Take a deep breath.
- Now you're all set to start walking. You basically do the same thing that you did the last time – follow the line. Only this time your feet should be moving in a zigzag manner. For example, let us start with your right leg. Move your right leg to the left over your left leg and then to the center. This is your first step. Repeat with your left leg moving it over your right leg, and then back to centre.
- As with the former technique, don't worry about your hips. They will move on their own as long as you are placing one foot in front of the other.

The one mantra to the proper pageant walk is, 'Less is more'.

Once you have understood this, congratulations! You have now mastered the basic pageant walk.

But wait, don't rejoice just yet. The feet are just the basics. Once you've mastered your feet, you need to master your hands, your stance and the pivot. They are equally important.

The Hands

Remember I said right at the beginning to take a deep breath? This is another place where it really helps. Once you take a really deep breath and let it out, you automatically relax your shoulders, and that's important. You want to look like a lady walking down the ramp, not like a robot. So what do your really do with your arms while your feet are being placed systematically in front of each other?

Well, the one mantra to the proper pageant walk is, 'Less is more.'! Normally, while walking, whether we are walking down the street or down an official corridor, we don't really pay any attention to our hands. Fair enough, actually. Because our hands are, more often than not, too busy to just swing forward and backward. We are constantly carrying something, or messaging someone or maybe just sipping a mug of coffee. But, on the ramp, your hands are free. You are expected to swing your arms in a 'natural' way as you strut down the ramp.

But as you guessed, 'natural' takes some work. It doesn't exactly come about naturally.

Have you ever observed a person walking? Have you seen how the arms swing from the socket like a pendulum, keeping time with the footsteps? That's what we have to emulate, but in a slightly more stylised form. Let us list the characteristics of a typical arm swing to begin with:

- It swings like a pendulum.
- It moves in the same rhythm as the feet.
- It moves forward to backward, not side to side.
- Each arm moves in the opposite direction of the leg on the same side of the body, i.e., if your right leg moves forwards, your right hand will inevitably move backwards.

These few characteristics listed above are also the do's. So now, let us combine these basic do's with proper style to get the proper walk.

- Put on some music, preferably electronic or anything that features some strong beats.
- Shake out your limbs, take a deep breath and make sure your entire body is relaxed. You will never get your arms to move right if you are not relaxed.
- Start walking your pageant walk. Before you start on your arm movement, you should have mastered the walk. All this time, keep your hands on your hips. Do a few rounds of the ramp this way until you feel confident enough.
- Now, let down your strong arm (for a right-handed person, this would be the right hand). Make sure your arm is relaxed at its socket. Just let it hang down.
- Observe your arm move in its natural course. Then correct it: -
- Your arm should stay close to your thigh (make sure it brushes against your thigh each time it swings either way).
- -Make sure your right arm moves forward only when your left leg is also moving forward.
- Your arm should move parallel to your body.
- Your arm should swing not more than one foot to either side of your body.
- While taking care of all the particulars above, try and keep your arm as relaxed as possible. It will be hard at first, but with practice, it will become second nature.
- Now put your right arm on your right hip and practice with your left arm. Practice like this until you feel confident enough.
- You can then let down both hands and try to synchronise them. However, if you find it hard at any point, just put one arm back on your hip and practise again with the other one (keep alternating arms though) until you feel confident enough to try both hands again.
- Remember! If you don't get it on your first try, don't fret! You will master it eventually. It's just a walk.

The Pageant Stance

In a pageant, you spend the majority of your time standing in one place. The walk might be an important component of pageantry, but your stance is an even greater one.

Throughout the pageant, whether you are on head-ramp or mid-ramp, whether you are answering a question or just waiting for the round to get over, you are standing. You might spend a maximum of five minutes on your walk, a maximum of two-and-half minutes on your answer, but what about the rest of the two hours and fifty-two-and-half minutes? What are you doing then? Sweetheart, you are standing on the spot that was assigned to you! And while you are standing there, you want to look good. You want to look alert and be on your guard all the time. You can't just stand there like you're waiting for the bus. You have to stand there like the crown is already on your head.

Remember, the judges might not be looking at you at that very moment, but at the same time, they might be. Why take a chance?

So what is this pageant stance that we keep hearing so much about? Simply put, it is one stance that has been universally agreed upon as the most flattering stance of them all. Indeed, it holds a monopoly in the pageant world. And why exactly? Unfortunately, no one has an answer to that! I guess we just have to comfort ourselves with the fact that not everything has an answer.

But that actually makes things a little harder for us. Because this stance holds such a monopoly that not knowing it or not adhering to the rule is treated as something of a blasphemy. I have found myself smirking at girls not

You want to look alert and be on your guard all the time. You can't just stand there like you're waiting for the bus. You have to stand there like the crown is already on your head.

holding the proper pageant stance. I'm not proud of it, but that's how ingrained it is in us. Just because it doesn't have an explanation behind it doesn't mean you reject it. Sure, I'm all for pushing the envelope, but in some cases it doesn't make any sense to do so. It's just a stance after all. And it's not going to bite you. So just do it!

They say that this stance is so popular because it has a slimming effect. I don't have a reply to that since I have never felt it makes much of a difference, but I have to admit, it definitely does look quite elegant.

So hold the pageant stance:

- Stand tall and in the proper posture (as explained in the previous pages).
- Let us assume you are standing on your left foot. Turn your left foot (the one that you are standing on) ninety degrees to the left while keeping your body facing forward.
- Place your right foot right in front of your left foot, making sure the two feet are joined at the heel.
- Raise your right heel by an inch or two at the most.
- Your weight will automatically be on your left foot, but do not sink downwards or push your hip out. Slightly tilt your hip to the left, but continue standing tall and straight.
- Your hands (both hands) should be on your hips. They should not be on your waist or near your pelvic bones, but somewhere exactly in between.
- The placement of your hands should be such that your fingers face forwards while your thumbs face backwards. Never have both your fingers and thumbs facing forward.
- Your wrist should be bent in order to portray casualness.

Remember, your body always faces forward in this position while your hips turn slightly to the left.

Pivot

Once you have your walk and your stance, you might think that the 101 is over. Far from it! Imagine this: You are standing at the base of the ramp in your correct pageant stance. Now you start to walk forward. You reach head-ramp. You stop and assume your pageant stance again. You look beautiful. Now what next? You have to turn and walk back—this is known in the pageant industry as the pivot. Sounds simple right? It is! But this is the part where most mistakes are made. It might be easy to carry out once you know how to, but it is equally easy to mess this bit up without the correct know-how.

You are standing at the base of the ramp in your correct pageant stance. Now you start to walk forward. You reach head-ramp. You stop and assume your pageant stance again. You look beautiful. Now what next? You have to turn and walk back—this is known in the pageant industry as the pivot.

There are two types of pivots. One is the head-ramp pivot and the other is the mid-ramp pivot. Let's deal with the head-ramp pivot first. It is the easier of the two.

- To start with, you will be standing in the pageant stance. Therefore, it is safe to assume that your right heel is still an inch or so above ground.
- First step is to step, literally. Put your right heel back on the ground, while at the same time turn it so that it is parallel to your left foot, and shift your weight to your right foot.
- You should now be facing sideways. However, rule of thumb—your face faces the audience. Always.
- Gradually take a step away from the audience with your left leg while slowly turning your body away first, and then, just when you are about to take the next step, turn your head. The rule of thumb applies here as well, your face is the last to turn.
- Walk back.

The mid-ramp pivot is harder and takes more coordination as this is done as part of the walk back. If you are a dancer, or have taken any kind of dance lessons, it should be easier.

- So now you are walking back up the ramp towards the wings.
- Once you reach the mid-ramp point (which should be pointed out to you by your ramp choreographer, but if not, it is safe to hazard a guess; after all, the mid-ramp point should be nowhere else other than the middle of the ramp length), make sure your left foot is in front. If it is your right foot in front, don't panic, don't try to shift your right foot back or left foot front in some sort of a hop. Just relax, and take another step. And your left foot will be in front then.
- As soon as your left foot touches the ground, twirl lightly on your toes as though you are doing a ballet pirouette. For the Kathak enthusiasts among you, don't twirl on your heel. You're wearing high heels and you don't want those to break.
- Do not twirl more than 180 degrees. Once you are facing your audience, stop! At this point your left foot should be in front facing your audience and your right foot should be behind and placed horizontally, i.e., at a 90 degree angle to your left foot.
- Hold that position for a maximum of two seconds.
- Now, place your right foot in front of your left and do the head-ramp pivot.

Walking the Walk

You're now done with the 101 of the ramp walk. Welcome to the next level, where you actually walk the walk, strut the walk or glide the walk, depending on the demands of the circumstances. By now, the basic walk should have been practised so much that the ramp walk is now second nature to you. It should be in your blood. You should be able to do it in your sleep by now! If you feel you can't, then you are not ready for this slightly more advanced level yet. Because, here you don't just walk the walk, you feel the walk.

Structure of the Ramp

Okay, this has nothing to do with feeling the walk. This and the next part are technical rather than aesthetic. But nevertheless, essential. It's time to understand clearly about ramps and their structures.

Watching Your Step

When I was learning how to walk the ramp walk, the ramp choreographer emphasised that all of us count our steps. By that, I mean, count how many steps you take to get from where you are standing backstage to the exact point on the head-ramp where you will pose.

To tell the truth, I scoffed at her inwardly. It's a walk, it's no rocket science, I thought. And true, it's not. But that doesn't mean you have an excuse to be sloppy. It always helps to be precise.

Walking the ramp is like dance. It is controlled, yet fluid. It is precise, yet spontaneous. The exact swing of the arm, the movement of the hips, the head held high, centred at the very centre of gravity… what else can it come under but dance?

So basically, you have to be precise about what you are going to do on that ramp. And part of that preciseness is counting your steps. Why? This is why.

Throughout that little piece about stance and pivot, I mentioned that you should end up at the head-ramp with your right foot in front. But how do you make sure it is the right foot that will end up in front? Both feet have a fifty-fifty chance, right? So what do you do? Suddenly start taking tiny steps near the head-ramp, or take a lunging leap across at the last minute, trying to get your right foot in front?

The answer is neither. During rehearsal, you walk up and down the ramp (the actual final ramp where the final walk is supposed to happen) and figure out which foot to start from in order to end up with your right foot in front. This is where counting also helps. If the total number of your steps is even, you start with your left. If the total number of your steps is odd, you start with your right.

Worst case scenario, you messed up and now the left foot is in front? Never mind, turn on your right foot. It's not the end of the world. Or even better—if you're good with your pivot, do the mid-ramp pivot here. You never know, that might impress the judges.

Swimsuit Walk

With the swimsuit walk and the gown/Indian-wear walk, it's really more about being in the moment. When you think of swimsuits, what does that remind you of? The beach, maybe. Goa, probably. That is the mood you try to bring here on the ramp.

For the swimsuit round, put a little bounce in your walk, plaster a grin on your face, up the energy level by a few notches and walk fast. Not too fast, you're not running a race out here, but faster than the neutral walk. If you have a sarong, play with it. Maybe mid-walk, you could untie it and let it drop, not entirely to the ground though. Hold on to it with one hand and drag it behind you. You don't want the next contestant to trip on it.

During rehearsal, you walk up and down the ramp and figure out which foot to start from in order to end up with your right foot in front. This is where counting also helps. If the total number of your steps is even, you start with your left. If the total number of your steps is odd, you start with your right.

The thing is there are no rules here. Except, don't keep your sarong on all the time; do, do, DO play around with it. And once your sarong is untied, don't try to tie it back on again. That just looks very clumsy.

One thing to remember though—the swimsuit round is all about fitness. So make sure you are always facing the audience and the judges head on. Show off your perfect ten figure, girl!

You know, someone once said to me, 'Models aren't hangers like people think we are, models are mime actors! Only much subtler!' And you know what? That's true.

There used to be this theatre practitioner named Konstantin Stanislavski. I highly recommend his books. He wrote three books called *An Actor Prepares, Building A Character,* and *Creating A Role*, all three of them outlining the methodology of acting which is today called, 'The Method'. In his books, he outlines something that he calls 'Emotion Memory'—a method in acting in which you recall emotions that occurred at a certain time and apply them to the present situation in the script. So here, the present situation is the swimsuit round, which requires you to be happy, energetic, maybe even playful, for want of a better word. So you imagine yourself in that scenario. Remember the last time you went to the beach. It doesn't even have to be the beach or have anything to do with the swimsuit. It could be your sixteenth birthday. Recall your emotions from then, imagine yourself in that scenario again and go out and do your thing!

The swimsuit round is all about fitness. So make sure you are always facing the audience and the judges head on. Show off your perfect ten figure, girl!

The more you practice, the more you will discover about yourself and what works for you. I can't dictate that.

A few technical things to take care of, though: do not forget your stick-on bras or double-sided tape. The reasons will be outlined in one of the upcoming chapters.

Gown/Indian-Wear Walk

Now, here is where you switch personalities. It really helps if you have any kind of acting background. From the bubbly young girl playing volleyball on the beach, you suddenly transform into a lady. This is your gala. And as you transform, so does your gait.

While the swimsuit walk is characterized by its high energy and playfulness, the evening gown walk is characterized by a serious somber elegance.

Many ramp choreographers emphasise certain differences between the evening gown walk and the Indian-wear walk. Some maintain that the evening gown walk is more energetic (thus more Western) than the Indian-wear walk. I beg to disagree. That to me is just creating a difference for the sake of creating a difference.

In my opnion, the evening gown walk and the Indian-wear walk are both one and the same. They are both elegant, ladylike and graceful. Above all, though, they are formal. The average Indian-wear is after all the Indian equivalent to the evening gown.

So this walk is more measured. Here, you don't walk, you glide. Imagine you're dancing the waltz… that's how you need to move.

The swimsuit walk and the evening gown walk are the exact opposite of each other. While the swimsuit walk is characterised by its high energy and fast-paced playfulness, the evening gown walk is characterised by a sombre elegance. A good way to practice might be to listen and walk to the music of Mozart or Beethoven. The pageant organisers will most likely not play music that will help you on D-day. The music they play will probably be very high energy and rhythmic. My advice to you is: ignore that music. Choose a piece of music that helps you get into the right frame of mind and keep playing that over and over again in your head as you walk up and down that ramp. Walk to that music.

A thumb rule is that you always stay a beat behind the music that the pageant plays. You might want to keep that in mind while choosing your own music.

A good way to practice the evening gown walk might be to listen and walk to the music of Mozart and Beethoven.

Another tactic that could prove helpful is to imagine yourself wearing the crown. You are now taking your first walk as the winner. Draw yourself up tall, breathe in, suck your tummy in and put your best foot forward. Walk slowly (but not too slowly, decide on a pace that feels natural) and deliberately. Feel like a winner and you will walk like a winner.

On a more technical front, when I was walking the ramp in the evening gown round at Miss India Worldwide 2012, I had a bit of trouble managing the train of my gown. It would pool around my feet and I almost tripped quite a few times. One trick you can try to avoid this is to surreptitiously kick the foot of your gown away from your feet with each step you take. Similarly, when you pivot, tactfully and covertly, kick the train of your gown away from your feet. This will keep you from tripping on your own feet plus make the gown look very elegant with the train trailing behind you as it should instead of around your feet.

CONCLUSION

A pageant D-day is like an examination. You have to prepare and prepare much in advance and then let it all go at the final moment. Relax, that is the only way you'll get anything done. And above all, remember mistakes happen. Nothing is ever perfect.

Did I tell you about my first ever ramp show? Ace choreographer Lubna Adams was choreographing it. And I, little old me, was to go first. I took a deep breath and started to walk out of the wings. At the point where the ramp meets the wings, they had smoke emanating from the top so that it would look like we were stepping out of the mist.

When you pivot, tactfully and covertly kick the train of your gown away from your feet. This will keep you from tripping.

But this smoke wasn't smoke. It was water vapour. And the moment it hit the ground, because of a certain temperature difference, it condensed. By the time I was supposed to walk and start the show, there was a pool of water on the ground at the entrance. And none of us knew about it. We assumed that the ground was dry, of course. FYI, it tends to be very dark backstage, you can't really see much.

So, the opening music struck it's first few chords. I braced myself, took a deep breath and took a step forward into the light. Suddenly, whoosh! I went into the air and landed flat on my butt, in front of maybe a couple of hundred people! I had slipped on the water! And comically enough, my first thought was not, 'Ouch! That hurts!' or even, 'That is embarrassing, what do I do now?' it was, 'OMG! Lubna is going to kill me!'

But you know what? That didn't exactly ruin the show. Far from it. I just got up and continued my walk, and the show, might I add, was quite a success.

So whatever happens, just remember, it doesn't matter. You could pick up a lesson from Crystle Stewart, Miss USA 2008. She tripped and fell at first at the Miss USA pageant. But did that stop her? Nope, she went on to win the pageant. A few months later, at Miss Universe, history repeated itself. But she remained unfazed, got up, clapped even, held her gown out of the way so she doesn't trip again, and carried on. And this time, she was placed in the top ten.

At the end of the day, it doesn't matter. Mistakes can be avoided, and they should be avoided. But if it happens, it happens. Get up, dust yourself off and carry on.

You could pick up a lesson from Crystle Stewart, Miss USA 2008. She tripped and fell at first at the Miss USA pageant. But did that stop her? Nope, she went on to win the pageant.

After all… the show must go on, right?

As a Judge

I was invited to judge Miss India New York 2013, Miss Teen India New York 2013, Miss Teen India USA 2013 and Miss India USA 2013, all held on the same day. Thanks to this, I actually got an insight into a part of pageantry that I had never been privy to earlier. Till then, I had only been a contestant and a winner. But now I was on the other side of the road, judging the contestants any of whom could have so easily been me!

I found this experience invaluable. And I only wish I had known how it is for a judge to judge a pageant before I had ever participated in one. Knowing how a judge thinks and why can help boost your performance so much.

This was my first time judging, so needless to say, I was rather nervous! But, that is the case with most judges. Most people don't make a profession of judging pageants. When it happens, it happens. And it usually doesn't happen more than once or twice in a person's lifetime. This is very important for you to remember. You, as a contestant are nervous. That is a given. Everyone knows that. Everyone expects that. But you must remember that the judge facing you there is just as nervous as you are. If this is the first time for you, well, it is the first time for some of them too. So help each other—this goes for all potential judges, too: smile at the contestants, make them feel at ease. Hopefully, this should calm your nerves a bit.

Since it was my first time judging (and remember, I speak for most judges here), I was very eager to do a good job.

I wanted the most deserving contestant to win. But I also wanted to ensure I was completely impartial and fair to each and every contestant. You have probably heard the saying, 'with great power comes great responsibility'. I never understood the meaning of that phrase as well as I did that day.

Let me begin with how my day started, because whatever happens before the judging process begins, does influence the judge's frame of mind. Do you remember how in Class 10 our teachers used to remind us to take into consideration the mood of the person who corrects our answer sheets? That person might have won a million-dollar jackpot that very day and so might be in a great mood, ready to give anyone and everyone a hundred on hundred. Or that person might have found out that their spouse wants a divorce and might feel miserly enough to give a student even ten on hundred. Well, nothing really has changed since high school. Gone are the school uniforms and Bata shoes. They have been replaced by evening gowns and six-inch heels!

So to start with, I miscalculated the amount of time I would need to drape a sari, but that really wasn't a problem as it turned out. The pageant was in Queens, one of the suburbs of New York. I lived in Manhattan. So I had called for a car to take me from Manhattan to Queens at 3.30 p.m. The reception of the pageant was supposed to start at 4.00 p.m. But soon it was already 3.40 p.m. and the car was nowhere to be seen. So I called up another car service, which a friend had recommended, only to be told that they don't have service in the area that I live in. So I hung up and Googled all the car services near me. I called every single number that Google came up with but none of them had any cars available. If you live in Mumbai, you probably know how I felt right then, since no car service in Mumbai ever seems to have any cars free ever, especially if you want to go to the airport. It was the same situation in New York. I guess it's just a big city thing.

So here I was, sitting at home, trying to figure out how I was going to get there on time when the cab service that had originally agreed to send me a car called me. Apparently there was a problem with the first car they had sent me, so now they were going to send me another car. Great, I thought! But wait a moment. There was a hitch. It would take that car about twenty minutes to get there. It was already 3.50 p.m. But I had no choice, so I decided to wait.

The driver turned out to be a young Pakistani boy who was in the country to study and was also working part-time as a taxi driver. He asked me where I'm from and we chatted for a bit about whether or not Indians speak Urdu, the economic problems of developing countries versus those of developed countries and Mao, among other things (hey, he was an Economics major, okay?). So he managed to make me feel quite relaxed by the time we reached.

However, there was one thing that was bugging me. I didn't have any cash on me. Most NYC taxis have a credit card machine in the car, so cash is usually not a problem. But this one, unfortunately, didn't. So I told him to stop at an ATM about five or six times. He didn't. By the time we reached the venue, I was at my wits' end. I had no idea what to do! So I told him my position clearly. Luckily, he was a darling and gave me his phone number to call him and pay him later.

Needless to say, that put me in a great mood and I literally waltzed into the venue.

If I had ended up in a sticky situation in New York that day, I might have subconsciously taken out my frustration on the contestants. For the girls involved in the pageant, it is just as important as the UN Security Council meeting.

Why am I telling you all this when I'm supposed to be telling you how a pageant is judged? Simply because had things not gone as they had and if I had ended up in a bad mood, I obviously wouldn't be able to show it publicly and

I might have subconsciously if not consciously, taken my frustration out on the contestants. I might have judged them very harshly, which would not have been fair.

But luckily, for everyone, things went just fine and I was in a very balanced and fair state of mind.

These words might seem a little too precautionary to you. You might think, 'Oh, what the hell! It's just a beauty pageant, not a UN Security Council meeting.'

Well, that might be so. But just so you know, for the girls involved in the pageant, it is just as important as any security council meeting in the world, maybe even more so. You might think of it as frivolous (in fact, if you think so, you should not be judging or participating in a pageant at all), but think of it as a final exam. These girls have devoted months, if not years, for this pageant. It is an important turning point in their careers. You have absolutely no right to play around with their dreams or careers. By accepting to be a judge, you owe it to them to judge as fairly as you can so that the most deserving contestant realises the dream she has been dreaming for so long.

I myself started preparing for pageantry as soon as I turned eighteen. It took me four years of hard work to win a pageant. And I intended to put in even more hard work in order to compete and win a grand slam pageant. I felt I had until I turned twenty-seven and I intended to make use of that.

It is fine if you can't accept pageantry as a serious business. That is your personal opinion and I will not interfere with that. But at the very least, you should appreciate the contestants' hard work, respect that hard work and reward them accordingly.

If you do ever judge a pageant, I sincerely hope you will keep my words in mind. It will mean a lot to the contestants if you do so.

Now, back to my potential contestants. I'm only halfway done. Till now, I've only gotten to my venue. The judging process is yet to begin.

Now the pageant that I was judging wasn't just one pageant. There were actually four pageants being held on the same date – two adult pageants and two teen pageants. That just doubled the number of contestants that I had to judge.

First of all there was the opening of the pageant, when all the contestants, wearing the sash with their name on it, performed an opening dance. Most pageants have this although not always in the form of a dance. At Miss India Worldwide, it was a flag round, where each one of us walked the ramp holding the flag of the country we were representing. Sometimes, it is a national costume round. Miss Universe actually does it twice, once as a national costume round and once as an opening dance number. I used to think that this was just for an aesthetic purpose—some twenty-five beautiful women coming and dancing for you, even if some of them can hardly move a limb gracefully, was a beautiful sight. I used to be against this round always, because to me it seemed like a meaningless exploitation of beauty.

Well, turns out I was wrong! This opening dance number was a blessing in disguise.

What happens in a pageant is that when each contestant walks up and down the ramp, we judges hardly have any time to register who the contestant is and how we should mark them. This is especially true for those few pageants in which the judges never get to meet the contestants beforehand. We glance at them for a couple of seconds and by then it is already time to punch in the scores because the next contestant is already on her way down the ramp. With this kind of rapid-fire scoring, there is an enormous margin for error. Yet, what can pageant organisers do? They have to wrap up the show in about three hours, or else the audience gets bored. And it is the audience who are paying to keep the pageant alive. Without them, there is no pageant. This is where the introduction comes into play.

The introduction gives us ample opportunity to observe the girls and make mental notes about each one. I used this introduction to note the beauty, grace and elegance in each contestant. It was, of course, too soon to make any notes on their intelligence and wit. That would have to wait until the final question and answer round. But there is still a lot you can tell about a person without them ever having to open their mouths. And how do you tell that? By observing the way they carry themselves.

One girl really caught my eye. She wasn't a glamorous beauty. In fact, she was pretty in a very ordinary way. Nothing so striking about her looks. Her make-up and hair were also done in such a way that all it did was accentuate her natural prettiness, which as I mentioned, was nothing more than ordinary. But from the moment she walked on stage, she was my favourite. I just fell in love with her.

Why?

Because of her poise.

Because of the way she carried herself.

Because of her confidence.

The minute she walked on to the stage, she looked at each of us five judges and smiled at us. And that smile wasn't your typical 'pageant smile' with all thirty-two teeth on display (girls, you're not horses on sale. No one needs to see all your teeth). No. It was a heartfelt, confident smile (I don't even remember if she showed her teeth, in fact) that warmed each one of our hearts, and said to us, 'I am the winner today. I'm walking away with the crown.' Yet, it wasn't overconfidence. It was the exact right mixture of confidence and humility. When she smiled, there was nothing that you could do but smile back at her. She really made sure she connected with us, the judges. She made us part of her experience. And she did that beautifully.

At the end of the day, she won! She was crowned Miss Teen India USA. And I really do believe that it was her confidence that helped her win. When she walked into the room, she owned it. And she didn't need her beauty to help her do that. Nope. It was her personality that helped her do that.

Don't believe me? Watch Lara Dutta at Miss Universe 2000, because she's exactly who this girl reminded me of.

So, yes. The first impression is indeed the most important impression. Just because the judges aren't scoring you for a particular round, doesn't mean that they are not judging you.

Being mathematically correct does not necessarily mean that you will win. You could have the perfect face, the perfect walk, the perfect poise, the perfect grace, the perfect answer, the perfect everything! But that doesn't mean you will win. And I'm saying this as a judge. At the same event, there was this other girl participating in one of the other pageants. She was perfect in every single way. The minute she walked on to the stage, all eyes were on her. She was wearing a beautiful lehenga. The way she held herself was impeccable. Her walk was to die for! The minute she walked on to the stage, I felt like I should do whatever is in my power to make this girl win. And in the first round, that's what I did! I gave her the perfect score. That is the other point I want to make. I was wrong

Being mathematically correct does not necessarily mean that you will win. You could have the perfect face, the perfect walk, the perfect poise, the perfect grace, the perfect answer, the perfect everything! But that doesn't mean you will win. And I'm saying this as a judge.

to be partial, to consciously award her more points than her competitors. But you have to realise that as long as you have human judges, that is what will happen. Sometimes charm plays a huge factor too.

But in the next couple of rounds, I noticed this other girl who really stole the cake. She had the perfect face, no doubt. Beautiful, wide-set eyes. And a very sweet smile which just lit up her entire face. She didn't have the perfect walk—far from it. Her sari was just average. It's definitely something I wouldn't have chosen to wear to a pageant. But she projected such a sweet and unassuming personality that she stole my heart. And I wasn't the only one! When her name was announced in the top five, the entire hall erupted in cheers. In a span of three hours, she had gone from 'who is she?' to the uncontested crowd favourite. Compared to her, the other girl felt a bit too la-di-da.

Whether you win or not also depends on the other contestants. It is not a game of absolutes. It's a game of relativity.

When the time came for the crowning, the first girl (with the perfect walk and lehenga) was crowned second runner-up for one of the four pageants held that day. The second one was crowned the winner. And believe me, the entire time, I was literally crossing my fingers and hoping she would win.

This brings me to my next point. Whether you win or not also depends on the other contestants. It is not a game of absolutes. It's a game of relativity. If these two girls I just spoke about had participated in two different years and not together, my guess is that they would have both won! But they didn't. They competed against each other. And one obviously had to lose. Such are the rules of the game.

So what can you do about this? You can't just say, 'Oh this is fate,' and sit there doing nothing. That's absolutely not an option. This is a contest and you are there to win. What you can do is when you first meet the girls, assess them fairly as if you were a judge. Recognise their strengths. Recognise what qualities they have that set them apart. Compare that to your own strengths and qualities. Recognise your weaknesses, especially in comparison to the other person's strength.

Concentrate on your strengths. Flaunt those strengths on stage and make sure they get noticed. And don't worry, every single girl in the group has a weakness, even if they seem perfect. And the judges know that. Even the best winners have had weaknesses.

See, I'm not trying to make you insecure. But let's say your weakness is your walk. And then you see another girl with a fabulous walk. Now you know she is going to score higher than you on that point. If she wasn't there, no one would have noticed your weakness. But because she is there, this certain weakness of yours will automatically be highlighted and compared to her strength.

Now, once you have made this assessment, check how much time you have left for the pageant. Most Indian pageants have a month-long training period. That's a lot of time for you to work on your walk. A month's continuous practice can work miracles! Plus, most Indian pageants have a specialist who will train you on different aspects of pageantry. Make use of that. Get extra help from that specialist. You can easily beat that girl with a month-long practice.

Most international pageants have a week-long, well, not a training period, let's call it a rehearsal period. Now, this is a really long time too! You can achieve a lot in a week. The downside is that most international pageants do not have a specialist to train you. But you can just put in extra work yourself. Or better still, go up to the girl and ask her to help you! Most girls would be more than happy to. Pageant contestants are not the bitches that movies make them out to be. They are just normal, simple everyday girls like you and me!

But the problem arises if you've got only a couple of days before the pageant. That is too late to relearn. You would be better off sticking to what you know. At this stage, it's just too dangerous. Concentrate on your strengths. Flaunt those strengths on stage and make sure they get noticed. And don't worry, every single girl in the group has a weakness, even if they seem perfect. And the judges know that. Even the best winners have had weaknesses. Some have had terrible walks, some have not really been beautiful, some have given miserable answers, and the list goes on. At the end of the day, your weaknesses don't matter as much as your strengths. If your strengths are strong enough, no one can stop you from winning!

Interview

It was 1997. Miss Universe was being held in Miami Beach, Florida, USA. The top three had just been announced. As is the custom, they were all put in a soundproof booth and asked the same question one by one, 'If there were no rules in your life for one day and you could be outrageous, what would you do?'

Marena Jimenez from Venezuela said, 'I think I would simply take a trip, I would travel around the world, I would go to Israel and since it would be in one day, I would just magically travel from place to place to place...'

Margot Burgeois from Trinidad and Tobago answered, 'I wouldn't wear clothes... I mean clothes, it is necessary... we know we have to be private and all that... but if we had no rules—I would like to be free.'

Brook Lee from the the USA just laughed and said, 'I would eat everything in the world. You do not understand. I will eat everything twice!'

By the end of the evening, Brook Lee had been crowned Miss Universe 1997.

As pageant contestants and aspirants, we spend months poring over newspapers and general knowledge books, practising answers to potential questions over and over again, but none of that can guarantee that you will score well in that round.

But, the fact is, in the pageant world in India, we have this obsession with 'studying'. I have seen so many girls cramming up the *Manorama Yearbook* two days before the pageant. Girls, that's not going to help. You're not attending your board exams, for god's sake. That's not to say you ignore current events and lack a basic awareness of the world around you. But the *Manorama Yearbook* will do nothing for you if you haven't mastered the art of public speaking.

Because that's what the interview round is all about—public speaking.

One thing that you have to understand: The judges are not looking for the next winner of *Kaun Banega Crorepati*. They are looking for the next brand ambassador for the pageant organisation, whatever pageant that is. They don't need someone who can spout random facts at a moment's notice. No! They need someone who is articulate enough to communicate her thoughts to the audience and convince them that she is right. And guess what? You have got all of ninety seconds to do that.

But, we're getting ahead of ourselves. Let's start at the very top: oratory skills and the art of public speaking.

PUBLIC SPEAKING

Contrary to what our school debate organisers seem to think (at least back when I was in school), public speaking is an art, a talent, a skill to be nourished and honed. It isn't something to be learnt by rote and spat out. No, it is to be delivered, to be performed. And trust me, if you perform something with enough confidence and skill, people will believe you. Forget believe! You'll have them eating right out of your hands!

The magic of oration is such that, if done properly, you can go in a skeptic and come out a believer.

It is not a coincidence that some of the most successful politicians and leaders have been extremely powerful orators. The magic of oration is such that, if done properly, you can go in a skeptic and come out a believer. That's what a good orator does to you.

But before you begin, there are some rules you need to know.

AWARENESS OF CURRENT AFFAIRS

They say, 'Write what you know about.' That's because when you write about something you don't know about, you end up looking like a fool. It's the same case with speaking. Speak about what you know. Or else you end up sounding like a fool. I'm being very blunt. But the fact is, the question/answer round, at this point of the competition, is the make-it or break-it stage. Let me explain how it works. Most pageants have three rounds. In round one, you will accumulate an X number of points. But if you make it to round two, your accumulated points will not be X+Y. It will just be Y. Confused?

Speak only what you know. Or else you will end up sounding like a fool.

Well, this is simply because in most pageants, the points you accumulate in one round do not carry into the next. You've made it from the Top 10 to the Top 5? Fantastic! But now the points you earned in the Top 10 round will be thrown away. For the Top 5, you will start from zero again. So if you make it to the interview round (this is usually either the Top 5 or the Top 3), whatever points you have earned are now forgotten again. You are back at square one and must start from zero all over again. So for you to

In most pageants, the points you accumulate in one round do not carry into the next. You've made it from the Top 10 to the Top 5? Fantastic! But now the points you earned in the Top 10 round will be thrown away.

win that crown, you have to be the best in this round. How you did in the previous ones does not count anymore. Not officially. Ergo, you cannot afford to look like a fool.

Understand that it's not a quiz round. No one is going to ask you the exact time down to the nanosecond that the Malaysian Airlines flight went missing or the name of the Germanwings co-pilot's psychiatrist's wife. But, inevitably, a few questions will be based on some of the latest and prominent events in the world.

Or the question might not even have anything to do with current affairs. Maybe your question is, 'Do you feel that popular media objectifies women? If so, how and what can be done about it?' Now, while answering this question, you have two options. Either talk about a hypothetical woman in a hypothetical project getting objectified. Or take a second to think and link that to something that really happened. For example, you could add a sentence about one of India's leading newspaper's headline from a few years ago about a popular actress's cleavage or about when Stephen Hawking said, 'Women are the greatest mystery known to man,' and all the popular news channels latched on to that!

Pageant questions are increasingly getting specific nowadays and you'll have to be prepared. A recent question at a Miss America pageant was: 'One of the biggest challenges facing the United States is social and economic inequality. So how do we narrow the gap between the rich and the poor?'

Wait… what?

People have spent their whole lives just trying to figure out the answer to that question! And you're supposed to provide them with a quick fix in just twenty seconds? While watching a part of this video, my gaze focused on a guy sitting in the audience, slowly sinking his head into his hands. I feel you, dude! But, and here comes the big bad but: What if you are faced with such a question? And what if you only have twenty, thirty or ninety seconds to answer it? You can't just sink your head into your hands like that dude in the audience.

Staying abreast of current affairs means that you care about the world around you. And to be a public figure, that is crucial. The above are just examples. And by the time you read this book, it will all be old news, forgotten and stashed away in some dusty corner of the brain. By the time you're on stage answering your question, there will be new news. Maybe humans would have landed on Mars by then. And if they ask you about that, please don't just look at them blankly and say, 'Mars? I would also like to go to Mars', except as a joke. Instead, talking about what this means for mankind might win you more points.

STUCTURING: THE BEGINNING, THE MIDDLE AND THE END

There is a very interesting sequence in one of my favourite books of all time written by Anita Amirrezvani. I would like to quote it word for word:

> *The charm maker stopped me. 'Imagine for a moment that you were the one telling a story instead of your mother,' she said. Let's say it's the one about Fatemeh, the spinner girl. At the beginning, you captivate your listeners by telling them how Fatemeh's father drowns in a shipwreck, leaving her to fend for herself. But what if, rather than waiting until the end of the story to tell them how she fares, you tell them right away?'*
>
> *'That would be silly,' I said*
>
> *'Indeed,' she replied, 'So how do you think a story should be told?'*
>
> *'When my mother tells tales, she puts the beginning, the middle, and the end in their proper place.'*
>
> *'That's right,' said the charm maker. 'The storyteller teases you with a little bit of information here and a*

little there. She keeps you in a state of wonder until the very end, when she finally sates your desire.'

I could not have put it in better words. The beginning belongs in the beginning, the middle in the middle and the end in the end. While answering a question, you are a storyteller telling a story.

But an answer has a different beginning, middle and end than that of a story. In a story, you are allowed to tease the reader/listener/audience with bits of information here and there. You are allowed ambiguity. But in an answer, not so much. Every bit of information that the answer should have, must be conveyed in a systematic manner, otherwise, you risk having an incomplete answer. And in an answer, there is no room for ambiguity. You have to let the judges know exactly what is in your mind. Whatever you are trying to convey must be conveyed. Ambiguity, which, in a story, would lead to various levels of meaning, only means inability to convey information in this case.

Every bit of information that the answer should have, must be conveyed in a systematic manner, otherwise, you risk having an incomplete answer. And in an answer, there is no room for ambiguity. You have to let the judges know exactly what is in your mind. Whatever you are trying to convey must be conveyed.

Yet, I call it storytelling. Why? Let's look at an example.

QUES: If you had the opportunity to live forever, would you want to and why?
ANS: I would not want to live forever because I don't believe one can live forever, so I don't think I'd like to live forever.

I have not made this up. This answer was given by a contestant at Miss Universe. In fact, this answer also made it to VH1's Top 40 dumbest celeb quotes. Not exactly an achievement to be proud of. So what's wrong with this answer structurally? Let's leave the content aside and just concentrate on the structure for now.

BEGINNING: 'I WOULD NOT LIKE TO LIVE FOREVER BECAUSE'

The beginning is perfectly fine. It's always wise, however, to repeat the question in prose form because:

1. It provides the introduction to your answer.
2. More importantly, it buys you time. In this case, say these two sentences out loud: (a) I would not like to live forever because... (b) If I had the opportunity to live forever, I would not like to do so because...

The second sentence obviously takes longer to read out loud. But why do we need to buy time? An answer should be short and sweet, right? Well, yes. But once you hear the question, that's when you start formulating your answer. And it's important that you have your answer formulated before you start speaking it. That way you don't blabber nonsense. But you also need time to think. So by simply paraphrasing the question, you are buying yourself time to think and formulate your answer and you are giving your answer an introduction.

So, as we have seen here, the beginning/introduction to this answer is fine. It could have been better and more useful, but it is quite passable. In the beginning of the answer, we have one sentence of introduction, which would ideally be the question itself. And let's not go beyond one sentence here since you have a very limited time to give your entire answer.

MIDDLE: 'I DON'T BELIEVE ONE CAN LIVE FOREVER SO—'

The middle section of the answer would ideally contain two

sentences. Because this is your answer. The beginning isn't the answer; it's the introduction. The end isn't the answer; it's the conclusion. But the middle, now here you not only have to give your answer, but also explain it. Sometimes, in a yes or no question, like this one, it makes more sense to give that yes or no in the introduction itself in order to avoid ambiguity. But you still have to explain why.

Now in this answer does the middle explain the answer? Her answer is, no, she does not want to live forever. So ideally, she should explain why she does not want to live forever. But does it do so? No. It does not. It just states her belief that one cannot live forever. That does not explain why she would not like to live forever since here we are assuming that immortality is possible.

The beginning isn't the answer; it's the introduction. The end isn't the answer; it's the conclusion. But the middle, now here you not only have to give your answer, but also explain it.

Therefore, we must conclude that the middle is poorly structured as it does not explain her position on the topic.

END: I DON'T THINK I'D LIKE TO LIVE FOREVER.

The conclusion is meant to tie up all loose ends, bring the middle and beginning together and end the answer. I would ideally limit it to one sentence. Does this answer do that?

Well, it's definitely one sentence. But it doesn't really tie up the loose ends and bring the middle and beginning together to end the question. And that's because there is no middle. There is nothing to tie up.

What this end does is basically repeat the beginning and that is not a good conclusion. Plus, it brings in ambiguity. In the beginning, she mentions conclusively that she would not like to live forever. Here, she changes that to 'I don't think'. When you're thinking, you're not decided. And the conclusion is meant to reaffirm your answer, not question it.

The conclusion is meant to tie up all loose ends, bring the middle and beginning together and end the answer.

So what would be a well-structured answer?

Let's look at the answer given by another contestant at a pageant.

QUES: If you could know one thing about your future, what would that be?
ANS: I think I'd wanna know if I'm going to remain as happy as I am right now. My heart is in my throat, my spirits are flying and if I can relive the rest of my life feeling the way I'm feeling right now, I think I'm gonna die with a big smile on my face (sic).

Once again, we are going to concentrate solely on the structure, alienating it as much as possible from the content.

BEGINNING: I THINK I'D WANNA KNOW IF I'M GOING TO REMAIN AS HAPPY AS I AM RIGHT NOW.

The beginning sets the tone for the rest of the answer. In fact, the first sentence, should give the answer itself. Does this sentence do that? Yes. Is it compact or does it stretch out meaninglessly? It is compact, to the point and succinct. Perfect. There's not much to be said here anymore. Let's move on to the next section.

MIDDLE: MY HEART IS IN MY THROAT, MY SPIRITS ARE FLYING AND

The purpose of the middle is to explain the answer given in the beginning. Does this do so? Well, there are two ways of looking at that. When you read the first sentence, the question that rises from that sentence is, 'Why?' This middle does not answer why she would want to know if she is going to remain as happy as she is feeling right now. Not directly anyway. However, it does elaborate on her happiness. She describes her happiness and what it is doing to her. And that, indirectly, gives us the answer to that 'why'.

The next issue, however, is the length of the middle. We stipulated while discussing the previous answer that the middle is preferably two sentences long as compared to the beginning and the end which are each one sentence long. This middle is arguably shorter than both the beginning and the end. However, does it really matter? My personal opinion, in this case, is that, no, it does not. The reason I laid out the rule of two sentences for the middle is because usually it takes longer to explain something than to just state that something. E.g: this is an egg (statement) An egg is the organic vessel containing the zygote in which an animal embryo develops until it can survive on its own, at which point the animal hatches (explanation as per Wikipedia). Well, in this case, it actually took longer than just two times the stating of the fact, but you get my drift.

The beginning sets the tone for the rest of the answer. In fact, the first sentence, should give the answer itself.

Coming back to the point, in this answer, the middle aptly explains the beginning. Therefore, the length or lack of length is a non-issue.

Thus, we must conclude that the middle is also rather satisfactory.

END: IF I CAN RELIVE THE REST OF MY LIFE FEELING THE WAY I'M FEELING RIGHT NOW, I THINK I'M GOING TO DIE WITH A BIG SMILE ON MY FACE.

Now, what did we say the purpose of the end was? 'The conclusion is meant to tie up all loose ends, bring the middle and beginning together and end the answer.'

Does this answer do that?

There really are not many loose ends in this answer, so that's pretty much taken care of.

It repeats the beginning in different words, thus reaffirming her answer (If I can relive the rest of my life feeling the way I'm feeling right now), combines it with the middle in the same sentence (since she told us exactly the way she's feeling right now) and effectively concludes it dramatically with 'I think I'm going to die with a big smile on my face'.

That checks all our boxes and thus, we must conclude that this is not just a satisfactory conclusion, but also a satisfactory answer as a whole.

You are, of course, more than welcome to disagree. And I look forward to receiving emails telling me just exactly how I am completely wrong.

The fact is, as much as I try to turn this into a science, it remains extremely subjective. One answer might be satisfactory to me, but to another, it could be sorely lacking.

DELIVERY

Let's look at the same answer that we were looking at just now.

'I think I'd wanna know if I'm going to remain as happy as I am right now. My heart is in my throat, my spirits are flying and if I can relive the rest of my life feeling the way I'm feeling right now, I think I'm gonna die with a big smile on my face.'

An answer should never be just recited, or even just said or spoken—it should be delivered. By delivered, I mean that stressors and intonations should all be in the right places.

Now imagine reading this in a robotic monotone without any punctuation. Do you think that's a winning answer? Not really.

An answer should never be just recited, or even just said or spoken—it should be delivered. By delivered, I mean that stressors and intonations should all be in the right places. Let me explain.

STRESSORS

One single sentence can be said in many ways. And each way will have a different meaning. So how do we say a sentence in various ways to mean different things? Well, that's where stressors come into play. A stressor is basically the word that you stress in a sentence. In any given sentence, we tend to stress a word or words to give shape to the sentence, to give clarity to the sentence.

Let's take a sentence for example: Mary had a little lamb. This one sentence can be said in numerous ways. For the sake of simplicity, let's limit ourselves to one stressor per sentence. Now, let's look at the numerous ways this one sentence can be said.

1. <u>Mary</u> had a little lamb.
2. Mary <u>had</u> a little lamb.
3. Mary had <u>a</u> little lamb.
4. Mary had a <u>little</u> lamb.
5. Mary had a little <u>lamb</u>.

All five sentences have their stressor in different places in the sentence. How exactly does that make each sentence different?

Here's how.

The first sentence lays stress on Mary, the subject of the sentence. By the simple act of stressing on 'Mary', the sentence tells the listener, 'Listen up, guys, it was Mary who had a little lamb, not John or Jane or George Washington. And it is this Mary that I'm talking about. And the lamb is only important because Mary had the lamb. So listen to what I'm saying about Mary.'

The second sentence lays stress on the word 'had'. Mary HAD a little lamb, not has or will have, but HAD. It implies that maybe something happened to the lamb. Because, it looks like she doesn't have her little lamb anymore. Or maybe, someone just argued that Mary never had a little lamb, she had a pet tiger. In that case, this sentence is saying, 'Nuh-uh. Mary had a little lamb. She told me so herself!'

In the third sentence, we are stressing on the word 'a'. A little lamb. Not THE little lamb. Or various little lambs just running about. Here, we are stressing the fact that Mary just had one random little lamb.

Now, the next one: Mary had a little lamb. Yes, you get the drift. The sentence implies that Mary had a 'little' lamb. Not a baby lamb, or a grown-up one, just merely a little lamb.

Last but not the least. Mary had a little 'lamb'. Yes, I hear you. This is getting a little repetitive. But this is the last one, I promise. So what did Mary have? A little 'lamb'. That's right. Not a goat or a cow or little pet tiger. She had a little 'lamb'.

That's it. I promise. Now we move on to the next topic.

PAUSING AND SPEEDING

This is a very common mistake that most of us make while delivering our answers. We either pause too much, or we speed too much. And over here, you have your time limit to keep in mind too. And the time limit can actually create more havoc than you might have imagined.

Organise your thoughts. When the question is asked, pause. Take a couple of seconds to organise your thoughts. Stick to one main point. And then answer.

If you have a lot to say in your answer, you are at the risk of speeding. Because you have so much to say and you have very little time, you just want to get it all out. But in the process, you risk stumbling over your own words and stammering incoherently.

The thing is, our brain works much faster than our tongue. While our tongue is still speaking the first sentence, the brain has already moved on to the third. That really does not help. What you need to do in such a case, is organise your thoughts. When the question is asked, pause. Take a couple of seconds to organise your thoughts. Stick to one main point. And then answer. But you can't take too long a pause. Any more than three seconds and you start looking as if you have no answer. So, now, buy time. Repeat the question in prose format. By now you should have your one single point. Stick to that one point and don't elaborate. Because you only get a minute or so. You might have written a thesis in your mind for the question, but here you need to give us a synopsis. This is where structure comes into play. One sentence for the beginning, two sentences for the middle and one sentence for the end.

What about pausing too much?

Well, that usually happens when we don't have enough to say. We pause to think. We pause because we are lost. By pausing, we are trying to force our brain to come up with something more. And that's when we resort to ums and ahs.

Ums and ahs really kill an answer because you are trying to show that you are an articulate young woman. But ums and ahs imply the exact opposite of that. If a random um or ah just slips into your answer, don't agonise over it. That's organic. I'm talking of a more chronic bout of ums, ahs and pauses. Let's take, for example, this answer, given by a contestant at an international pageant.

QUES: Do you think a woman is unfulfilled if she does not have children? Why or why not?

ANS: Yeah, I think that, uh, I think that for me it's very important, a family. And I think also for woman, uh, the work of woman is that she must have children and think that if, uh, she has children, a good man and family, it's for me, will be so great.

Alright, first of all, let's just ignore the content. It's pretty much nonsensical (probably there's a huge language barrier at play here, but we'll get to that in a while).

But apart from that what I can deduce from it is that she really doesn't have an answer to that question, or rather, not enough of an answer. She has tried desperately to think on her feet but could not do a very good job of it.

It could have probably been cold feet. It happens to the best of us. You're on stage with 200 odd people looking up at you, waiting for you to speak, knowing well enough that this answer might cost you that crown. So what do you do in such a case? Well, the same thing you would do if you were speeding. Take a second, take a deep breath, organise your thoughts (you could always repeat the question in sentence form to buy time) and then, just go for it. Speak your heart. Plunge in head first.

Now if even that doesn't work, let me tell you of about a pet trick of mine. Look at the lights. Don't keep staring at them. Just look at them for a couple of seconds. And guess what? It will blind you. Suddenly, you won't be able to see anyone around you. You're all alone. No one's watching you. No one's judging you. So just go. Speak your heart. And it might just fetch you the crown.

Weirdly enough, even if you don't have a perfect answer, just saying it with confidence can create the illusion of the perfect answer. For example, Lara Dutta's answer at Miss Universe 2000 was a great answer.

BODY LANGUAGE/ CONFIDENCE/SELF-ASSURANCE

I don't know how to tell you to be confident. It's easy for me to say. But confidence can be the hardest thing to gather on stage sometimes. But you know what the good news is? Yes, there is good news.

The good news is that it's all in the mind. You just have to decide.

Confidence, or the lack of it, can play a major role in either winning you the crown, or losing.

Weirdly enough, even if you don't have a perfect answer, just saying it with confidence can create the illusion of the perfect answer. For example, Lara Dutta's answer at Miss Universe 2000 was a great answer. But it was by no means, perfect. What really won the crown for her that day was her confidence. I would highly recommend every pageant aspirant to go watch her interview and question/answer round at Miss Universe 2000. Unfortunately, it is not possible to embed a video on a printed piece of paper, otherwise, I would have done so!

If your body does not speak of your confidence in every move, you are going to come across as under-confident.

There are many things that contribute to confidence or at the very least, the illusion of confidence.

BODY LANGUAGE

You might be a very confident person. But if your body language does not affirm that, no one but you is going to know of your confidence. If your body does not speak of your confidence in every move, you are going to come across as under-confident.

In order to truly project your confidence, you have to have complete control over your body.

First of all, stand up straight. As we discussed in Chapter 5, posture is extremely important to give out a message of self-confidence. For more pointers on posture, please refer to Chapter 5.

Second, stay in the pageant posture for the duration of the answer. However, don't keep both your hands on your hips. That just looks way too posturish. Relax a little. You're making conversation. You're communicating. So take one hand off your hip. That leaves you with one hand free to communicate while still maintaining your attitude. You can use this hand to hold the mike, or just to communicate. To know more about the pageant pose, please refer once again to Chapter 5.

Third, don't flail your hands around too much. We usually use our hands to talk, to communicate. Our hands take a life of their own when we're communicating. But you need to keep a check on whether or not they're too lively. Sometimes, we don't realise it, but the way our hands move can become a bit too much. You might want to control that, because that can give the impression of under-confidence, or trying to force an answer out.

Many pageant trainers encourage students to rehearse before a mirror. This poses one inherent problem. It will make you focus more on analysing your performance than focussing on your performance.

One good way to counter that, is to record yourself. I have provided some sample questions in the latter part of this chapter and in the last chapter of the book, all of which have been asked at a pageant. Make use of those and rehearse. Set up a camera on a tripod, stand in front of it and just rehearse your answers. Once you're done, rewind and watch yourself. No one is a better judge than you.

You could also do the same in front of a mirror. Many pageant trainers encourage their students to rehearse in front of a mirror. But this poses one inherent problem. When you're rehearsing in front of the mirror, you are focusing more on analysing your performance than focusing on your performance. That will inevitably bring down the level of your performance. And that is rather counter-productive. When rehearsing, we'd like you to focus on your performance rather than observing yourself. That's where a camera comes in handy.

Fourth and last, smile! You may be absolutely stunning, drop-dead gorgeous. But you know what a smile is going to do to you? It's going to make you look even more beautiful. And that can't exactly be bad now, can it?

SELF-ASSURANCE

Confidence doesn't just come from nowhere. It comes from self-assurance.

In order to convince the judges that you are indeed the one they should pick for the crown, you need to believe in yourself, that you are indeed the one, among all the others, who deserves the crown.

In order to convince the judges that you are indeed the one they should pick for the crown, you need to believe in yourself, that you are indeed the one, among all the others, who deserves the crown.

If you believe that, you are halfway to that crown already.

Remember, every minute that you are on stage, you deserve to be there more than anyone else. Any doubts, any insecurities you might have had are things of the past. This moment, right now, facing the lights and the cameras, you are the best that the judges can pick.

You need to know that you are a winner to have reached the final stage. Thousands of girls would have applied for the pageant. Among those, only fifty will make it to the auditions. Out of those, only twenty-five make it to the finale. And out of those, only five make it to this point. You are among that elite group of the handpicked five. That in itself is quite an achievement. You have come this far. Nothing can stop you now.

Believe that you are a winner. And you will be a winner.

FLUENCY OF LANGUAGE

Plenty of times, pageant finalists, in a bid to impress the judges, try to over-reach themselves. That's not going to work. A girl might be intelligent and perfectly articulate in one language, but she might not be so in another. Just because it is a pageant does not mean that you must speak in English. Venezuela doesn't always speak in English, but Venezuela almost always wins.

It's a pageant, not an English exam. No one cares about your fluency in English or lack of it. What they care about, however, is your answer and how well you are able to communicate your thoughts.

English has nothing to do with your crown. Not anymore than Swahili, or Mandarin.

Imagine this scenario: You are at a major international pageant, one of the grand four, in fact. Now you are asked a question in Afrikaans. You understand Afrikaans. But you don't speak it. Would you really attempt to answer that question in Afrikaans. I thought not.

Similarly, if English is a language that you are not fluent in, avoid the language altogether. Answer in a language you are comfortable with. The pageant will provide you with a person who will translate your answer for the judges. That way, you will get your point across. But if you decide to speak in English and fumble, then you might not. Worse, it could look like you don't have an answer. You might have the best of answers, but if you are unable to communicate it across to the audience and the judges, what use is it?

So stick to the language that you are comfortable with and get your point across. That's the most important part. It's a pageant, not an English exam. No one cares about your fluency in English or lack of it. What they care about, however, is your answer and how well you are able to communicate your thoughts.

DEALING WITH COMMON VERSUS INDIVIDUAL QUESTIONS

In pageants, you will often come across two types of questions:

i. Individual questions
ii. Common questions

INDIVIDUAL QUESTIONS

Individual questions are usually not the final questions. Most times (though you should check up on this, as pageant structures change all the time), the individual questions are asked by the judges to the top ten contestants.

Sometimes, there might be a twist in this. For example, for a while in the 2000s, Miss Universe would not have the judge ask a question. Instead, they had all the contestants write a question each. The questions were shuffled. And each judge, would be assigned a question from this pool of questions at random. So effectively, the contestants were asking other contestants their questions.

Either way, you are each asked a question and expected to answer it.

This type of question can probably be dealt with in the most straightforward way. However, one word of caution: like the common questions, the individual questions also have a time limit. Usually, it is around thirty seconds (however, you should confirm this with your pageant well in advance, as this differs from pageant to pageant). And it is in your best interests to stay within this time limit. Anything over and above the time limit is usually discarded. Once your time is over, you will be allowed to finish your sentence but anything more than that is frowned upon, and might even work against you.

However, if you take care to keep yourself calm, structure your answer and organise your thoughts, you should do just fine. Above all, however, practise! Structuring one's answer and organising one's thoughts doesn't come to us as naturally as breathing. You must practise answering questions within a time limit. Get someone to time you as you practise or use your phone. For this purpose, you will find a bunch of sample questions at the end of this book. If you need more, well, the World Wide Web is at your service!

COMMON QUESTIONS

A common question is the one that is asked of all contestants. Usually it is asked in the final round, when only the final five are around. Common questions are primarily of two types.

The piece of paper given to you is usually equipped with carbon paper under which there is another blank sheet. Once you are done writing, the carbon copy is taken away and given to the judges, who will compare it with your answer while you speak.

WRITTEN COMMON QUESTION

The written common question is the original common question. Once upon a time, it was the only kind of common question at pageants. Today, however, it is a dying breed.

The written common question is asked by the judges to all the five (or sometimes three) contestants. Each contestant is expected to write their answer on a piece of paper and when their turn comes, read it out word for word.

For written common questions, you need to read out exactly what you wrote—word by word. You cannot make changes to it while reading.

And mind you, when you read it out, it has to be word for word. That means that you must properly frame and structure your answer and then write it down. Because once you write it down and read it out, you cannot make any changes to it. And I'm sure you don't want to read a list of random points for your answer. The piece of paper given to you is usually equipped with carbon paper under which there is another blank sheet. Once you are done writing, the carbon copy is taken away and given to the judges, who will compare it with your answer while you speak it. So if you do improvise, you will be caught and that will be used against you.

Since writing takes significantly more time than speaking, the time allotted for this is one-and-a-half minutes. You must put your pen down as soon as the time ends, even if it is mid-sentence. Unlike the spoken answer, where you are allowed to finish the sentence even though the gong has sounded, that is not an option here. And we all belong to a generation which is not really accustomed to writing, so what we must do, lest our hands cramp in the middle of our answer, is practice, practice and practice while, of course, timing ourselves.

ORAL COMMON QUESTION

The oral common question is gaining more and more prominence over the written common question, gradually replacing it.

The theme is the same. As in the written common question, all the five (or three, as the case may be) are asked the same question. However, instead of bringing in podiums and handing out sheets of paper and pens, four contestants are led to a sound-proof cabin made of glass or plastic and is transparent. So while you cannot hear the world around you, you definitely can see it, and more importantly, they can see you.

Once the contestants are securely shut in the sound-proof cabin, the fifth contestant, who was left behind on stage is asked a question. This question is treated exactly like the individual question. Once the contestant is done answering it, another contestant from the sound-proof box is asked to come out. She is then asked the same question.

And so, each contestant is asked the same question one by one. In this manner, since no contestant ever knows the question coming to her (unless there is something wrong with the sound-proof box structurally, which I doubt would happen), this question/answer round is treated exactly the same as the individual question round, and rules applied also remain the same.

ANALYSIS OF A FEW ANSWERS GIVEN BY PAST CONTESTANTS

1. Question: 'What is the most memorable thing you've learnt from any one of the other contestants?'
   Answer: 'Well, not only from the contestants, mainly them, but from other people who surround us, I've learnt that circumstances and people don't put barriers to us. And that is why I'm here because I want Bolivia to see that if they want something, they can make it and that's a great I – uh – emotion, when you reach something and you say I'm happy, because I've made it. The contestants that haven't made it, I think it's because they really didn't want that.' (Miss Bolivia at Miss Universe 1990)

Analysis: Ouch! That's the first word that comes to my mind when I read this. Just ouch! That last sentence is really hurtful. Everyone on that stage has really worked hard. But the structure of any competition is such that there is only one winner. And if you are lucky enough to be that one winner, the least you could do is win gracefully. The other girls have also, just like you, worked for years to achieve this goal. Their failure to make it would have disappointed them enough. I've seen girls crying backstage at their name not being announced. Hey, I almost cried onstage! You really don't need to rub it into them again. And trust me, no one is going to take kindly to that. Especially, not the judges.

And I haven't even gotten into the real analysis part of it. Apart from content, there is just so much that's wrong in this answer. Miss Bolivia, with all due respect to her, is just fumbling along her answer. The whole answer is spoken in a very 'stream of consciousness' manner. And that doesn't work when you have a time limit to deal with. Within the first sentence, we must know what the answer is. And you, the contestant, must know exactly what you are going to say after that sentence ends. Your brain works faster than your mouth. Make use of that.

2. Question: 'If you were a judge tonight, who would you vote for as Miss Universe and why?'
   Answer: 'Well, all of the girls who were here tonight were all qualified and were very unique and special in their own way. But I'm very partial to my roommate, she is a wonderful woman and I wish her the best. So I'd have to say I vote for Miss Trinidad.' (Miss USA at Miss Universe 1990)

Judges are not looking for answers that will save the world. It definitely used to be the case once upon a time. Today, they are looking for an answer that tells them more about you.

Analysis: This, being a common question round, had a twenty-second time limit. What I like about this answer is that it is sharp, concise and honest. Usually, when you are training, people will tell you that the best answer in such a case is no answer at all. They mean that the best answer is something along the lines of, 'Every single girl here is a winner for having reached this stage. They are all special and unique in their own way and therefore, I would just like to say, "May the best girl win".' That's really not an answer at all. That's just a diplomatic way of wriggling out of the situation. And once upon a time that might have worked. But not anymore. Judges are not looking for answers that will save the world. It definitely used to be the case once upon a time. Today, they are looking for an answer that tells them more about you. And that's where Miss USA's answer succeeds. It is a an honest answer. But it is not brutal like the earlier one. It is still very diplomatically phrased. And thus, it strikes a chord. It works.

However, the question specifically says, 'if you were a judge'. If you are a judge, you are not allowed to be partial. This answer is charmingly honest and just diplomatic enough, but what follows is just her opinion as a contestant, not as a judge. Since she was asked to step into the shoes of the judge, she should have evaluated the girls as per the requirements of the crown and given her answer. Most likely, the girl you consider your greatest competition is the answer to this question. Choosing a person just because she is your roommate is a very poor way of judging, and there this answer fails.

3. Question: 'If you become the leader of your country tomorrow, what is the first thing that you would do?'
   Answer: 'I think the first thing I will do is uh, I'll open up a big, biggest, I can say, sports track and field ground in India because we are lacking there and that's the first thing I would do.' (Miss India at Miss Universe 1993)

   Your answers do not always need to be politically correct. Answers today need a little bit of personality. It needs to be YOU who speaks the answer, therefore, it needs to contain a little bit of YOU!

   Analysis: Before I start my analysis, I would just like to quote Madhu Sapre, Miss India 1993, on what she had to say about her own answer. Ms Sapre says, 'All the officials had told us that our answers had to be truthful and coming from the heart. Nobody told us we had to be politically correct. I said what my heart told me and I lost. According to me, India has been in poverty for many years, so it was not going to suddenly change in one year by my becoming the prime minister. But there are other areas like art and sports in which we can improve. And being a sports girl I had suffered because we don't have the equipment and the grounds in India. In the brief time you get to answer I wanted to say all this but perhaps because of my inadequacy in English, I could not express myself.'

This answer was probably one of the most honest and heartfelt answers in the history of beauty pageants. Your answers do not always need to be politically correct.

Answers today need a little bit of personality. It needs to be YOU who speaks the answer, therefore, it needs to contain a little bit of YOU!

But where this answer failed was in its composition. Ms Sapre, while being comfortable with the content, was not very comfortable with the language used to deliver it. Let me explain. She was a sportsperson, primarily. Her field of expertise was sports. And yes, we are a country that treats sports as something that is so low on our list of priorities that it never even comes into the spotlight (unless it is cricket). We barely even emphasise physical fitness for growing children in schools—schools that are supposed to be responsible for the overall growth of children. As a sportsperson, Ms Sapre would have obviously noticed it. It would have been more obvious to her than if she had been, say, a physicist. A physicist, in her place, would have probably emphasised the need for more research in our country. And that answer would not have been wrong either. But that is the issue. When we are talking about our field of expertise, we cannot expect everyone to identify with the answer. It is easier to achieve that when you talk about more general issues. That is not to say that you don't make your answer specific. It just means you have to do a better job of explaining your answer than you would otherwise. If Ms Sapre, had articulated the need for better facilities for sports and physical education in general (as human beings, we cannot exist without our bodies after all), she would have had a perfect answer. But she did not do so. She just mentioned that she would want to open a sports track and left it at that. She did not explain it. And there the answer failed.

There are many reasons as to why that might have happened. Maybe she froze in the moment. Maybe she was unable to think of anything else. Or maybe, it is as she said, that she was not comfortable in English. Fair enough. But herein lies a very important lesson for all of us. You must choose your language of communication properly. There is no law that states you are only permitted to use English on this stage. No. Venezeula has won Miss Universe a total of seven times so far (beaten only by USA which has won eight times), Miss World a total of five times (beaten by absolutely no one), Miss Earth a total of two times (might not sound like a lot, but it is the highest) and Miss International a total of six times. Venezuela has one of the highest number of wins overall and yet, I can count on my fingers the number of times they have spoken in English. Basically, it all boils down to this—if you are not fluent in a certain language, you will not be able to communicate properly. And over here, communication is everything, and I mean everything!

We Indians have a chip on our shoulder when it comes to speaking English. We act as though it is the be all and end all of everything. The proof is in the pudding. I don't think I have seen a single Indian contestant speak in any other language but English at any international pageant. But I most definitely have seen many Indian contestants fumble their way through their answer in nearly broken English. They might actually be better at it than they were on stage. But nervousness is not the best companion to fluency. And so they mess up their answer, one that might have actually been a winning answer if delivered properly in a language they are more fluent in. That is an issue. If you do not speak English well enough, gasp, we act as though we have failed in life. And it's high time we put this in perspective. English might be one of the most common languages in the world and mastery of it is definitely very useful. But mastery of it is not a judge of you as a person. It is merely a tool used for efficient communication, just like any other language on earth. Use it as a tool. And if you are not fluent enough in English, use whichever language you are comfortable in. It is the answer that matters, not the language.

4. Question: 'If you could change one of your physical characteristics, which one would it be and why?'
   Answer: 'Thank god! I'm very well satisfied with the way that god has created me and I wouldn't change a thing! I

think of myself as a woman with talent and inner beauty. I have my principles. I have acquired many wonderful principles from my family and I plan to follow them for the rest of my life and now, I would like to give all you a piece of advice, respect one another...' (time runs out) (Miss Angola at Miss Universe 2011)

Analysis: I think we're beginning to sense a pattern here. Some of the best answers have also been some of the most heartfelt and truthful. But we also established in the previous example that a truthful and heartfelt answer is not everything. So what is it that you need to add to that answer? What was it that led to Ms. Angola's triumph? Well, the little thing that led to her triumph (by the way, this is what I mean by repeating the question in your answer) was something that I like to call fluency of thought and fluency of language.

Now, you might be very clear in your mind as to what your answer is, unlike example number one. But unless you can translate that properly into words, you're fighting a losing battle. There's a reason I'm not providing you with lists of homonyms, synonyms and antonyms and asking you to learn them by heart. You can find them in your thesaurus any day. What you need is to be in touch with your heart and your brain. And translate that into human language. Fluently. And that, sweetheart, only comes with practice.

When you answer a socially relevant question, you have to have a take on it.

5. Question: 'Who should be held accountable for the prison abuse scandal in Iraq?'
   Answer: 'I believe that um... I believe that um... that our president and the people of our country are doing all we can to help Iraq and I just believe that the prisoners that were held in Iraq should... I just believe that we should do our best to help... to help reach our goal in that country.' (Miss Alabama 2007)

Analysis: Okay, this does not happen very often at pageants (though the way things are now, it might just be more and more common in the next few years), but sometimes, you might be asked to take a stand on a currently relevant issue. And you need to be prepared. The lady here was not. In fact, with all due respect, she has no idea what she was talking about. She is answering for the sake of answering, not for the sake of communicating her thoughts and opinions. And that is exactly what is wrong with the answer.

As I said, you need to be prepared. You need to know what is happening around you and that includes reading the newspaper everyday. Make a habit of it. And you need to have an opinion. You can't afford to sit on the fence. Not in today's day and age. When you answer a socially relevant question, you have to have a take on it. Otherwise the judges, won't be able to see your personality come out through that answer. Questions are asked to know more about you. You've got to give them that.

Sometimes, it so happens that a question is asked and you really don't know anything about that topic... What do you do then? Well, Sushmita Sen (Miss Universe 1994) once gave me some fantastic advice on this topic. Tell the judges that you are not familiar with this topic and ask for another question.

But sometimes, it so happens that a question is asked and you really don't know anything about that topic. Like with this answer. What do you do then? Well, Sushmita Sen (Miss Universe 1994) once gave me some fantastic advice on this topic. Tell the judges that you are not familiar with this topic and ask for another question. Now that sounds counter-productive at first. But think about it. It makes a lot of sense. If you pretend to be knowledgeable about a topic that you know next to nothing about, you'll just end up making a fool of yourself. But if you confess that you really don't know much about this topic and ask for an alternative question, sure, you might raise some eyebrows. But you'll also gain a tremendous amount of respect. It takes courage to come out and say I don't know. That can only work in your favour.

6. Question: 'Who do you think is the most successful woman living today and why?'
   Answer: 'There are a lot of people I admire, but one of the most admirable people is Mother Teresa, who has been so compassionate, considerate and kind.' (Miss India at Miss World 2000)

Analysis: Alright! I'm going to get some haters with this one for sure. But here goes!

First of all, let's read the question again: Who do you think is the most successful woman living today and why?

Now, the answer is impeccably framed and structured. Full marks to that. But the key word here is 'living'. The question asks who the most successful woman 'living today' is. And Ms Chopra answers Mother Teresa. This was in 2000. Mother Teresa passed away in 1997. Three years ago. That's a big blunder to make. Ms Chopra was pretty lucky to get away with it. You might not be so lucky.

The point that I'm trying to make, as you might have guessed, is listen to the question carefully before answering. If you didn't hear it, ask again! No problem with that. And get your facts right. Especially the basics. When someone asks you this question, Mother Teresa might be the first person to jump into your mind. Or maybe Madam Curie, or Sylvia Plath or whoever. But take a second to think. Are these people alive? Because this question is specifically asking for people still alive. If there is even a flicker of doubt in your mind, stay away from that answer.

But there's also another lesson to be learnt here. Say something confidently enough and you probably will get away with it. What Ms Chopra said doesn't make much sense in accordance with her answer. But go on YouTube and check out her delivery. It is quite flawless. The judges probably didn't even realize the factual error until much later, most probably. Now if you say something with so much confidence, and the judges believe it... imagine what if you have the perfect answer. You'll have them eating out of your hands! Figuratively, of course.

7. Question: 'If you could be beautiful and not so smart, or brilliant and not so beautiful, what would you be and why?'
   Answer: 'Well, quiet please! Well, I'd rather choose to be beautiful, um because, to be beautiful it's natural. But being smart you can learn... you can learn, um a lot of things... a lot of things from the experience... you can learn from a lot of things to be smart.' (Miss Philippines 2001)

Analysis: Yes, you read that right. She actually asked the audience to quieten down before starting on her answer. That's actually not a bad move. Sometimes, it so happens that the audience gets over-excited over something. Now you can't just start shouting at the top of your voice just to make yourself heard over the babble. In such cases, it is always a good idea to wait for the audience to settle down. Usually they settle down within a second or two. But in the case that they don't, like what happened here, it is really not a bad idea to request for their silence and co-operation. But you need to be more polite. You cannot go up to the audience and order them to quieten down. No. Phrase it in a nice manner, 'Ladies and gentlemen, may I please ask you all to settle down. Thank you.' Or something like that. You have a job to do, after all, and you need their cooperation.

Anyway, moving on to the rest of her answer. I, for one, do not quite understand what she is trying to say. Is she saying she wants to be beautiful or is she saying she wants to be smart?

See, it's easy enough to panic and blank out on stage. It happens to all of us from time to time. At Miss India Worldwide, during the final answer round, we were supposed to pen down our answers. For a couple of seconds, I blanked out. Nothing came to my mind. Zilch. It happens. But if you want to win that crown, you need to know how to snap out of it.

If you blank out on stage, just request the judge to repeat the question. Take a few deep breaths. Calm yourself down and take the plunge. There is really no harm in asking them to repeat the question. You might have heard the question. But guess what? It buys you time. Precious few seconds to really think and organise your thoughts. But I don't recommend that all contestants start buying time through this approach!

Just don't panic. You've come this far and you've only got a few more steps to go. The crown is just within your reach. Reach out.

8. Question: 'Which profession deserves the highest salary and why?'
   Answer : 'Since I am very close to my mother, I think … uh … a mother deserves … uh … the highest respect. And when you talk about salary, I don't think it's just about … uh … about cash. But I feel it's the love and respect that you give to someone. And I think, uh, my mom has been the biggest inspiration in my life and, all mothers, they just sacrifice so much for their kids, so the profession that deserves the highest salary, the highest respect and love, should be of a mother.' (Miss India at Miss World 2017)

Analysis: This was the question asked to Manushi Chhillar at Miss World 2017, a pageant that she won, making it India's first win in nearly two decades. Let's analyse her answer, since it is quite different from the answers we have encountered so far.

Okay, so like always, let's look at the structure first. The beginning, middle and end. 'Since I am very close to my mother, I think ... uh ... a mother deserves ... uh ... the highest respect.' She doesn't include a prelude or anything, but it gets the point across just fine. She has understood the question and here is the answer, that parenthood or motherhood is that profession. Clear enough.

Now getting to the body of it, the middle: 'And when you talk about salary, I don't think it's just about cash. But I feel it's the love and respect that you give to someone. And I think, uh, my mom has been the biggest inspiration in my life and, all mothers, they just sacrifice so much for their kids'—Okay, not the best way to put together a few sentences, but it does get the point across. It does get her reasoning for the answer across. It could have been done a lot more efficiently definitely, but it gets the job done.

And now the end: 'So the profession that deserves the highest salary, the highest respect and love, should be of a mother.' And that wraps it up nicely.

But do you notice something? She doesn't really answer the question. She mentions that she feels motherhood is the most deserving profession but then immediately dismisses the salary saying that it is not about the cash. Most probably, she was back-footing, but instead, it ends up adding to the emotional nature of the answer. And that works for her. And that is an important lesson in itself. Appealing to emotions can be a risky bet, as you run the chance of making your answer too dramatic, or too self-conscious. But motherhood is an emotional subject for most. And it worked for Manushi. She judged her risks well.

If you watch the pageant, you will see that Manushi's was not actually the best answer. It was England who gave a much better answer to her question which was, 'If you could speak in front of all the world leaders of the world, what is the topic that you would want to talk about?' England was diplomatic and framed her comprehensive answer well. Sure, it was a bit superficial, but you can't solve problems like universal health-care (which was the topic she said she would want to talk about) in thirty seconds. But Manushi's answer was more personal. It was more heartfelt. It told the judges more about the person that she is. And so, she won. Even though it wasn't perfectly framed. Even though she ummed and ahhed a bit. Like I've mentioned earlier, no one is looking for an answer that saves the world. They are only looking at the person you are and what you will bring to the table as you. Not as a diplomat. But as the personal person that you are.

Now, that's not easy. But that's not that hard either, is it? After all, you hang out with yourself all day. All you've got to do is get to know yourself better.

ONE LAST WORD

So it's question-answer time. You're prepared. You're calm. You're collected. You've practised all you can and now is the time to awe everyone with your speaking skills and prance away with that crown? What could possible go wrong now, right?

Oh, so much! And the fact is, there is only so much that we can do wrong. The rest is all, let's say, 'circumstances beyond your control'.

Let me give you an example. You remember I told you that at the finals of Miss India Worldwide, we were given about a minute or so to pen down our final answer? Well, for the first couple of seconds, as I told you, I blanked out. But that's okay. That's in my control and I got over that soon enough. And I penned down a pretty good answer, even if I say so myself. They had asked us, 'There are many women who are socially oppressed and are victims of human trafficking. What would you say to these women to help them get out of that situation?'

Now, I don't remember the exact structure and wording of my answer, but I said something along the lines of, 'I would encourage them to learn how to help themselves. Unless you are willing to help yourself, there is only so much that the outside world can do. Unless you yourself are willing to get out of the situation, the vicious circle will forever go on. Thus I would embolden them to step out, and take their lives into their own hands.'

You can control what you say and how you say it. But you cannot control what others say. And you cannot know beforehand what someone else is going to say. And that can win or lose you your crown.

A bit simplistic, but it covers the main points. It is uplifting, optimistic and practical. I was convinced that I had a winning answer. But still, this was only on paper so far. We had not yet delivered our answers to the judges. The time ran out, the host came around to collect the carbon copies to give to the judges. My heart was pounding. Now, I just wanted to get this done with. Then the host came around with the mike. The order in which we were standing, from left to right was Australia, Kuwait (me), Guyana, United Kingdom and Suriname. This was the order in which we would be questioned. So Australia went first. And imagine my surprise and horror at realising that her answer, not just in content, but also in structure and wording, was almost exactly the same as mine! It wasn't enough that she and I looked more or less like twins (I myself had gotten confused on seeing a photograph on Facebook, so when I say we looked like twins, I mean we looked like twins), we also had identical answers.

Panicking, I considered changing my answer while I spoke it. But that would be impossible. It was too late for that. The judges had a carbon copy of my answer. It didn't look like they were comparing, but that would be a foolish risk to take. The best bet would be to go on with my answer as planned and hope that the judges realised I wasn't copying any answer. I just hoped they understand that it just so happened that we had a similar thought process.

Of course, once I had heard all the answers, I knew the outcome. From the answers, it was obvious that Guyana would win (she did have the most extensive answer) and that Australia and I would be placed as runners-up. And that is exactly what happened. Guyana won. I was first runner-up and Australia was second runner-up.

But I still believe that if I or Australia had given a different answer, I would have had a much better chance of winning. I will always believe that.

This is what I mean by being in circumstances out of your control. You can control what you say and how you say it. But you cannot control what others say. And you cannot know beforehand what someone else is going to say. And that can win or lose you your crown. I don't believe in destiny. I don't believe in fate. But if such a thing really exists, this is it!

And this is not the only way that circumstances can trip you over. There are many inexplicable ways. Maybe you gave a perfect answer, but the judges disagree. Maybe you were asked to take a stand on a currently relevant issue, and the judges don't like the stand that you took. What you can do about it is try to be diplomatic (this need not be politically neutral) when answering a question, especially if it is a controversial subject. But the judges are also, at the end of the day, human. And that disagreement (which is a result of a stand that they asked you to take) might translate directly into lower marks.

Or maybe, the judges are just in a bad mood. Maybe they had a fight with their spouse, and the said spouse went ahead and scratched the new Ferrari with their initials. Hey, you never know! But what this translates into is that they might take out all that on you. Why you? Maybe you look like their spouse, I don't know! There is no answer. Just that there is absolutely nothing you can do about it.

Or in a common question round, your answer might be absolutely perfect. But another contestant might come up with a take that makes much more sense. It is something that you just hadn't thought of. Even though this one is pretty much in your control, it does happen that sometimes we don't think of a certain thing in a particular way and someone else might. It happens. And sometimes, just sometimes, there is absolutely nothing you can do about it.

Your Pageant Wardrobe

Fashion is a mighty fickle thing.

What is 'in' today is 'out' tomorrow. The eighties were the time of the enlarged shoulder pads, the nineties shunned them. The nineties were the haven for crop tops and high-waisted denims, the millennials shunned them. 70s style bell-bottoms (or flared jeans as they were renamed) were the go-to for the millennials but the 2010s shunned them in favour of skinny jeans. So far, skinny jeans look like they are here to stay, but it won't be long before we throw them out in favour of something else. And now we are coming back to crop tops and high-waisted denims.

So what we are going to concentrate on instead are some comparatively timeless rules that have governed clothing as we know it. Still, despite the fact that it is supposed to be 'timeless', I would ask you to take whatever I say with a pinch of salt and rely on your own better judgement.

KNOW YOUR BODY

The fact that different body types need to be draped in different styles is a relatively new science (that is, if you can call it a science at all). Once upon a time, the only purpose of clothing was to cover you and protect you from natural elements. True, there was always a decorative side to it. But it was never as commercialised as it is today (and that is why no one knows the name of the stylist of Queen Elizabeth I).

Frankly speaking, categorising a human body into a set of geometric shapes is a bit derogatory (using the name of fruits, instead, only makes it a teeny bit better). Every human body is unique and special. But I suppose it is useful for our purpose now, and for the luxurious times we live in.

And remember, these are only guidelines. You and your mirror are your best judges. If you find that any of these tips don't help you, just chuck them and make your own rules.

Apple

Even though I just said I feel categorising a human body into a set of geometric shapes is a bit derogatory, I must admit, it does make the job a lot easier. The names are pretty self-explanatory!

So if you are 'apple-shaped', what that basically means is that you carry your weight mainly around your waist. Note that I said weight, not fat. Body shapes are determined by your bone structure, not fat percentage. You could be size zero and still be apple-shaped. For clarity, think Catherine Zeta Jones or Bipasha Basu.

If you have an 'apple-shaped' body, you probably have

- Rounded shoulders
- Average to big bust
- A wider bone structure around your waist
- Fantastic legs

What to wear:

- Empire line dresses
- Longer length tops
- Low-ish necklines if you feel comfortable.
- Anything streamlined that skims over your body.
- Softer fabric, so that nothing bunches up around your midsection
- Slender strappy stilettoes

What to avoid:

- Short jackets
- Shrugs
- Pleated skirts or any kind of gathered or tiered skirts
- Anything with a lot of frill and ruffles (especially around the midsection)
- Petite shoes/kitten heels

As for swimsuits:

- Thicker straps for your bikini tops
- Make sure the cup has wired support
- Brighter and more detailed bottoms
- Side ties and sashes for the bottom to give the impression of curves

Pear

You've seen a pear plenty of times. So I don't really have to explain what being pear-shaped is. Being pear-shaped is when you have a fuller bottom than waist and bust.

For clarity, think Jennifer Lopez or Kim Kardashian.

If you have a pear-shaped body, you probably have:

- Narrow shoulders
- An average to small bust
- A defined waist
- Fuller hips and thighs

What to wear:

- Bold bright tops to balance out your bottom
- Large collars, lapels, shoulder pads or puffed sleeves (but don't overdo this)
- Jackets and tops that finish just above or below the widest point of your hips
- Fitted styles around your waist, e.g.: empire lines, wraps, etc.
- Flowy dresses (knee-length would be perfect)
- Straight leglines

What to avoid:

- Narrow-legged pants, pinstriped trousers, wide or flared leglines.
- Details around your hips and thighs
- Miniskirts
- Dropped waistlines
- Tube, pencil and fishtail skirts

As for swimsuits:

- Halter necks to maximize your bust and broaden shoulders
- Bandeau swimsuits
- String bikinis (but be careful with this, as some string bikinis can be inappropriate for a pageant)
- High-cut bottoms
- Boyshorts
- Avoid side ties and sashes on the bottom

Strawberry

Now, strawberries are usually fuller on the top and smaller on the bottom. Essentially, it is the exact opposite of a pear-shaped body.

For clarity, think Renée Zellweger or Dolly Parton.

If you have a strawberry-shaped body, you probably have:

- Broad shoulders
- Average to large bust
- Little definition between waist and hips
- Comparatively flat hips and bottom.

What to wear:

- Fuller skirts
- Wide-leg trousers
- Low-ish necklines characterised by v-shaped or scoop necks if you feel comfortable
- Straight streamlined dresses that skim your body but don't cling to it
- Wide belts

What to avoid:

- Skinny jeans or any kind of tapered-leg trousers
- Big straps and halter necks
- Pencil or fishtail skirts
- Detail (frills/ruffles, etc.) around the top

As for swimsuits:

- Darker tops
- Lighter bottoms
- Bright, ruffled or patterned bottoms
- Waistlines that cut straight across the hips

Hourglass

An hourglass-shaped body is more symmetrical than most. It basically means having the top part of your body balanced with the bottom part of your body. Hourglass figures are curvy, to put it simply, with an equally full bust and bottom contrasting with a tiny waist.

If you have an hourglass-shaped body, you probably have:

- Broad shoulders
- A fuller bust
- A defined waist
- A fuller bottom/hips

For clarity, think Marilyn Monroe or Katrina Kaif.

What to wear:

- Wrap dresses
- Waist-cinching belts
- Structured dresses that complement your natural curves
- Wider and lower necklines
- Wide-leg and flared trousers

What to avoid:

- Straight shapes that hide your waist
- Extra details (frills/ruffles, etc.) around your waist
- Double-breasted jackets

As for swimsuits:

- Tops and bottoms in matching colours, textures and designs
- Bottoms that cut right across your hips
- High-waisted bottoms
- Basically, anything that maintains the natural symmetry of your figure.

Rectangle

Rectangle-shaped bodies are also very symmetrical. Although it can be argued that it is a very boyish structure, it is the body structure most suited for the field of modeling.

For clarity, think Kate Moss or Kangana Ranaut.

If you have a rectangle-shaped body, you probably have:

- Narrow shoulders
- Average to small bust
- Very little waist definition
- Narrow hips

What to wear:

- High-necked tops
- Wide belts to cinch the waist
- Structured clothing cinched at the waist
- Straight cuts with softer fabrics that skim your figure.
- Skinny jeans

What to avoid:

- Low-rise jeans and trousers
- Sheath dresses
- Straight lines from top to toe (mix it up with something, like a straight top with a pencil skirt)
- Dropped waistlines

As for swimsuits:

- Colour-blocked tops and bottoms
- Wide-set straps

- Waistlines that cut right across the hips
- Bandeau swimsuits
- Strapless tops
- Avoid high-waists, halter necks and string bikinis

KNOW YOUR STYLE

At a pageant, the last thing you want to do is get lost in the crowd. And a lot of factors play a very important role in that, such as your personality, and confidence, your opinions, your presence and how you present yourself.

How you present yourself plays a crucial role. And a huge part of that is styling yourself.

In order to create a good first impression, you must be able to speak through your clothes. You must be able to make a statement through your styling: This is who I am! And to do that, you must closely examine yourself and the statement that you'd like to make.

When you see a person dressed in a grey pinstriped business suit, you form a certain opinion of them. When you see a person dressed in torn jeans and a T-shirt with a logo, you form a particular opinion of them too. You must analyse what exactly your clothes are saying about you, and if that is what you would like them to say. Because even though I would usually advise you to not care about what other people say, pageantry doesn't work like that. You are there to be judged. Thus, you must be very careful as to what image you portray of yourself through your clothes.

Different styles say different things. I do not know you, thus I cannot analyse what styles would be best suited for you. But to help you do that yourself, I have included a brief introduction to a few different styles of clothing and what exactly they say about you.

Classic

The classic style is characterised by straight lines and extremely structured clothing. Think sheath dresses, silk blouses, heeled pump shoes, etc., in sober colours. Classic outfits are timeless and never go out of style.

What this says about you: It portrays the image of an independent, organised career professional. On one end of the measure, it could come off as extremely corporate (something you might want to be careful about) but on the other, it could be quite glam! Personally, this is the style that I identify with the most.

Bohemian

This is a nice, fun look to portray. It is typically represented by long flowy skirts and dresses, organic textiles and bright pop colours.

What this says about you: This style basically tells people that you are an independent woman who knows exactly what she wants. You're outgoing, confident and opinionated.

Sporty

Ultra casual. If you don the sporty style, we'd probably see you lounging around in a comfy pair of jeans, a well-fitted t-shirt and sneakers to boot.

What this says about you: You love comfort. You love your space and you don't give a damn about what others think. That's great! But unfortunately, dressing very casual at a pageant could give off a lazy vibe. So you might want to reinvestigate your wardrobe and maybe throw in some other styles to balance it out.

Fashionista

This one is quite trendy and up-to-date. Fashion changes every four months. And the fashionista is well aware of it. The fashionista is not about any one style, but comprises whatever is 'in' at the moment.

What this says about you: You're very conscious about what you say with your clothes. You would not be caught dead with a bag from the last season. And that's not exactly a bad thing either. Because beauty pageants are very intricately linked with the fashion world. And an inside knowledge would definitely work in your favour. But it can get very tiring, refurbishing your wardrobe to stay in style, and it can get pretty heavy on the pocket too. So you might want to mix this up with some other styles also.

Romantic

This one is a misnomer. But I couldn't think of a better title. The romantic look is characterised by soft silhouettes, delicate patterns (maybe floral) and pastel colours.

What this says about you: That you're a romantic at heart. You're probably the sweet 'girl-next-door' who enjoys rom-coms and Jody Foster novels.

Now, you might be completely different from what I've 'predicted' about each clothing style. In fact, I expect you to be. Because no person ever fits into any labels. But the problem is, despite that, we humans insist on giving out labels. I've just listed the ones I have observed. You will not fit into any of them perfectly, but that doesn't mean you can't use those labels to your advantage.

DRESS FOR THE OCCASION

Now, you wouldn't wear a T-shirt and a pair of shorts to a formal gala, would you? And nor would you dig out your silks for a get-together next door. It would probably be the opposite, right?

If you said yes, then half my job is done.

This is a useless section, you would probably think. Most of us know how to dress for the occasion. We've been taught that since our childhood. But whenever I was at a pageant,

I never ceased to be shocked by the thoughtlessness of some of the contestants. I have seen girls slap on full make-up for their morning workouts. And some who donned their best leather miniskirts for a day out at the local orphanage.

Now what is the trouble with that, you ask? Well, make-up clogs your pores. And when you work out, you sweat. That sweat needs a clean outlet, which make-up absolutely hinders. If you wear make-up to the gym, sweetie, you're just begging for skin problems. And a leather miniskirt to the orphanage? Don't get me wrong, I'm not being a prude. But at the orphanage, you are being judged on your interaction with the children. You will run around, play tag and hopscotch with the kids. You cannot do that with a leather miniskirt. And yes, leave your stilettoes behind for this as well. Wear some pretty flats. Not only will it be kinder to your feet as you chase those kids around, you will also project the right image.

There would be many other occasions and places or organisations that you'll have to visit, and would require you to dress appropriately. These are only examples. But whenever you are dressing for the day, plan it out carefully. Pay attention to what the day's schedule is like and dress accordingly.

SUNDAY IS LONGER THAN MONDAY (AND OTHER FASHION FAUX PAS)

Fashion faux pas are very easy to make. But they take a while to be forgotten. I'm not going to spend any time on the more 'aesthetic' faux pas like matching your bags and shoes. At a pageant, that's just being picky. And it's very subjective. I will try to steer away from the subjective. Because subjectiveness doesn't mean faux pas, it merely means a difference in opinion.

CHECK YOUR HEMLINES

I have this really beautiful dress. I bought it a few years ago. It's very 1960s, complete with a high stiff collar. I fell in love with it the minute I saw it at the store. But the first time I wore it (after buying and removing the tags), I noticed something I hadn't earlier. The lining at one point was a little longer than the hemline. And no, it was not deliberate. It was an obvious manufacturing defect. It was tiny, hardly noticeable, but that dress is still lying untouched in my wardrobe (mainly because I'm just too lazy to fix that one little blip).

What I mean to convey is that your dress might have something wrong with it. Manufacturers are not perfect. However tiny that defect may be, don't ignore it. Don't assume that people will not notice it. They will. And even if you feel they won't, your pageant is not the place for you to test your theory. Remember, at a pageant, there is not a single moment that you are not being judged. Better to err on the side of caution.

TAGS, TAGS, TAGS!

Oh tags! The bane of the absent-minded. I cannot begin to tell you just how many times I've confidently walked out of my house only to be reminded by the first person I walk past, that my clothing tags are hanging out.

Yes, I periodically forget to remove the tags from my clothes!

In day-to-day life, that is nothing but a minor embarrassment. But at a pageant, well, you just want to avoid any sort of embarrassment. Pageants are stressful enough without all this.

So, please, just make your life easier for yourself and remove those incriminating tags while packing for your pageant.

SHOE LABELS

Yes, I'm talking about those little stickers stuck on the sole of your shoes. Those ones that you never bothered removing, because, hey, who notices them, right? They're below your feet. Under your shoes. You can't see them!

Uh...no. Judges can see them. Unfortunately. You know when you lift your foot to take your next step? Then! Judges can see them clear as day. And it does not look nice. But we're like three-year-olds, sometimes. We assume that if I can't see it, others can't either. But they can. They so can!

Removing those tags can be tricky. Those little stickers can really stick! But remove them. Arm yourself with some soap and water or some rubbing alcohol and get rid of them. It won't take more than fifteen minutes, I promise. But do get rid of them.

BALANCE YOUR OUTFIT

Okay, this one is subjective. I'm going against my own decree. But I feel very strongly about this, so I'll make an exception.

If you are wearing something short on the lower half of your body, make it a point to dress conservatively on the upper half. If you are wearing something revealing (oh how I hate this word, it gives all the wrong vibes) on top, make it a point to dress conservatively on the lower half. That balances your outfit and helps you draw the fine line between showing some skin to showing a bit too much of skin. Very few people can dress 'skimpily' (another word I hate) on both the top and bottom and manage to carry it off in a very classy manner. Most of us can't and we just end up looking very innapropriate.

So judge yourself objectively and assess if you can really carry off that style and not look inappropriate.

I, personally, would take this 'rule' very seriously. And the only exception to this rule, in my eyes, is:

i. The pageant itself has specified the outfit to be worn
ii. The swimsuit round (obviously)

SHOES AND BAGS

You know the one mistake I made at most of my pageants? Carrying fifteen pairs of shoes.

I love shoes. At the last count, I had about sixty pairs (and that's after I had just cleaned out my cupboard). I have a shoe rack that extends from the floor to the sky. Did I mention I really do love shoes?

But when you're going to a pageant, you need to pack wisely. Shoes take up a lot of space. So stick to the basics and they will serve you well. You might need a different outfit for each day of the pageant duration, but you definitely do not need a pair of shoes a day. Stick to the basics: white/silver heels, black heels, nude heels, gold heels, sneakers, a pair of basic flats and a pair of heels in a nice pop colour or a floral pattern (something that makes a statement basically). That's all you need. And that itself adds up to seven shoes.

But the basic list I have just mentioned is not indispensible. You will need those. You will need every one of the shoes that I have just mentioned. And remember, the heels must be at least three inches high.

As for bags, I would really forget the rule about matching your shoes and bags. That's all well and good in real life, but at a pageant, you need to be practical. Frankly speaking, one nice tote bag in a neutral colour should suffice. If you absolutely must, you carry another bag in addition to this. But I wouldn't recommend it. It takes up unnecessary space and chances are it will return untouched. However, do make sure your bag is roomy enough because you will be stuffing all kinds of things into it during the pageant (that's why I recommend a tote).

What Shoes to Carry

I have already listed the types of shoes that you must carry. I will list them once more over here just for the sake of clarity:

1. White/Silver heels
2. Black heels
3. Nude heels (This is what you will most probably be using with your swimwear
4. Gold heels
5. Sneakers/Sports shoes
6. A pair of basic flats (Ballet shoes or sandals, whatever is more comfortable. In case you are carrying sandals, make sure you carry two pairs, since sandals can easily break, especially in the rains.)
7. A pair of heels in a nice pop colour to break the monotony
8. Blister plasters. These are not shoes, obviously. But you will need them if and when your shoes pinch you. Better go prepared.

Remember, all your heels must be a minimum of three inches high.

But how do you go about choosing these heels? Unfortunately, there is no healthy or ergonomic version of high heels, and thus there is no healthy or ergonomic way to ensure that you are buying the best you can. The only parameters here are looks and comfort. I will deal with each parameter individually to help you ensure that your shoes (especially the heels) are the most comfortable and look great.

Looks

There is not much to say here, except that less is more. When you are buying heels for your pageant, the simpler the better. Remember, you will be wearing these heels with practically everything—from jeans, to sarees, to evening gowns. So you must pick a pair that will look equally at home with anything that it is worn with. That means nothing that is heavily worked upon. Rhinestones, embroidery are all pretty much thrown out of the window here since you cannot guarantee that it will look equally good with whatever you wear.

So go for the simplest and most elegant footwear you can find.

Also, as much as possible, try and stick to strappy open-toed heels, especially for silver, gold and nude footwear. The silver and gold heels are most likely what you will end up wearing with Indian wear, and usually (not always though), open-toe strappy heels tend to look better with Indian wear. As for the nude heels, they are what you will be wearing with your swimsuits. You are basically emulating a beach look there. And wearing closed-toe heels would only take away from that illusion. Of course, you are effectively breaking the illusion by the simple act of wearing heels with swimwear, a trend that I am yet to see emerge on beaches. But that is where you take things with a pinch of salt. You are walking the ramp, thus heels. But you are emulating a beach look, thus strappy nude heels. Yes, it doesn't make sense. But sometimes, that's how the world is.

Lastly, stick to stilletoes rather than clogs or any other type, simply because stilletoes lend themselves towards a more malleable look.

Comfort

First of all, heels are not meant for comfort. Period.

The primary purpose is looks, not comfort. But you are competing in front of thousands of people, and you need to have at least a minimal level of comfort in order to perform to your utmost ability, right? So let's figure out how to make the most of the little bit of comfort that your heels provide you.

When it comes to buying heels for your pageant, don't order online. That's okay for random shoes you might buy, but not for this. Go to a store, and before you do anything, get yourself measured. You might be very sure that you are a size 7, and for many brands, you might be. But though every brand says they follow a standardised size, when it comes to fashion, there is rarely any standardisation. Different brands have different parameters for measuring their sizes. So at every store you go, get your shoe size checked. Don't take it for granted.

Once you get your foot measured, shop around for a look that you like. If you have a model you like, try it on, of course. But don't just try it on to look at it in the mirror. Walk around in it for a bit. Make sure it is comfortable to wear for long hours at a stretch. Only if you are sure of all that, only then, buy it. But once you have bought it, don't just let it remain in the box. You will be tempted to preserve them for the pageant. And that is fine. You don't have to wear them outside. But just wear them for some time every few days inside the house to let your feet get used to the heels, and to break in them. If you don't do that, on the first day of the pageant, when you're wearing your heels for an extended amount of time, your shoes might pinch you. And trust me, that hurts. Those blisters really hurt, especially in heels. And you do not want that.

So moral of the story, break in your shoes completely before you head for your pageant.

But sometimes, it so happens that for the finale, the pageants want you to wear shoes that the sponsors provide.

What then? Well, if you are lucky, you will be asked to try out the shoes that they will provide well in advance. And if that happens, then fine. You are ensured the right size and fit. Yep, the shoes haven't been broken in, but it is only for one day. And it is only for a few hours on that one day. So it will be fine (just stock up on those blister plasters, just in case though).

But what if they mess up and you don't get your size? Or what if they bring in the shoes at the last minute, without a prior trial, and your size and fit isn't available? The answer to that depends on whether the shoe is larger than your size or smaller.

If it is larger, and if it is a closed toe, then you are lucky. Simply stuff the toe area of the shoe with tissue paper or cotton, until the extra area is all filled up and the shoe effectively shrinks to your size.

If it is larger, and it is an open toe, then you're not so lucky. But you still have a way out. Remember those blister plasters I asked you to pack? Layer them up on the part of the strap that goes around the back of your ankle. You'll tighten the fit up somewhat. It is not the most convenient, but it is something.

But if it is smaller, then you really don't have that many options. One advantage of being stuck with a smaller size than a larger one is that at least your foot will not slip out! But at the same time, your chances of the shoe pinching you go up dramatically. And there is not much you can do to avoid it. But you can try one thing. Put on your shoes and contract and flex your toes continuously for a while. If your toes grow tired, rest them. And then, once they are rested, start again. The movement of flexing your toes will stretch the shoe somewhat. And by the time you go on stage, your shoes will be at least marginally comfortable.

But still, for this more than anything, stock up on those blister plasters.

INNERWEAR

Trust me when I say that your innerwear is just as important as your outerwear.

Actually, no. Scratch that. Your innerwear is way more important than your outerwear. Outerwear just has to be pretty. Your innerwear has to be much more. So please, heed the following words.

Before you head out to your pageant, stock up on your inners. And not just any inners, mind you, but well-fitting inners. That is of utmost importance. Why? Because if your inners do not fit you well, it shows on your clothes, and it does not look good.

Innerwear stores like La Senza, Women'secret, Victoria's Secret, etc., usually provide help in choosing the right size for you (especially bra size). You might think you know your size, but there is no harm in making sure. Just head to your local store and get yourself measured. And if you are indeed wearing the wrong size, stock up. It can only help.

Before heading out to your pageant, make sure you have the following:

i **Nude Bra**: For all those times you are wearing a white or opaque top. And yes, do not ever wear a white bra underneath a white shirt. The outline will be visible, and it does not look good. For a white shirt, stick to a nude bra. There are various shades of nude. So be careful while shopping to select the one closest to your skin tone. Also, make sure you carry more than one. This will be the most handy of all your bras. Your go-to solution. And one more thing, get the ones in which the straps are detachable.

ii. **Black Bra**: The straps for this too should be detachable.

iii. **Transparent straps**: For all the times when your top poses the danger of exposing your bra strap.

iv. **Silicone/Stick-on Bra**: This is great for all those strapless and backless outfits. For those of you not in the know, silicons or stick-ons are basically bras that have an adhesive underside to them. You stick them on. These have got no straps and no back. It's also great for swimsuits.
v. **G-string:** The problem with normal innerwear is that you can see the outline of it if the dress is figure-hugging. G-strings can get rid of those unsightly panty lines for you.
vi. **Shapewear**: Even those of us who are blessed with the perfect figure, sometimes, don't look toned in certain outfits. A decent shapewear will always make sure you look toned.
vii. **Seamless underwear**: For the exact same reason as the G-string. G-strings are not always very comfortable. Seamless underwear can be the more comfortable alternative to that.
viii. **Black Opaque Pantyhose**: Good quality black opaque pantyhose can quickly turn a day outfit into an evening outfit. But make sure you carry more than one as pantyhose tends to be very delicate and easily tears.

WARDROBE MALFUNCTION

At the Miss Venezuela pageant in 2008, Miss Guarico was walking down the ramp during the swimsuit round, when, suddenly, her bikini came undone. It was a string bikini. And one of the knots came undone. Miss Guarico was obviously unable to finish her walk and rushed backstage.

These things seem like they might only happen to others. We always feel that such things won't happen to us—until it does. As I always say, it's better to err on the safe side.

String bikinis can be extremely tricky to handle. A light tug and the whole thing will come off. It doesn't even need to be a tug. The friction from your arms as they brush against it while walking can easily loosen it. The same thing goes for halter necks. Clothes are not motionless. As you move, they also move against your body. Therefore, any knots can easily come untied, provided there is enough friction. Pins can get unpinned. Stiches can break… you get the drift.

Thus, whenever you wear something, make sure you have fastened it properly. Tug against the knots to make sure they are secure. In fact, double knot them to be on the safe side. Check if the pins are too weak for the fabric. Try and stick with reliable strong fabrics. In other words, be careful.

WHAT YOU MUST CARRY TO A PAGEANT

By now, you would have got a fair idea of what you need to carry to a pageant. Later on in the book, I have also provided for you a checklist that you can use while packing for your pageant. However, pageants also usually tell you what they expect you to carry. Given on the next page , is a copy of the lists of things to carry that I was provided by the pageants that I participated in. Also included is the list from I AM She–Miss India Universe. The pageant does not exist anymore. However, it was the most detailed and extensive list among all the others and therefore, I have included it.

FEMINA MISS INDIA SOUTH 2010

Dear Contestant,

I would like to congratulate you and confirm that you have been selected to participate in the training and thereon the finals of The Pantaloons Femina Miss India South 2010.

I would request you to please note down all that is mentioned in the mail because these details are extremely important.

In order to participate in the final rounds of the contest you will be required to attend a compulsory residential training and grooming session from the 12th of December 2009 to the 24th of December. The residential training would take place at Novotel in Hyderabad.

Please note that it is compulsory for you to check into the hotel by 12th morning 7.30 am.

As soon as you reach the hotel you will be required to meet the management of the contest who will be present at the Femina Hospitality desk.

There are a number of things that you will have to bring to your training

1. *A two-three skin tone 'sheer to waist' pantyhose (ones that do not have horizontal or any seams at the thighs).*
2. *There may be a contest for the most talented participant. If you wish to participate, please bring music cassettes or any other instrument/equipment that you may require for your prepared act. If there is anything that you would like us to arrange for the audition, please let us know at the earliest.*
3. *You will be filmed and photographed during the training period, for which you are required to carry short cocktail or evening dresses that brings out the best in you, a variety of tops of various colours and designs. It is compulsory for you to bring a white top that brings out the best in you. This white blouse could be an off-shoulder, a peasant blouse or any design and cut that suits you best.*

4. *Shoes:*
- *Black heels*
- *Strappy skin tone shoes*
- *White/Silver heels*
- *Gold heels*

Please carry a lot of casuals along with accessories, and shoes to be worn everyday during the training program.

Please bring along a well-fitting swimsuit, which can be a one-piece or a bikini. It can be of any colour and design. Well fitted jeans, dupatta, long gown.

Please ensure you carry all the necessary inner wears including silikons, panty-liners, thongs, etc.

You will also have to bring ethnic attire to the training. This can preferably be a saree, must look dignified and elegant.

5. *For training and rehearsals casual clothes comprising leotards, shorts, T-shirts, short skirts, etc., and comfortable flat shoes/keds have to be carried. You will also be attending two-three functions so you will have to carry two-three party clothes. Cocktail dresses. Please carry fitness wear for thirteen days for the work-outs, etc.*

MISS INDIA UNIVERSE

Preparing For The Pageant

Rehearsal Clothes

For training and rehearsals casual clothes comprising shorts, T-shirts, short skirts, work-out clothes, track suits, jeans and comfortable sport shoes/ keds /flat shoes/ slipon sandals or similar have to be carried. It is essential that you wear what will be most comfortable for movement, dancing, and stage practice. It is also suggested you keep a light sweater or jacket with you at all times. For fitness and yoga sessions ideally carry a yoga floor mat, well-fitted track suits, shorts and bustier/t-shirts in bright colours as most sessions are captured on camera. You will need comfortable and well-fitted sports shoes and a few pairs of thick cotton sports socks for your training sessions with the Physical Fitness trainer. You should bring items such as jeans (at least three pairs), sweaters and comfortable shoes for indoor/ outdoor activities. You will be traveling from one city to another, and the season can be very warm or very cold, so please pack keeping both extremes in mind. Non-crushable clothes that can be layered and can work multi-shifts is a good idea. For shoots, rehearsals and choreography sessions please carry comfortable pairs of medium- and high-heeled shoes. Please carry complimentary accessories for your outfits. We suggest you carry the following pairs of shoes and clothes with you:

Shoes

1. Black heels
2. Silver/White heels
3. Gold heels
4. Sports shoes
All heels/stilettos to be at least 3 inches high

Interview / Pre-Judging Outfit

You may wear clothing that you feel is appropriate for an interview and presents you in a sophisticated and confident manner. We suggest you wear a nice suit or daytime dress, Indian or Western, as you wish. Please ensure that you are carrying the necessary accessories and shoes to match the outfit.

Special Events Wardrobe

There will be about four to six cocktail events during the course of the grooming tenure. Four to six informal dresses or pants will also be necessary. There may be about two formal gala events planned during this tenure. Hence, you are advised to carry about two evening gowns for these events.

Indian Clothes

Please bring a few ethnic attires for this tenure, especially two chiffon sarees with blouses and petticoats, along with their matching accessories. They must look dignified and elegant.

Swimwear

Please bring along a well-fitted two piece swimsuit, preferably a bikini. It may be of any colour or print.

Innerwear

Please carry skin-one strapless Bras, Silicon Bras, cups, thongs in skin and black, panty liners and other options. Kindly ensure that you carry sufficient clean and well-fitting lingerie (g-strings, slips, etc.).

Personal Hygiene

If you have any special dietary requirements or allergies, it is imperative that you include this information on your Medical Form. If you require special medications, be sure to bring sufficient quantities for at least three weeks. Please carry tampons, sanitary napkins and all necessary articles of personal hygiene.

During the Miss India Worldwide pageant special dress codes apply for the contestants. Please find these below.

<table>
<tr><th>No.</th><th>Day and date</th><th>Morning</th><th>Afternoon</th><th>Evening</th></tr>
<tr><td>1</td><td>Monday 20-02-2012</td><td>Jeans with branded T-shirt</td><td>Same</td><td>Saree</td></tr>
<tr><td>2</td><td>Tuesday 21-02-2012</td><td>Leisure wear for outdoor photo shoot</td><td>Same</td><td>Colorful Churidaar</td></tr>
<tr><td>3</td><td>Wednesday 22-02-2012</td><td>Jeans with branded T-shirt</td><td>Casual Dress for official lunch in Hotel</td><td>Will be supplied</td></tr>
<tr><td>4</td><td>Thursday 23-02-2012</td><td>Jeans with branded T-shirt</td><td>Same</td><td>Talent outfit</td></tr>
<tr><td>5</td><td>Friday 24-02-2012</td><td>Jeans with branded T-shirt</td><td>Same</td><td>Will be supplied</td></tr>
<tr><td rowspan="5">6</td><td rowspan="5">Saturday 25-02-2012</td><td rowspan="5">Jeans with branded T-shirt</td><td rowspan="5">Same</td><td>Flag round: White churidaar will be supplied</td></tr>
<tr><td>Western Gala Round: Own outfit</td></tr>
<tr><td>Indian Gala Round: Own outfit</td></tr>
<tr><td>Own Talent outfit for top 10</td></tr>
<tr><td>Afterparty: Own choice of outfit</td></tr>
</table>

Preparing for your Pageant

There is this book titled *What Would You Do To Save The World?* written by Ira Trivedi, a finalist at Femina Miss India 2005. The book details the fictional story of a 'could-have-been beauty queen' at a national pageant. Let me quote a passage from the book: '2 April – The day it all finally began. The Miss India Beauty contest, the place where dreams are built and shattered… I have never been in such a constricted environment at any point in my life. I felt as if I was back in my Catholic all girls' boarding school, though this time around instead of ribboned plaits we had styled hair – sprayed puffs, and instead of knee-length, starched, pleated skirts, we had racy, revealing swimsuits. Though the Grand Hotel was a top of the line, brand new seven-star hotel, every morning I woke up thinking of the concrete walls, alarm clocks and curfews of grade school.'

I could not have summed up the pageant experience better.

When I was charting out the basic outline of this book, I designated this chapter to tell you about what to expect at a beauty pageant. But now that I've finally gotten to this chapter, I find that I'm lost. I can't tell you what to expect at a pageant, actually. No one can. Because at a beauty pageant, you never know what to expect. I'll prepare you the best I can… but know that anything can happen. Anything. You are going on the roller-coaster ride of your life, so be sure to buckle up.

First of all, I'm going to start with the acceptance letters that I received from Femina, Tantra (I AM She) and Miss India Worldwide Organization. That will give you a fair idea of what a pageant expects from you and will provide me some ground to start off. I highly recommend you go through them all diligently.

FEMINA MISS INDIA SOUTH 2010

Dear Contestant,

I would like to congratulate you and confirm that you have been selected to participate in the training and thereon the finals of The Pantaloons Femina Miss India South 2010.

I would request you to please note down all that is mentioned in the mail because these details are extremely important.

In order to participate in the final rounds of the contest you will be required to attend a compulsory residential training and grooming session from the 12th of December 2009 to the 24th Dec. The residential training would take place at Novotel in Hyderabad.

Please note that it is compulsory for you to check into the hotel by 12th morning 7.30 am.

As soon as you reach the hotel you will be required to meet the management of the contest who will be present at the Femina Hospitality desk.

There are a number of things that you will have to bring to your training

[...] (Points 1 to 5 as mentioned on p.317-18)

6. *Upon registration in Hyderabad, you must submit a cash deposit of Rs. 5,000/- to allow for expenses to be charged to your room for phone calls, room service*

etc., if applicable. The balance amount, if any, from the deposit will be returned to you (after settlement of your bill) on checkout in Hydearabad itself.

7. *You will also have to get the following tests done and need to get the reports by Sunday, i.e. 13th December:*
    a. CBC
    b. ESR
    C. LFT
    d. Serum Cholesterol & Triglycerides

Please note that lodging, local transportation and meals during the training period will be taken care of by us. Any other cost incurred over and above this will have to be borne by you.

TANTRA (I AM She–Miss Universe India 2011)

My beautiful one,

They say, one moment of glory is worth an age without a name! Your moment has arrived.

You are not just one of the 20 most accomplished women of India... but also contenders for bringing back the Crown and the Glory...

On you lies the setting of a precedent that women will follow in the years to come.

From this moment on, you tread a path, an iconic one... So, choose your direction well.

To help you on your path to greatness... I have personally chosen grooming stalwarts, who shall chisel, mould and hone your inner potential... to give it the polish you so richly deserve. Your days will be full of sessions, activities, media interactions, photo and video shoots, hence, I have listed a few guidelines that are mandatory and would need your strict compliance.

But, most of all your victory will lie in you getting in touch with your I AM quotient, and revealing it in all its inherent glory!

For me, each one of you is already a winner... and I am here only to witness how a winner behaves!

Love and god bless

Sushmita Sen

Important dates

2nd July, 2011 – check in to hotel, Mumbai & orientation

2nd July to 14th July, 2011 – grooming sessions, social & media interactions, technicals & travel

15th July, 2011 – finale

16th July, 2011 – check out

The detailed grooming schedule will be shared with you at the time of check in.

PREPARING FOR THE PAGEANT

Rehearsal Clothes

For training and rehearsals, casual clothes comprising shorts, T-shirts, short skirts, workout clothes, track suits, jeans and comfortable sport shoes/keds/flat shoes/slipon sandals or similar have to be carried. It is essential that you wear what will be most comfortable for movement, dancing, and stage practice. It is also suggested you keep a light sweater or jacket with you at the all times. For fitness and yoga sessions ideally carry a yoga floor mat, well-fitted track suits, shorts and bustier/t-shirts in bright colours as most sessions are captured on camera. You will need comfortable and well-fitted sports shoes and a few pairs of thick cotton sports socks for your training sessions with the Physical Fitness trainer. You should bring items such as jeans (at least 3 pairs), sweaters and comfortable shoes for indoor/outdoor activities. You will be traveling from one city to another, and the season can be very warm or very cold, so please pack keeping both extremes in mind. Non-crushable clothes that can be layered and can work multi shifts is a good idea. For shoots, rehearsals and choreography sessions please carry comfortable pairs of medium- and high-heeled shoes. Please carry complimentary accessories for your outfits. We suggest you carry the following pairs of shoes and clothes with you:

Shoes

1. Black heels
2. Silver/white heels
3. Gold heels
4. Sports shoes
All heels/stilettos to be at least 3 inches tall

Interview / Pre-Judging Outfit

You may wear clothing that you feel is appropriate for an interview and presents you in a sophisticated and confident manner. We suggest you wear a nice suit or daytime dress, Indian or Western, as you wish. Please ensure that you are carrying the necessary accessories and shoes to match the outfit.

Special Events Wardrobe

There will be about four to six cocktail events during the course of the grooming tenure. Four to six informal dresses or pants will also be necessary. There may be about two formal gala events planned during this tenure. Hence, you are advised to carry about two evening gowns for these events.

Indian Clothes

Please bring a few ethnic attires for this tenure, especially two chiffon sarees with blouses and petticoats, along with their matching accessories. They must look dignified and elegant.

Swimwear

Please bring along a well-fitted two-piece swimsuit, preferably a bikini. It may be of any colour or print.

Innerwear

Please carry skin tone strapless bras, Silicon bras, cups, thongs in skin and black, panty liners and other options. Kindly ensure that you carry sufficient clean and well-fitted lingerie (g-strings, slips, etc.).

Personal Hygiene

If you have any special dietary requirements or allergies, it is imperative that you include this information on your Medical Form. If you require special medications, be sure to bring sufficient quantities for at least three weeks. Please carry tampons, sanitary napkins and all necessary articles of personal hygiene.

Baggage

Most airlines allow one carry-on and one check-in bag not weighing more than 5 kgs and 20 kgs respectively. Hence, please pack keeping the same in mind. Kindly be advised that any overweight/oversize baggage charges will have to borne by you. Please attach the baggage tags with your complete details on the luggage. We recommend that anything valuable be left at home. Tantra Entertainment Pvt Ltd (TEPL) will not be responsible for any losses.

PROCEDURES

Arrival at the venue, Mumbai, on Saturday, July 2nd 2011
All Contestants will be met and welcomed at the VENUE by TEPL team members at the "Wadhawan Lifestyle I AM She-2011 Miss Universe India Pageant" desk.

Every contestant must register at the desk. At registration, you will be assigned to a chaperone who will be your supervisor for the entire grooming duration. Also, you will be asked to deposit any registration documents pending till then, like the pending original passport, affidavits, etc.

Post registration, your respective chaperones will hand over your contracts (copies of which will be shared on arrival) on stamp papers to be signed by you. You will be given a sash and a badge, which will denote your contestant number for all practical observation and judging purposes. Either the sash and/or the badge are to be worn at all times during the grooming tenure, sub contests/events and finale. This is your credential and you must never leave your hotel floor without it. You will not be admitted on any transport or internal facilities including grooming sessions, without your sash.

HOTEL ACCOMMODATIONS/MEALS/INCIDENTAL EXPENSES

Two contestants share a pre-assigned room and will have a pre-assigned supervisor nearby. Please know that there can be no roommate changes. The contestants' rooms and hotel floors will be secure from public access.

Lodging, food and local transportation during the training are furnished by TEPL. You will be responsible for all personal incidental expenses like laundry, tips or any other out of pocket expenses. Breakfast, lunch, dinner and other meals as suggested by the dietician will be provided each day. Hotel room service will not be available.

Upon registration in Mumbai, you must submit a cash deposit of Rs. 3,000/- with the hotel to allow for additional personal expenses that you may incur, to be charged to your name and room. The balance amount, if any, from the deposit will be returned to you (after settlement of your bill) on checkout in Mumbai itself. Additionally, Rs. 2,000/- is to be handed over to the TEPL Team for any expenses to be incurred on your behalf. All personal expenses must be cleared before you leave the hotel. There will be no exceptions to this rule. If your incidental personal expenses at the hotel exceed Rs 5,000 at any time during the Pageant, you may be asked by the hotel to pay, to bring the balance to zero. This is a long-standing rule for your protection, as well as for the hotel and TEPL. Any portion of your cash deposit that is not used, will be refunded.

There will be no mobile phones allowed and all calls will be monitored and can only be made at the time allotted by Wadhawan Lifestyle I AM She-2011 pageant organizers in their presence.

Personal guests are not allowed to visit contestants, neither is outside food permitted.

Friends and family may write to you at the address provided by TEPL. The letters will be delivered to your rooms by TEPL team.

On departure on 16th JULY, 2011 you will be asked to sign a release form releasing you as a contestant (if you do not win) upon the conclusion of Wadhawan Lifestyle I AMShe-2011 and relieving TEPL of any and all liability.

SECURITY

Security will be extremely tight during the grooming tenure. Security officers will be with your group at all times, including backstage, outside dressing room areas, and at the hotel. This is done for your comfort and safety, so please cooperate with all security personnel.

The contestant floors at the hotel will be closed to the public. With the exception of selected Wadhawan Lifestyle I AM She-2011 staff, no one, including family, friends, or sponsors, will be permitted on the contestant floors. Contestant supervisors and security will be with you from the time you arrive at the hotel until immediately following the Finale Event.

You can assist in limiting security problems by following all instructions carefully and by reporting any unusual circumstances immediately to your supervisor or a Wadhawan Lifestyle I AM She-2011 official.

You will be given the option to open a security deposit box at the hotel. Again, even though security measures are provided, we strongly suggest that you leave valuables, such as jewellery and other personal items, at home. Please also mark all your belongings with your personalised NAME TAGS to avoid confusion and loss of property. TEPL AND VENUES WILL NOT BE RESPONSIBLE FOR ANY LOSSES.

CONTESTANT SUPERVISORS (CHAPERONES) AND SCHEDULES

The Contestant Manager will supervise the contestant supervisors and coordinate your daily schedule. A contestant supervisor will be assigned to you for your security and assistance.

In addition to making your stay pleasant and lending a helping hand throughout the pageant, your contestant supervisor is also charged with enforcing the rules and regulations of Wadhawan Lifestyle I AM She–2011.

At no time is any contestant permitted to attend or leave any function, her hotel floor or the venue without a contestant supervisor, unless specifically authorised by the contestant supervisor and contestant manager.

Your contestant supervisor will be given an updated schedule each day. He/She will review your schedule and wardrobe needs with you daily. Please be respectful of his/her reminders – they are for your benefit.

It is imperative that you adhere to the schedule and we cannot stress enough the importance of discipline and being ON TIME. Flexibility to schedule changes is also important. Weather conditions may necessitate last minute changes during location videotaping. In these instances, your cooperation and attention to any new instructions given to you by the staff or your contestant supervisor is crucial.

It is also imperative that you be on time for assembly with your luggage according to the times given to you, so you can catch assigned transport on time. Instructions on when you need to keep your luggage packed for transport to airport and such other important details will be instructed well in advance, and need to be followed to the letter.

Your contestant supervisor is your guide and counselor. Shall there be any queries or problems, they need to be addressed to your supervisor who will help and ensure that they are handled for you. In case your supervisor fails to be helpful, you may approach the Contestant Manager with your problems. Always remember that the team of Contestant Manager and Supervisors are Wadhawan Lifestyle I AM She-2011 Staff and must be treated with respect and dignity.

Your contestant supervisors are pleasant, responsible people who we trust will help you make your Wadhawan Lifestyle I AM She-2011 experience smooth. Please remember that they are also away from families and friends and anything you can do to make their assignments easier will be appreciated and will make your stay, and theirs, more enjoyable. Remember, we are guests of the hotel and we shall, therefore, conduct ourselves respectfully at all times, and at all venues.

MEDICAL AID

A medical advisor will be available to the contestants at all times. Report any illness or emergency to your contestant supervisor or medical advisor immediately.

REHEARSALS

Throughout the grooming tenure, there will be many rehearsals to ensure that you are comfortable with the stage patterns, formations, lighting, etc., you will be performing to during the preliminary show and telecast. These rehearsals are hard work, but necessary and mandatory. The people guiding you through your rehearsals are highly respected professionals who know exactly what it takes to make you look your best. Your success and stage confidence will depend upon your willingness to BE COOPERATIVE. Please listen to directions, follow instructions, and BE ON TIME. When rehearsing on stage, there will be times that you will be split into groups and your group may be asked to sit out while another is rehearsing. It is important that, while sitting out, you pay attention to what is happening on stage. Lack of concentration and attention will affect your performance.

TALENT ROUND

There may be a contest for the most talented participant. If you wish to participate, please bring costumes, props, music cds or any other instrument/equipment that you may require for your prepared act. We would only be providing a sound system, CD player with mic for the same.

FINAL CONTEST AND PAGEANT

This will be the final evening of the competition in which the contestants are announced and compete for the title of Wadhawan Lifestyle I AM She–2011 Miss Universe India Crown. During this telecast, special awards will also be given out in accordance with rules and procedures determined by TEPL in its sole discretion.

CORONATION BALL PARTY

A party will be held immediately following the crowning of Wadhawan Lifestyle I AM She–2011 Miss Universe India on the 16th of July 2011. This event is designed to be your party - a time to relax, dance, unwind, and visit with guests. All contestants are invited to attend this event. A brief ceremony will be held at this time to present gifts and scholarships to the winners and finalists.

IF YOU ARE SELECTED WINNER OF WADHAWAN LIFESTYLE I AM She–2011

Immediately following the Pageant, there will be photos, interviews, and the After Party. The morning after the event, the winner and her family will be briefed on what can be expected in the upcoming year. Following any press responsibilities the morning after, the winner will immediately begin her duties along side I AM Foundation initiatives.

If she wins the International title, the 2011 Miss Universe, the winner will be under contract to Miss Universe L.P., LLLP for which she will be paid a salary for her services. Her responsibilities will include travel throughout the United States and abroad and living in New York City for the duration of her employment.

ADDITIONAL NOTES

- *You are required to carry a book along for reading. This may be fiction or non fiction in any language you are comfortable with.*
- *You are required to get yourself abreast with current affairs and global news.*
- *Please note that our TV Partners as a part of the Curtain Raiser will be filming you for which you need to be dressed with make-up and a decent hair-do at all time. Therefore mplease respectively carry your make-up & hair kit.*
- *Photographs for the program book will be taken during your training and you may be interviewed by our television production staff, radio team and members of our website team. You will also be asked to verify the correct spelling and pronunciation of your name for print and broadcast. Kindly cooperate with the team to ensure the best results.*
- *We will be conducting a photo shoot during your training. The photographs will be used in the judging process.*
- *All the video shooting footage, photographs and profile shoots will be the property of the TANTRA ENTERTAINMENT PVT LTD. (TEPL)*

RULES AND REGULATIONS

In order for 'Wadhawan Lifestyle I AM She–2011' to run smoothly and in the interest of fair competition, we require all contestants to observe a few simple rules. Always keep in mind that our host community and millions of people throughout the world, via television and newspaper coverage, will be watching you. Please remember the following:

1. *Any misconduct or violations of the rules, regulations, terms and conditions imposed by TEPL in connection with the Wadhawan Lifestyle I AM She–2011, including, but not limited to, those contained in this handbook and in the Official Entry Form/Contract for Wadhawan Lifestyle I AM She–2011, may result in issuance of a BLACK CARD. The same issued twice would lead to immediate disqualification and dismissal from the Pageant, in the sole discretion of TEPL. All rulings by TEPL will be final.*
2. *For conducting as per the Wadhawan Lifestyle I AM She–2011 norms & attributes, and supporting a sporting spirit, a GOLD CARD will be conferred to the most deserving contestant, chosen by the expert panel and Wadhawan Lifestyle I AM She–2011 team, on a daily basis. The higher the number of GOLD CARDS received by an individual, the closer the contestant would find herself in the top 10 finalists.*
3. *You must wear your identification sash/badge (provided by Wadhawan Lifestyle I AM She–2011) at all times – from the time you leave your hotel room in the morning until you return to your hotel room at night.*
4. *The consumption of alcoholic beverages and drugs (other than prescription medication legally prescribed by an authorised physician) is strictly prohibited during the grooming tenure.*
5. *Smoking is not permitted in public.*
6. *Panty hose or stockings are prohibited during swimsuit competition.*

7. *No cell phones, laptops or PDA devices (e.g., Blackberrys, Treos, etc.) are permitted during the duration of your stay with TEPL.*
8. *Contestant supervisors are to be present with you at all times that you are away from the contestant floors of your hotel. For your own safety, you are not allowed to leave the hotel floor without a contestant supervisor, unless specifically authorised to do so by your contestant supervisor.*
9. *Discipline is vital, and hence, please be on time for all activities.*
10. *No family, friends or sponsors will be allowed backstage or in dressing rooms at any time.*
11. *No member of your family, friends or any guests will be allowed in your hotel room or on the contestant hotel floors during the entire grooming tenure. There will be a designated time to meet with the parents and family members. The same shall be communicated to the contestants well in advance.*
12. *No contestant, member of her family, friends or any affiliate of any national pageant organization may communicate in any fashion with the judges or their guests – whether by phone, correspondence, with gifts, or anything of the like. Any contact or communication with the judges by or on behalf of a contestant may result in immediate disqualification of the contestant from Wadhawan Lifestyle I AM She–2011. This decision will be under the sole discretion of Tantra Entertainment Private Ltd. All rulings by TEPL will be final.*
13. *Contestants are not permitted to solicit or sell any products or goods during the grooming tenure to any other contestants, friends, family or Wadhawan Lifestyle I AM She–2011 staff.*
14. *Contestants are not permitted to have any appliances not supplied by the hotel, e.g., microwaves, refrigerators, tanning beds or exercise equipment such as treadmills or stairmasters, in rooms at any time*

15. *Contestants must check out on time from the hotel/s on the advised date/s.*
16. *All contestants are governed by the rules, regulations, terms and conditions set forth in the Official Entry Form/ Contract for the Wadhawan Lifestyle I AM She-2011 pageant, which you will sign on arrival at the hotel.*
17. *Please direct any questions or concerns regarding the rules of Wadhawan Lifestyle I AM She-2011 to your contestant supervisor (details of which will be shared with you on arrival at the Hotel).*

Welcome to An Experience of a Lifetime!!
-Team Tantra

MISS INDIA WORLDWIDE ORGANISATION (Miss India Worldwide 2012)

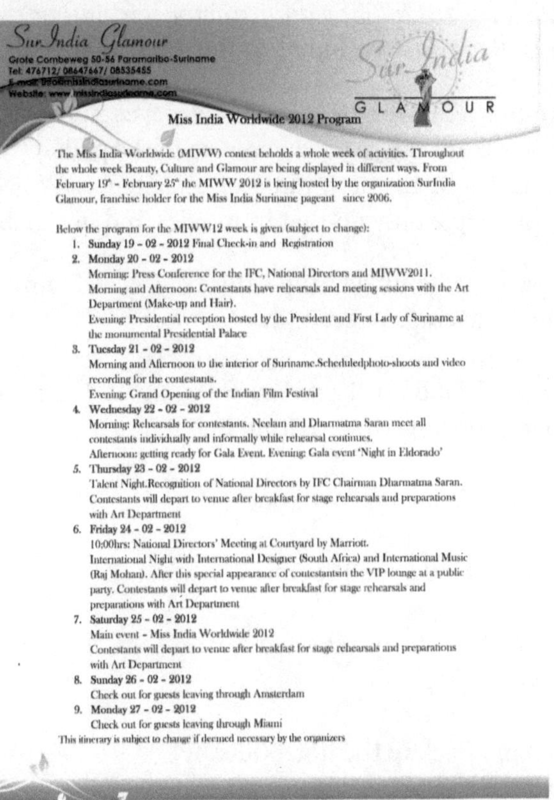

SurIndia Glamour
Grote Combeweg 50-56 Paramaribo-Suriname
Tel: 476712/ 08647667/ 08535455
E-mail: info@missindiasuriname.com
Website: www.missindiasuriname.com

Sur-India GLAMOUR

Miss India Worldwide 2012 Program

The Miss India Worldwide (MIWW) contest beholds a whole week of activities. Throughout the whole week Beauty, Culture and Glamour are being displayed in different ways. From February 19th - February 25th the MIWW 2012 is being hosted by the organization SurIndia Glamour, franchise holder for the Miss India Suriname pageant since 2006.

Below the program for the MIWW12 week is given (subject to change):

1. **Sunday 19 - 02 - 2012** Final Check-in and Registration
2. **Monday 20 - 02 - 2012**
   Morning: Press Conference for the IFC, National Directors and MIWW2011.
   Morning and Afternoon: Contestants have rehearsals and meeting sessions with the Art Department (Make-up and Hair).
   Evening: Presidential reception hosted by the President and First Lady of Suriname at the monumental Presidential Palace
3. **Tuesday 21 - 02 - 2012**
   Morning and Afternoon to the interior of Suriname.Scheduledphoto-shoots and video recording for the contestants.
   Evening: Grand Opening of the Indian Film Festival
4. **Wednesday 22 - 02 - 2012**
   Morning: Rehearsals for contestants. Neelam and Dharmatma Saran meet all contestants individually and informally while rehearsal continues.
   Afternoon: getting ready for Gala Event. Evening: Gala event 'Night in Eldorado'
5. **Thursday 23 - 02 - 2012**
   Talent Night.Recognition of National Directors by IFC Chairman Dharmatma Saran.
   Contestants will depart to venue after breakfast for stage rehearsals and preparations with Art Department
6. **Friday 24 - 02 - 2012**
   10:00hrs: National Directors' Meeting at Courtyard by Marriott.
   International Night with International Designer (South Africa) and International Music (Raj Mohan). After this special appearance of contestantsin the VIP lounge at a public party. Contestants will depart to venue after breakfast for stage rehearsals and preparations with Art Department
7. **Saturday 25 - 02 - 2012**
   Main event - Miss India Worldwide 2012
   Contestants will depart to venue after breakfast for stage rehearsals and preparations with Art Department
8. **Sunday 26 - 02 - 2012**
   Check out for guests leaving through Amsterdam
9. **Monday 27 - 02 - 2012**
   Check out for guests leaving through Miami

This itinerary is subject to change if deemed necessary by the organizers

WHAT TO EXPECT...

Let's deal with this in a systematic manner.

Luckily, I maintained a diary religiously every time I was at a pageant. The only time I actually stuck to writing a diary, in fact. Let's look at that diary and figure out what to expect from this once-in-a-lifetime opportunity of yours.

An Average Day in a Pageant Contestant's Life

From my diary spanning two different pageants (I AM She, Miss India Universe 2011 and Miss India Worldwide 2012):

3 July 2011: 'It's already 11pm and we still haven't...'

5 July 2011: 'We were lining up before the press conf...'

21 February 2012: 'She's an attractive girl in her own way. Not exactly attractive, but quite hot. She's quite the se...'

(Quite the se... what? I guess we'll never know. These are examples from my diary where I fell asleep, diary and pen in hand. Right in the middle of a sentence. Wow! And I thought people only do that in movies and not in real life.)

At a pageant, your day typically begins at 5 a.m. Let me outline an average pageant day for you:

5.00 a.m.: Wake up (I used to wake up at 4 a.m. so that I could spend some time writing my diary.)

5.30 a.m. – 7:30 a.m.: Workout

8.00 a.m. – 8:30 a.m.: Breakfast

8.30 a.m.: Day starts: rehearsals, trainings, photo ops, press conferences, etc.

10.00 p.m.: Back to the hotel (ideally)

This probably doesn't feel like much to you. Yes, it doesn't feel like much to me either, now that I put it down on paper. But look at it this way, starting from the top of the list.

Once you're done with your workout, you get half-an-hour to get ready for breakfast. If that sounds reasonable to you, consider this. You don't actually get half-an-hour to get ready. You get fifteen minutes to shower, wash your hair, dry your hair, style it, put on make-up and basically doll up. Fifteen minutes. Now where did the other fifteen minutes go? Well, you do have a roommate, you know, and she needs to do the same. I really can't tell you any tricks for this. The only thing I can tell you is shower as fast as you can and learn how to speed up your make-up routine. After these pageants, I can now put on my make-up, all the way from foundation to mascara in under five minutes. You just have to learn how to do that. And please don't even consider going without a shower. There are many girls who do that seeing that there isn't much time. But please, no! You've just had two hours of strenuous working out. No amount of deodorant can hide that. However, what you can try is carry dry shampoo. I've personally never used it, but it could come handy on the days that you don't have time to wash and dry your hair.

What you could also do is be the one to go to the bathroom first. Don't give in to your laziness. Not only will your roommate love you for that, you also get an edge. You get fifteen minutes in the bathroom and fifteen minutes outside the bathroom to get ready. Therefore, you get an entire thirty minutes. And that brings me to my next point: carry your hairdryer. Yes, most hotels provide a hairdryer in your room. But those are usually permanently fixed in the bathroom. If you carry your own, you don't have to hog the bathroom. You can let your roommate use the bathroom while you go out to the bedroom and finish your routine. Trust me, she will love you for this too! And it is very important to have your roommate on your side. Why? I'll get to that later.

Now that you're ready, you're off to have breakfast. Usually, you would have had a newspaper delivered to your room in the morning. But so far you wouldn't have found time to even touch it. See, you leave your room at 5-5.30 in the morning, and the newspaper would probably not have been delivered by then. Plus, you haven't had a chance to relax either. You will look forward to this half-an-hour of breakfast as a chance to just sit back, chill and relax. Nuh-uh. Please don't do that! This half-an-hour is the only free time you will have in your long day. Use that constructively. That newspaper you haven't yet touched? Pick that up. And don't just skim through the headlines, read them properly. Study them. And yes, the *Economic Times* can be pretty boring, but you know what? So was Math in high school. You still suffered through that, didn't you? So put yourself through it and read that newspaper. Trust me, you will thank yourself for it at the end of the pageant.

Now you start your day. Like really start it. You begin with your rehearsals, appearances, photo ops, press conferences and whatever else that the organisers might have planned for you. In one average day at Miss India Universe, we might have had rehearsals with Lubna Adams, a press conference, an appearance at a popular radio station, a photo op at the clothing brand(s) that were sponsoring us and to round it off, a personal session with Sushmita Sen. All of this in a little more than twelve hours.

And at each of these you are expected to be this bubble of energy, smiling and laughing the whole time (except for the personal sessions where you are allowed to be a little grumpy).

And if that's not enough, at Femina Miss India South, we had all that rounded off with a personal session with Marc Robinson who would sit with us and analyse former contestants and winners till 2 a.m. All this is very important and informative, but quite tiring too.

So on an average, you might get to sleep for anywhere between three and seven hours. That might not sound bad. And it isn't, for the first few days. But as the days draw on, and you keep doing the same thing again and again without a break (remember, the concept of weekends does not exist in a pageant)... that's when it really starts taking a toll on you.

I'm not trying to scare you. I'm trying to prepare you. And the more prepared you are, the better you'll be able to perform.

So on an average, you might get to sleep for anywhere between three and seven hours. That might not sound bad. And it isn't, for the first few days. But as the days draw on, and you keep doing the same thing again and again without a break (remember, the concept of weekends does not exist in a pageant)... that's when it really starts taking a toll on you.

ISOLATION

Pageants are isolated. They are experiences in lonliness. You are uprooted from your usual life and airdropped into an antiseptic tank. Like literally. Let me elaborate on that.

When you are at a pageant, you are away from friends and family. You are in a foreign environment, on alien territory. You are not in your comfort zone anymore. And to make that worse, at most national pageants, you are not allowed any sort of contact with your comfort zone. By that I mean, for the duration of the pageant, you might as well forget that you have any friends or family outside of this organisation, because chances are, you will have zero contact with them.

For the duration of the pageant, you might as well forget that you have any friends or family outside of this organisation, because chances are, you will have zero contact with them.

At Femina Miss India South, I was a nineteen-year-old girl who had seen absolutely nothing of the outside world. As far as I knew, the outside world might have had rivers of milk flowing at everyone's doorstep and angels and demons paying social calls and I might just have lapped that all up. So my mother decided to stay for part of the duration of the pageant, at the same hotel that we were parked at. I still remember, after a tough rehearsal session, I made some excuse saying that I had to go to my room for something. Instead, however, I ran to my mother's room and cried my heart out over a (forbidden) cup of coffee. Of course, when I finally got back, I was ticked off for being late.

All this sounds contradictory to what I said? Well, here's the twist. No one knew that I had my mother there with me. No one was ever supposed to know. By having my mother there, I was breaking rules. I was not supposed to have any form of physical contact with the outside world. However, thankfully, we were allowed to keep our mobile phones with us. So we could phone home whenever we wanted. Thank god for small mercies!

But at I AM She Miss India Universe, we didn't even have that little source of comfort! Any kind of contact with the outside world was banned. Phone calls, physical meetings, emails—nothing. Only snail mail was allowed. Snail mail? In 2011? Really?

At these pageants, we were hardly ever even allowed out of our rooms or floors without a chaperone. We were guarded from the outside world like a 16th century harem.

And sometimes, this was even taken to an extreme. On 13 July 2011 there was a bomb blast in Mumbai. A lot of us were worried because we had family in the city. My own parents had just arrived the day before. Now this blast was in an area that they would not normally be in, but you never know.

I was extremely worried. I approached a chaperone and asked her if I may call my parents. As expected, she said no.

I explained that this was no social call. There had been a bomb blast and I just wanted to be sure that they were fine. The chaperone stuck to her guns. By this time, it wasn't just me asking. All the other contestants had joined. They all had friends and family that they were worried about. But the management didn't budge. We were getting pissed, to put it mildly.

Finally, the management relented, just a tiny bit. They told us that they would place a call themselves and let us know. We were mollified. This was all we had wanted. This was at 9 in the morning. Throughout the day, I kept approaching the chaperones and asking them if they'd been able to get through to my parents. They kept brushing me off. Finally, by noon the next day, I got an answer. I had asked for the umpteenth time, and they had grudgingly told me, yes, they are fine.

A few days later, the pageant ended and I was reunited with my family. While discussing the entire last month, I told them about this bit too. They were shocked. They had not received any phone call from the pageant. The pageant had bluffed to me by saying that they are fine. On the contrary, my parents had been the ones to call the organisation over and over again only to have their calls not answered. Finally, a lady had answered the phone and curtly replied that everyone was fine. She had not even bothered taking down their names, leave alone their message.

This was shocking and absolutely unethical. But the fact is, this was an extreme, not a common occurrence. And the only reason I'm telling you this is for you to be aware of the level of isolation that these pageants can sometimes trigger.

What they always said is that this is so that we can concentrate on the pageant and on our performance with undivided attention. But no. This is a PR move. They don't want anything getting out that they have not sanctioned themselves. By restricting your movement and communication, they are trying to gain greater control over the image that they portray to the outside world. And as an outsider, you are a liability. Fair? No. But the fact is, pageants are commercial ventures and if you want to win, you'll just have to play by their rules. However, be sure to draw that line in the sand. The pageant might be a commercial venture, but you are not. You are an individual. And you have the right to have any serious concern addressed.

GOSSIP GIRLS

Put ten people together in a room and you are sure to have gossip and rumours flying out of the window before the day is over. We've all seen Bigg Boss.

Now your pageant world might seem to be a far cry from the highly rated reality show, but guess what? They're isolated, you're isolated. They're contesting for one single prize, you're contesting for one single prize. They're in the public eye, you're in the public eye. The only real difference and the absolute main one, might I add, is that they are rewarded for controversy, while you are punished for controversy.

But human nature remains human nature. Thus, any beauty pageant is a fertile ground for gossip.

At Femina Miss India South 2009, I had created history of sorts by walking out of the pageant, convinced that it was rigged in the favour of one of the contestants. It was not only me who felt so, but also a majority of the other contestants. I was nineteen, idealistic and felt I could change the world. So I took a stand and stuck to it. Whether or not I was right, I don't know. But little did I also know that this would come back to haunt me at I AM She–Miss India Universe.

My diary entry from that period reads:

4 July 2011: Yeah, so Day 3. The Press Conference day. The fact that I had walked out finally came out. PH told everyone. Actually it was after the press conference. She was sitting, talking to U. I was walking past and PH stopped me. She was like, 'Anvita, you were really good!' Then she introduced me to U and told her that she was with me in Femina Miss India South and that I had walked out because I felt it was rigged. So then, U asked me if it really was. PH replied to that [and] we all know what happened in the end.

5 July 2011: I couldn't even finish my entry last night, I was that tired! So anyway, to continue with the story, U turned to me and said, 'You are an example to all of us. I really admire what you did.' Then she went on to clarify, 'But you'll find there is no fairer pageant than this one'... yeah, the cat's out of the bag now. The girls crowded around me asking about it. Only T seemed to be a bit belligerent about it. More about that later.

6 July 2011: V and T started arguing about whether or not N was a good winner at Femina. I kept quiet. Didn't want to get dragged into it. Can't get labelled as a troublemaker.

One discovery turned into a huge discussion that was to last for days! It wasn't really that big a thing. I had done what I considered best for myself at that moment. But when you are closeted within four walls, insecurity rises and everyone becomes a suspect. To stress on that, another diary entry. I overheard this conversation between two contestants. As usual, no names will be disclosed.

9 July 2011: I overhead this conversation earlier today.

P: V! Congratulations!
V: Huh? For what?
P: Congratulations for winning the pageant.
V: What are you talking about?
P: That's what people are saying. That you'll be winning the pageant.

V: Who's saying that?
P: No, I just heard someone say it.
V: That's just a rumour, who was it?
P: I don't know. I was getting my make-up done so I had my eyes closed. I don't know if it was one of the contestants or one of the make-up people.
V: It's just a rumour. If it was a contestant, it's just a rumour. In any case, I haven't been told anything about it.

Fact is, at pageants, names will be pointed. There will be rumours. You have a bunch of girls who have all worked extremely hard to win that crown. No one wants another person to steal it away from her. If you're really serious about that crown, everyone is a suspect.

Also, it is true that there are rigged pageants in the world, and there are fair pageants in the world. And while you are at the pageant, you have no way of knowing which one it is. So it's best to turn a blind eye and a deaf ear to such rumours. You are there to win that crown. Concentrate on that. I know I myself haven't followed that advice. As mentioned in one of the earlier paragraphs, I walked out of Femina Miss India South 2010 because I thought it was rigged. It was not exactly a wrong decision. But it was not the wisest either. In fact, it might have been rather foolish. Because however strong my suspicion was at the time, the fact remains that I did not actually know whether it was rigged. There was no way for me to possibly know! So if it was a rigged pageant, I never had a chance anyway, but at the same time, it couldn't do me any harm either. It would have just been back to square one. But if it was not rigged, I might have had a chance of winning. By walking out, I just ensured that I lost that chance as well.

When you are running a race, keep your eyes on the finishing line. The minute you look back to see if you are winning, you've already lost the race.

Idealism is a good thing. It can do wonders for the world. But sometimes you have to be practical as well. Sometimes, you have to ask yourself, whether your idealism is doing you any good or is it actually harming you? Because at the end of the day, you are the vehicle through which your idealism can function. On its own, it can't do anything, it just remains a belief. But with you, through you, it can achieve a lot. It's like the logic behind helping a child put on his/her oxygen mask only after you've put on yours in a flight. If you're not around, you can't really do anything for anyone. Or in this case, if you're not in a position to, you can't do anything for anyone.

I read a phrase in a book once. It went something along the lines of, 'when you are running a race, keep your eyes on the finishing line. The minute you look back to see if you are winning, you've already lost the race.' Just keep that in mind. There will be rumours galore abounding around you. But pay them no attention. Not because the world is fair. No. But to keep your own sanity. Oh, listen to them for sure. They can be most entertaining. But the moment you start taking them to heart, you start messing up your own mind. You need to keep your cool. You need to concentrate on your own game, not on someone else's. That's the only way you can perform.

As I said, there are rigged pageants and there are fair pageants (like anything else in the world, really). If it is a rigged pageant, you never had a chance anyway, but at least you gained valuable life experiences. If it is a fair pageant, you'll only ruin your own chances of winning if you don't focus all your energy on your performance. And you have no way of knowing which it is while you are in the thick of things. So just give them the benefit of the doubt and work on your game. Don't let anyone else ruin your game.
After all,

Kuch toh log kahenge
Logon ka kaam hai kehna.

Let that be your mantra.

BFFS

So far, I've only stressed on the negative side of the pageant experience. But you know what? A pageant can be a beautiful experience as well. The people you meet, the experiences you gain, can truly be memorable and exceptional.

At I Am She–Miss India Universe, I met a wonderful young woman. I will not name her, but she knows who she is. She was my roommate. Frankly, on the first day, I was terrified to think of who might be my roommate. For all I knew, she could be an extremely insecure and vindictive person who would do everything in her power to make my life a living hell. Basically, I was thinking of a Balaji serial vamp. But 'A', my roommate, was nothing like that. She was a year younger than me and her birthday was just one day before mine. And let me just say, 'A', you made my life wonderful for those fifteen days by just being there. Thank you.

At the same pageant, something else extraordinary happened. 14 July was A's birthday. And on 15 July was mine. On both those nights, several contestants and chaperones smuggled in 'forbidden fruit', namely, chocolate—and even fruit actually, since fruit was not allowed on the pretext that they contain too much fructose. It doesn't make sense, but when you've got only two weeks to get twenty girls in shape, I suppose desperate measures are the order of the day! The contestants actually bribed hotel staff to get them chocolate bars they could gift to us. This could have disqualified the contestants and cost the chaperones their jobs (one chaperone actually brought in a slice of chocolate cake, though he did insist that we could only have one bite each). But despite that, they strived to make the day special for us. They knew how it wasn't an ideal birthday for either of us, away from friends and family, and they did their bit to make it special, despite all odds. I will never forget that selfless gesture. It truly opened my eyes to the goodness that exists in the world.

Goodness is all around you. You just have to reach out, recognize it and reciprocate it. That is a very important lesson that pageantry taught me. At every pageant that I have contested at—which numbers to four—the crux was the same: a bunch of girls competing for one crown.

Goodness is all around you. You just have to reach out, recognize it and reciprocate it. That is a very important lesson that pageantry taught me.

You would have thought that it would be anarchy. Catfights, name-calling, hey, I'd even heard a story about one particular contestant who sneaked into her competitor's room and destroyed the girl's finale gown! And yes, we did have our spats. There was a lot of gossip (as illustrated in the previous section) that disrupted our peace of mind for at least a while. But for the most part, I only saw girls going out of their way to make life easier for each other. And it was an eye-opener. Here we were, in a rat race, each one for themselves, yet, you take out time to genuinely lend a shoulder to a younger girl who's homesick because she has never been away from home earlier. Your position in the top ten might completely depend on how stunning you look, yet you spend ten minutes fixing another girl's make-up because the make-up man didn't have enough time to do her beautiful eyes justice!

Truly, it was an enriching experience and I wouldn't exchange it for the world!

Throw twenty-five girls together in a room and you can expect the room to blow up is what conventional wisdom says. But no. The room did not blow up. What I say is throw twenty-five girls together in a room and at least a bunch of them will come out as friends for life.

OVERWORKED AND UNDERSTAFFED ORGANISERS

Simply put, the pageant staff is usually overworked. They're usually just as old as you, maybe a couple of years older and for them, this is their daily bread and butter. And usually, there just isn't enough staff, at least, not as much as the pageant usually needs (just like any other organisation, really). So each person ends up doing more than one person's job.

Let's start from the top.

Pageant staff mainly comprises two groups: the organisers and the chaperones.

The organisers are usually a little higher-up in pageant hierarchy. As the name itself says, they organise stuff.

The chaperones are a little lower down the rung and their main job is to take care of you. Of course, their side job is also to help the organisers organise the happenings of the pageant.

Of course, there are also the trainers, the publicists, the PR people, etc., but let's concentrate on these two groups now because they are the ones you'll be dealing with every waking moment of your average pageant day.

And no, I'm not exaggerating—I mean it. Every waking moment. Literally from the moment you wake up to the moment you sleep. The chaperones will be the ones banging on your door at 5 in the morning, trying to get you to wake up, banging on your door again half-an-hour later because you're late for workout, monitoring your food, making sure you don't smuggle any fruits to your room (this is actually true, we tried to smuggle oranges, got caught and had the oranges confiscated) making sure you sleep on time, etc. They are basically running your lives for the duration of the pageant.

Believe me, you will hate them.

But whenever you feel that hatred coming on, take a deep breath. Yes, they have more control over your life than you do at that moment. But they're just doing their job, you know. And by the simple act of participating in the pageant, you effectively gave them that job. So sit back and just let them do what they are supposed to.

And frankly speaking, if you are feeling stressed out, they're probably doubly stressed. If you have to get up at 5, they have to get up at 4, because they have to be up and ready by the time you're up. If you go to bed by 12 a.m., they can only go to bed at 1 a.m., because they have to get the next day's schedule out. They are extremely sleep-deprived and overworked. And they are the weakest links of the pageant hierarchy. If anything goes wrong, they are the ones who will be blamed. Regardless of whether or not it is their fault.

So to get through the pageant while remaining sane, I have a simple mantra:
Hope for the best, but expect the worst.

So the next time you see them hurry past you with a harried expression on their face, give them a nice smile and enquire after them. Remember, you're all in this together. You need each other. So you might as well make that easier by just the simple act of being nice and kind.

MENTAL STRENGTH

From everything I have outlined above, it is obvious that pageantry is stressful business. From the hectic schedules to the competitiveness to something as simple as running in 4 inch heels (which, trust me, is actually not simple). So to get through the pageant while remaining sane, I have a simple mantra:

Hope for the best, but expect the worst.

Remember that pseudo documentary that came out a few years ago, *The Secret*? Well, that's absolute rubbish. The whole universe is not working to bring to you your one singular wish. The whole universe has better things on its hands to do, like expanding at an exponential rate and figuring out ways to puzzle us mere human beings with its seeming randomness—like, a supervoid, seriously? Anyway, I digress.

What I'm trying to say is that you need to be prepared for the eventuality that things might not work out exactly the way you planned them. You might not win the pageant. It happens, you know. You have anywhere between 20 to 90 girls, but only one crown. Someone's got to lose.

And it might just be you.

You must prepare yourself for that eventuality.

Because, when you find out that you have lost on a stage facing two hundred people, it will hit you hard. Despite all my efforts to maintain my composure and dignity, I found a stray tear rolling down my cheek when my name wasn't announced at I AM She-Miss India Universe. The dream was over.

Except that it wasn't. It is important to lose as well. When you lose, you discover how to pick yourself up and move on again, a lesson that is much more important than anything that winning can ever teach you.

Keep a Level Head

The past few sections have not only told you about what to expect at a pageant, but also informed you about any potential distractions. Keep those distractions at bay. You are here to win, that should be your singular focus. Nothing else really matters. Those fights with your chaperone, that one time someone cried foul for favouritism, the other day when you weren't allowed to have that extra helping of dal even when you were tired to the point of exhaustion, that time the designer yelled at you in front of everyone for forgetting your silicones—none of that matters. None. Of. That. Matters. At. All. Move beyond it. The thing that does matter is the crown. Keep your eyes on it.

It is important to lose as well. When you lose, you discover how to pick yourself up and move on again, a lesson that is much more important than anything that winning can ever teach you.

But for that, you must mentally discipline yourself. And one trusted time-tested tool for that is meditation. Yes, I can hear you groaning. But do me a favour, just try it out. Just clear your mind and direct your thoughts in the direction that you want. Just try it once. And if you don't feel any calmer by the end of it, I'll give you a million bucks (though it's a different matter that the cheque would bounce).

There are many ways to clearing your mind. For some, it is traditional meditation. For some, it is a good adrenaline-rush-causing workout (in which case, don't bother, you'll be getting plenty of that, I assure you). For me, it was the simple act of recording my thoughts. I made it a point in all my pageants to write in my diary every morning and every evening. And that really helped me organise by thoughts and feelings. Without that, I would have been a nervous wreck by the end of it.

I don't know which mind-clearing device will help you the most. You know yourself better and thus would be a better judge of that than I could ever be. But just to get you started, I'm listing below a few popular methods:

1. **Traditional meditation:** If you know yoga, all the better. Nothing like good old Pranayama to start your

day. But even if you are not a yoga fan, a few deep breaths assisted by an attempt to control and streamline your thoughts (it will be difficult in the beginning, but you'll get better with practice) will take you a long way.

2. **Morning pages**: Jot down your thoughts, just a few pages every morning. Whatever comes to your mind. Don't filter it. Just be honest with yourself.

3. **Doodling/Sketching:** Again, similar to the morning pages, whatever comes to your mind. Don't filter this either. Be honest with yourself.

4. **Going for a walk:** This one might be a little tough as most pageants don't let you go anywhere without a chaperone. But if your pageant does allow you a little more freedom, there is nothing like taking a little me time to focus on your task.

5. **Confide in a person:** You know what they say, 'A problem shared is a problem halved.' That is so true! If your pageant allows you to keep your mobile phone with you, then use that. Schedule a time to talk with your mom or your best friend. And warn them in advance that this is your time to rant. If you hit it off with your roommate, even better. Talk to her. Confide in her. Share your fears and insecurities; chances are she feels exactly the same way. There's nothing like getting your negativities out of you in order to look at things in a more positive manner. But be careful. Do not attempt that unless you feel you can absolutely trust her 110 percent! If she's just looking for ammunition, don't just spoon-feed her. Use your better judgement and take that call.
6. **Physical exercise:** Any form of physical exercise releases endorphins. Endorphins are feel-good chemicals your body releases. They act as painkillers. They act as sedatives. They are basically your body's way of drugging you to make you feel better. And you could

really use that pick-me-up if you're really stressed. And the best part of using this as your stress buster is that pageants will give you loads of physical workout. Every morning at 5 a.m. So win-win!

Physically

In today's world, winning a pageant is more than just being a pretty well-spoken young woman. Fortunately or unfortunately, your figure plays a major role in you walking up to that crown. And the more commercial your pageant, the more your chances of winning depend on your figure.

So you have to prepare well. And the only way you can do that is by planning well in advance.

For example, if you plan to participate in your national pageant next year, start working on it now. Right now.

Find a good gym, find a good personal trainer. Start working out every morning. Or start yoga. If you choose yoga, do keep in mind that yoga takes more time to tone you, but also retains the toned effect for longer. So you will have to start planning this much more in advances. Your trainers might tell you that three times a week will suffice, but go five times a week. Get your diet in order. Stock up your refrigerator with the right food. Hire a dietician, if necessary. Start your weekly manicures and pedicures NOW.

And for god's sake, please start reading the newspaper, right now!

How much in advance do you need to start, you ask.

Well, most pageant aspirants who have done well in pageants start grooming themselves six months in advance. For Miss India Worldwide, I had started one year in advance. It takes effort. And it takes consistency.

So stop putting it off, and start planning.

Sample Questions for your Interview

1. What has been the most significant accomplishment of your life? Why?
2. At what point does a girl become a woman?
3. Do you consider yourself to be a giver or a taker? Why?
4. Who do you feel is the most popular person in the world?
5. What would you like to see done to improve the public's understanding of the importance of organ donation? Why?
6. How can we promote better volunteerism?
7. What do you want to do in life?
8. What would you say is the biggest problem facing our educational system today? Why?
9. What are the best qualities a parent could share with their children? Why?
10. If you showed me around your state, where would you take me?
11. What do you expect to gain by participating in pageants? Why?
12. Tell me about the cultural activities in your state.
13. What is important to you now that was not important to you when you were younger?
14. What has been the biggest disappointment in your life? Why?
15. What is your message to young women today?
16. Which song best describes your outlook on life?
17. You just found a deflated helium balloon with a note inside from a student in another state. What do you hope the note will say?

18. What do you think makes your country special?
19. If you could interview anyone in the world, who would it be?
20. Women have been elected to many high level government posts. If you could choose a government post, what job would you choose and why?
21. As a possible Miss Universe, you would travel around speaking to a lot of people. What is your message?
22. If you were invited to be a guest on one of those late night talk shows, what would you want the host to discuss with you?
23. Is it important for the husband to help do chores, such as cooking and cleaning? Why or why not?
24. How important is winning to you?
25. There is an increasing sentiment that we should not continue to fund the space program. Why should our space program be a priority?
26. What sort of people seem to rub you the wrong way?
27. What do you want in your next boyfriend that you do not have now?
28. How can education of our children be enhanced by parental involvement?
29. Name an example from your life where you turned a negative into a positive?
30. What do you think is the most important change taking place in your country today?
31. What are the advantages or disadvantages of being beautiful?
32. What do you think is the best thing about living in your country?
33. If you had the opportunity to live forever, would you want to and why?
34. Tell us something about yourself that you haven't already told the press.
35. If you were to become Miss Universe (or any other pageant winner in its place), what is the single most important thing that you would wish to accomplish?

36. What do you consider is the greatest problem facing young people of today?
37. If you could be a fictional film or literary character, who would you be and why?
38. If you had the time and money to embark upon a great adventure, what would it be?
39. What relevance do you think pageants such as this have for a woman today?
40. Everyone has a mission in life. What do you think your mission is?
41. What do you think is the essence of being a woman?
42. If you were to have a son or a daughter one day, what is the most important lesson you'd teach him or her?
43. Do you think the world would be a better place if we had just one world government and no separate countries?
44. If you had the power to do anything you wished to improve the status of women in your country, what would you do?
45. Who do you think should make birth control decisions? The government or individual women? (A question where the recent cases of Purvi Patel from Indiana and Bei Bei Shuai can be referred to.)
46. Would you marry a man who wants to stay home and take care of the children while you support the family?
47. Other than this pageant, what is the greatest challenge in your life at this time?
48. Do you think it is important for women to have equal opportunities to participate in sports and if so, why?
49. If you could choose only one, would you choose: smart, rich or beautiful and why?
50. Who do you think is the greatest woman and why?
51. What do you think men can learn from women?
52. How would winning this pageant help you with your career goals?
53. What's the most important decision you've had to make in your life?
54. Other than being Miss (name of country/city you

represent), what achievement in your life are you most proud of?

55. If you knew one of the delegates had received the questions in advance, what would you do?
56. If you could do one thing to change the status of women in your country, what would you do?
57. If there were no rules in your life for one day, and you could be outrageous, what would you do?
58. A woman has awakened after being asleep for twenty years. What do you tell her she missed?
59. Right now, there is a protest going on calling this pageant disrespectful of women. Convince them that they are wrong.
60. What motivates you and why?
61. How would you best describe your family?
62. If you could invite one famous person, living or dead to a dinner party, who would it be and why?
63. How would you let a man know that you are attracted to him?
64. What is the most important thing in life for you?
65. What is the biggest misconception about beauty?
66. Aside from winning your title, what was the best day of your life?
67. What are you most afraid of?
68. If you were stranded on a desert island, what one thing would you bring with you and why?
69. Tell us something about your country that most people don't know.
70. If you had to change one thing about your past, what would that be?
71. If you had to represent another country, which country would that be and why?
72. What is the biggest misconception people have about your country?
73. What is the one thing you need to overcome?
74. What is the most important thing that you have learnt about yourself by participating in this pageant?
75. If your life was videotaped, what would you erase and what would you replay?

76. What makes you blush?
77. If you could change anything in history, what would you change and why?
78. If you could have only one of the five senses, which one would you pick and why?
79. What is the most important thing in your life?
80. What is the most precious gift that you have given to someone?
81. If you could be either water or fire, which would you be and why?
82. If you could interview any female leader in history, who would you interview and why?
83. What do you think has been women's greatest contribution to today's world and why?
84. Give us three words that would describe you and why?
85. If you could choose what time period to be born in and what sex to be, what would you choose and why?
86. What is the one failure in your life that you have learnt the most from?
87. If you ever recommend a book to someone, which book would it be and why?
88. What can men learn most from women?
89. What is the biggest challenge in your life?
90. What is one of the most difficult situation that your country is going through and what would you do to solve it?
91. What is your biggest fear?
92. What values would you like to teach your children?
93. If you had the opportunity of changing something in humanity, what would you change and why?
94. What would you say is one of your major flaws?
95. What is your definition of success?
96. Would you rather have a relationship with a man who is spontaneous and wild or with one who plays it safe?
97. If you could have any type of superpower, what would it be and why?
98. Is it better to live life following your heart or following your mind?

99. What is the one lesson that you learnt as a child that still affects your life today?
100. If you could go back in time and change a moment in your past, what would that be and why?
101. Do you believe men or women have it easier in life and why?
102. What is the biggest sacrifice you've ever had to make and how did you handle it?
103. When is a woman truly satisfied?
104. Is there still discrimination against women and if so, what can be done about it?
105. According to WHO, there is a dire need for HIV testing across the globe, do you believe that HIV testing should be made mandatory?
106. Tonight you were judged on how you look in a swimsuit, but in some countries, women are not allowed to wear swimsuits. How does that make you feel?
107. Has being a beautiful woman made your life easier or has it prevented people from taking you seriously?
108. In many parts of the world, obstacles still exist that impede women from attaining success in some corporations. What can women do to overcome this?
109. Justin Timberlake once said, 'The worst thing about being famous is the invasion of your privacy.' What is it about fame that makes many people, including you, want to be famous?
110. In your opinion, what effect is unsupervised internet usage having on today's youth?
111. Legislation against religious clothing has caused a controversy around the world. What role should a government play in determining such a personal preference?
112. Some countries still practice death penalty—is it acceptable and why?
113. Many airports are now using full body scanners. How do you feel about going through a scanner that can actually see through your clothes?
114. What is the one big mistake that you've made in life and what did you do to make it right?

115. If you could trade your life with anyone in history, who would it be and why?
116. Would you change your religious belief for the person you loved? Why and why not?
117. Nudist beaches are common in some parts of the world. Is public nudity appropriate or inappropriate?
118. What would you do to avoid fighting a war if you didn't agree with it?
119. If you could change one of your physical characteristics, which one would it be and why?
120. What is the one thing guaranteed to make you angry? How would you deal with it?
121. What is the most memorable thing you've learnt from one of the other contestants?
122. What do you think is the greatest problem in the world for today's people?
123. Who or what makes you laugh?
124. What has been the most difficult moment of your life and what did you learn from it?
125. If you were a judge tonight, who would you vote for as the winner and why?
126. Do you think it's really possible for a male/female relation to have an equal partner?
127. If someone hired you just for your looks, would you take the job?
128. If smart women become world leaders, what special quality will they bring with them?
129. Everyone wants to be successful. How will you know when you are successful?
130. What is the most important advice your mother ever gave you?
131. Could you ever marry someone your parents disapprove of?
132. If you were banished from your own country, where would you go and what would you do?
133. If you could go back into the past and change any event in history, which event would you choose and why?

134. If you could know one thing about your future, what would you like to know?
135. If you had the chance to go into space accompanied by one other person, who would you want to take and why?
136. Would you prefer to have a life full of passion or one of serenity?
137. If you became the leader of your country tomorrow, what is the first thing you would do?

Photo Credits

1. May Queen from the 1910s: The University of Missouri Archives
2. Margaret Gorman, the winner of the first Miss America pageant in 1921: https://en.wikipedia.org/wiki/Margaret_Gorman#/media/File:Margaret_Gorman_4.jpg
3. Bess Myerson, Miss America 1945: http://www.latimes.com/resizer/YtNi742N9IsuvZWD8Xg4h7IqPfA=/1200x0/www.trbimg.com/img-54ac02ad/turbine/la-me-bess-myerson-20150105]
4. Yolande Betbeze, Miss America 1951: Neal Boenzi, New York Times
5. Lisl Goldarbeiter, Miss Universe 1929: https://commons.wikimedia.org/wiki/File:Miss_Austria_1929_(Lisl_Goldarbeiter),_by_Hermann_Schieberth.jpg#filelinks
6. Armi Kuusela, Miss Universe 1953: http://www.fernandomachado.blog.br/novo/wp-content/uploads/2017/06/a-mu-52-armi-coroada-piper.jpg
7. Armi Kuusela, Miss Universe 1953: http://www.tpmum.com/uni14th.html
8. Kiki Hakansson, Miss World 1951: https://i.ytimg.com/vi/aZ2TwJ_nDC0/maxresdefault.jpg
9. The Vitruvian Man by Leonardo da Vinci: https://en.wikipedia.org/wiki/Vitruvian_Man#/media/File:Da_Vinci_Vitruve_Luc_Viatour.jpg
10. The Marquardt Mask of Beauty: http://www.beautyanalysis.com/wp-content/uploads/2014/10/the-facial-masks-01-repose-frontal.jpg, © Marquardt Beauty Analysis
11. The Marquardt Mask of Beauty on Nefertiti: http://www.beautyanalysis.com/research/evidence/former-eras-beauty/ , © Marquardt Beauty Analysis
12. The Structure of Skin: https://en.wikipedia.org/wiki/File:Skin_layers.png, Author: Madhero88
13. 'My daytime look' and 'My evening look': Anvita Sudarshan
14. Face chart: https://s-media-cache-ak0.pinimg.com/736x/c3/d4/99/c3d49989a67dfacaa5e2dbd4c28ab31b.jpg, https://in.pinterest.com/publicphotos/
15. A strand of human hair at 200x magnification: https://en.wikipedia.org/wiki/Hair#/media/File:Menschenhaar_200_fach.jpg, Source:

Wikimedia Commons, Source: Wikimedia Commons, Author: Jan Homann

16. The structure of hair: https://en.wikipedia.org/wiki/Hair_follicle#/media/File:Hair_follicle-en.svg, Source: https://commons.wikimedia.org/wiki/File:HairFollicle.png
17. Cross section of hair: http://www.ecobyte.com.au/a_Basic_Hair_struc_Xsec.jpg
18. Highlighted Hair: https://pxhere.com/en/photo/619152
19. Lowlighted Hair: https://pixabay.com/en/lure-hair-blond-wave-long-1407256/
20. Streaked Hair: https://pxhere.com/en/photo/836692
21. Dip-dyed Hair: https://pxhere.com/en/photo/56189
22. Flaviana Matata, Miss Tanzania 2007: https://bongocelebrity.files.wordpress.com/2007/05/flaviana.jpg
23. All hairstyle illustrations: Anjali Sakleshpur
24. Structure of a tooth: https://en.wikipedia.org/wiki/Human_tooth#/media/File:Human_tooth_diagram-en.svg, Author(s): KDS4444 - Human tooth diagram-en.svg from Wikimedia Commons - License: CC-BY-SA 4.0]
25. The Golden Ratio of teeth: Though every effort has been made to obtain the source/permission for this image, it has not been possible to do so. If the source is brought to our notice, it will be added in future editions.
26. Aligned teeth, misaligned teeth, gap teeth, yellow teeth: Anvita Sudarshan
27. Clear braces: https://en.wikipedia.org/wiki/Dental_braces#/media/File:Transparent-Bracket.JPG

www.ingramcontent.com/pod-product-compliance
Lightning Source LLC
LaVergne TN
LVHW100508110826
845146LV00002B/557